Praise for the Melofonetica Method and the author's work

'Astonishingly helpful! The method gives you a clear vision of the building blocks of Italian, which is demystifying and very empowering. You realise that if you sing the text in the right way, good Italian releases good technique and gives authority to dramatic expression.'
— MADELEINE HOLMES, soprano

'Brings the text to life and encourages vibrant tone quality as well as incisive diction. The whole performance gains conviction as a result.'
— JENNIFER HESLOP, singing teacher

'As a trained singer, Matteo absolutely understands what is helpful vocally so not only are students able to deliver much clearer language but they are also able to sing the music with greater ease. I have learnt so much from him and it has really influenced the way I work as a vocal coach.'
— LIZ MARCUS, pianist and vocal coach

'The Melofonetica Method really works: I've seen at first hand the difference that the tools and techniques make to singers, pianists and conductors.'
— MALCOLM MARTINEAU OBE, pianist

'The Melofonetica Method is refreshing: it cuts through complexities and helps make clearly articulated Italian achievable.'
— MARK SHANAHAN, conductor

'Revelatory! I really enjoyed finding new vocal colours in my singing.'
— SEÁN BOYLAN, baritone

'The Melofonetica Method has enabled me to understand my own support system through the use of consonants, as opposed to a vowel-to-vowel "*legato*" mentality which has driven my technique for many years.'
— STEPHANIE PEAT, mezzo-soprano

"Un plauso a Matteo Dalle Fratte, il vocal coach che fa cantare tutto il cast in un ottimo italiano." [Applause to Matteo Dalle Fratte, the vocal coach who helped the whole cast to sing with great Italian.]
— ALESSANDRO CAMMARANO, review of the 2020 Opera Rara recording of Donizetti's *Il Paria*, *Le Salon Musical*, January 2021

'Another boon to this issue is the forensic clarity of the singers in their projection of the text [...] the consistency and naturalness in their enunciation of the Italian text is a real joy. The language coach Matteo Dalle Fratte [...] has clearly done a wonderful job.'
— RICHARD HANLON, review of the 2018 Monteverdi Productions recording of *Il ritorno d'Ulisse in patria*, *MusicWeb International*, March 2019

'It is thanks in large measure to the insights of language coach Matteo Dalle Fratte that this performance is every bit as vivid (in many respects more so) as any DVD production might be.'
— EUROPADISC, review of the 2018 Monteverdi Productions recording of *Il ritorno d'Ulisse in patria*, October 2018

'The stagings are simple and direct, arising naturally from the singers' delivery of the all-important text – bravo to the language coach, Matteo Dalle Fratte – and Monteverdi's sublime music.'
— HUGH CANNING, review of Monteverdi's Triptych, performed by the Monteverdi Choir and Orchestra and English Baroque Soloists at Teatro La Fenice, *The Sunday Times* (News Licensing), 25 June 2017

'It's a joy to hear well-projected and clearly well-understood Italian [...] Language coach Matteo Dalle Fratte has done excellent work here.'
— DAVID NICE, review of *Le donne curiose*, performed by the Guildhall School of Music & Drama, *The Arts Desk*, 5 November 2015

MATTEO DALLE FRATTE
Foreword by Sir Mark Elder

The Melofonetica Method

A complete guide to
clear and expressive
Italian diction
for singers

Copyright © 2023 by Matteo Dalle Fratte

All rights reserved. No part of this publication may be reproduced, stored in a retrieval system or transmitted, in any form or by any means, electronic, mechanical, photocopying, recording, web distribution or otherwise, without the prior written permission of the copyright owner. The moral right of the author has been asserted.

Although the author and the publisher have made every effort to ensure that the information in this book is correct at the time of going to press, and while this publication is designed to provide accurate information in regard to the subject matter covered, the author and the publisher do not assume and hereby disclaim any liability to any party for any loss, damage or disruption caused by errors or omissions, whether such errors or omissions result from negligence, accident or any other cause. In particular, the author and the publisher make no guarantees concerning the level of success the reader may experience by following the guidance contained in this book, and the reader accepts that results will differ for each individual. The testimonials provided in this book are not intended to represent or guarantee that readers will achieve the same or similar results. Readers are encouraged to seek advice from a competent language, vocal or music coach in accordance with their individual needs.

Every effort has been made to trace copyright holders and to obtain their permission for the use of copyright material. The author and the publisher apologise for any errors or omissions in the acknowledgements printed in this book and will be happy to incorporate any corrections into future reprints or editions.

All translations are the author's, unless otherwise indicated.

Cover design: Tom Howey

ISBNs
Paperback: 978-1-7392622-0-4
Hardback: 978-1-7392622-1-1
E-book: 978-1-7392622-2-8

First print edition April 2023
Published by Lyric Arts Press, UK
The Melofonetica Method is a trademark
For more information, visit melofonetica.com or contact info@melofonetica.com

*To Jamila,
whose genius, love
and patience made
this book possible*

La Musica Scienza deve aver le sue regole,
e [...] bisogna far tutto quello, che si può per iscoprirle.

[Music as a science must have its rules,
and [...] we must do everything we can to uncover them.]

— Pier Francesco Tosi, 1723

CONTENTS

Foreword	xi
Preface	xiii
Acknowledgements	xix
Introduction	xxi

Prologue: Italian, a language built to be sung   1

Chapter 1: Consonants   15
   1.1 The distinctive duration of consonants   16
   1.2 Short vs. long consonants   17
   1.3 The onset, hold and release of consonants   18
   1.4 Identifying short consonants   19
   1.5 Short consonants in notation   24
   1.6 Identifying long consonants   26
   1.7 Long sung consonant categories   32
   1.8 Length, not strength   35
   1.9 Long consonants in notation   36
   1.10 Groups of consonants   42
   1.11 Coarticulation of consonants   51
   1.12 The three musical effects in sung Italian   62
   1.13 The technical benefits of long consonants   65
   1.14 Vocalising with text   70
   Chapter summary   71
   Vocalising exercises   74

Chapter 2: Vowels   83
   2.1 The five archi-vowels   84
   2.2 Vowel modification   87
   2.3 Open and closed vowels   89

2.4 Groups of vowels and vowel prioritisation	94
Chapter summary	107
Vocalising exercises	109

Chapter 3: Expression — 111

3.1 The *attacco del suono*	113
3.2 Melo-gemination: the lengthening of short consonants for emphasis	118
3.3 The agogic accent	129
3.4 Stressed syllables	134
3.5 The incorporation of rests and punctuation into diction	135
3.6 The Michelangelo effect: the essence of Italian style	144
3.7 *Notes inégales*	158
3.8 The colour palette of vowels	161
3.9 *Canto legato* and *portamento di voce*	162
3.10 Line, phrasing and anchoring	177
Chapter summary	178
Vocalising exercises	181

Appendices

A The Italian melophonetic alphabet and notes on pronunciation	189
B Guide to melophonetic transcription	201
C How to prepare Italian text: a quick guide	205
D Melophonetic transcriptions of Italian arias:	209
1 *Giunse alfin il momento ... Deh vieni non tardar*	210
2 *Una voce poco fa*	213
3 *Che gelida manina*	217
4 *Bella siccome un angelo*	220

Glossary	223
Bibliography	235
Index	249
About the author	260
Further guidance, resources and training	261

FOREWORD

Beautiful singing. Beautiful song. In Italian, *bel canto*. The dream of every singer – whether faced with a tiny Baroque aria or a grand Verdi opera. But what are the secrets we all need to uncover in order to truly master *bel canto*?

Knowing how to 'sort of' pronounce the words is a first step. But it is by no means the end of the road. With this new book, Matteo Dalle Fratte has at last found an appealing and accessible way to map it all out for us. His Melofonetica Method is a major achievement that I am sure will be welcomed by singers, teachers, coaches and conductors. I have so enjoyed delving into it.

Matteo is certainly a master in his field. With immense clarity, he describes the essence of sung Italian – as opposed to spoken Italian – from the fundaments of the language to its greatest, most intense utterance.

While the examples and exercises are inevitably pedagogical, the book is so thorough and so passionate, the understanding so profound, that I urge everyone remotely interested in *bel canto* to embrace it and dive in!

Sir Mark Elder

PREFACE

This is a guide to the science and art of sung Italian. My aim is to help singers and their coaches to understand and achieve clear and expressive Italian in opera and classical music.

The findings and guidance I set out here are the culmination of over a decade of research and my work, since 2009, as an Italian language coach with singers of all levels and nationalities.

In the early stages of my coaching career, I became aware that there was something missing in the methodology for teaching Italian diction to singers. The adoption of the International Phonetic Alphabet (IPA) and the study of Italian phonetics, introduced into singing pedagogy from the 1980s onwards, had certainly been useful for singers, but there remained uncertainty and contradictory opinions on various aspects of sung Italian language. Most importantly, I observed that simply applying the rules of spoken Italian pronunciation to singing was not enough for singers to achieve the level of clarity and expression needed in a performance space.

Reflecting on my own training, I realised that, like many other students of singing, I had learnt through mirroring. From 1998 to 2008, I trained in Italy as a tenor with Paolo Badoer, an international bass and pupil of the great Gilda Dalla Rizza, Puccini's favourite soprano. Often, after my singing lessons, Maestro Badoer would select an LP record from his vast collection of opera recordings and talk me through how the great singers used their vocal technique and expressivity. While he did not focus specifically on their diction, it was evident that their ability to articulate text clearly and with conviction was interwoven into their artistry. Clear and expressive diction was an inherent part of their craft – a craft that had largely been handed down orally over the centuries by skilled artists and teachers.

Following the completion of my degree in Italian Literature and Musicology at the University of Padua in 2003 and a master's degree in Music in Performance at the Guildhall School of Music & Drama (GSMD) in London in 2009, I began working with singers as an Italian language coach. Among other aspects, students were particularly seeking clarity on how to correctly articulate double consonants, how and where to apply open and closed vowels, how to achieve 'pure' Italian vowels, and the perceived conflict between the use of stop consonants and maintaining *legato*.

Listening to the best performances of Italian repertoire by the world's leading opera singers, past and present, I wanted to understand, scientifically, what made them so good in order to communicate this to my students. I consulted singing methods and previous studies of phonetics in singing but could not find the definitive answers I was seeking. There seemed to be a gap in the literature examining the phonetics of Italian in the context of music and singing – particularly operatic performance in large acoustic spaces.

This marked the beginning of my research journey. In 2012, I embarked upon a two-year research fellowship at GSMD to investigate the phonetics of sung Italian. Drawing on the fields of linguistics, phonetics, musicology, performance practice and vocal science, I set out to answer the following two broad questions from a phonetic perspective:

- What does it mean to sing well in Italian?
- What do singers need to know about the language in order to sing it well?

In parallel to empirical observation through my work with singers, I conducted a review of a wide range of key texts relating to the evolution and structure of the Italian language, the role of Italian language in opera, and the teaching and learning of Italian diction for singers. This led me to examine the very roots of the Italian language and gave me a new understanding of its evolution as a language for artistic use, its fundamental characteristics, how it has shaped composition and how it has been taught to singers over the centuries.

A key element of my research was an in-depth study of Italian phonetics, particularly the work on *italiano neutro* [neutral, standard Italian] conducted by Luciano Canepari, a prominent Italian phonetician and professor in the Department of Linguistics at the University of Venice.

The study of the phonetics of spoken Italian in recent years has undoubtedly helped singers to improve their pronunciation, but language changes in singing. As Appelman points out, 'all sung sounds are modifications of speech sounds', because 'duration, pitch, and vocal force demand a larger opening of oral and pharyngeal cavities and prevent the sound from being the same' (1986: 221).[1] Sung language is modified by the intonation, rhythm and accents of music, yet it must remain clearly audible in a performance space. It therefore has to be, to some extent, a reinvention of spoken language.

Discussing this at length with Professor Canepari, it became clear that sung language needed its own branch of phonetics to examine and transcribe the way that sounds, diction and expression adapt in singing. Professor Canepari suggested that a suitable name for this area of study might be 'melophonetics' – *melos* in Ancient Greek meaning a melody or a lyric poem intended for singing – and so the term 'melophonetics', or *melofonetica* in Italian, was born.

My early investigation into Italian melophonetics and coaching work with singers thus far had revealed two key findings:

- Firstly, I had observed that the correct use of consonants, in particular long consonants, played a fundamental role in the quality of sung Italian. With the correct identification and production of long consonants, singers consistently achieved clearer and more expressive sung text, better engagement of the breath support, more resonant vowels and more effective collaboration with their pianist.
- Secondly, attempting to open and close *e* and *o* vowels in accordance with spoken Italian, or brighten or darken vowels according to an

---

1. Used with permission of Indiana University Press, from *The Science of Vocal Pedagogy: Theory and Application*, Ralph Dudley Appleman, 1986; permission conveyed through Copyright Clearance Center, Inc.

idea of how an Italian vowel should sound, was of no help to singers endeavouring to achieve clearer or more idiomatic sung Italian.

These findings served as an important catalyst on my research journey but prompted further questions. From 2014 to 2023, I continued my exploration of Italian melophonetics with an expanded literature review and further observation through my work with singers. This enabled me to develop a much more refined understanding of key aspects of sung Italian, including:

- The inherent patterns of musical rhythm in the language
- The essence of 'Italian style'
- The metrical representation of text in notation
- The benefits of consonants for singing technique
- The freedom in sung vowels afforded by the language
- Expressive tools, including the use of the agogic accent (emphasis through duration) and *portamento*

The Melofonetica Method, presented here, distils my key findings. While the framework of rules that underpins the method provides a scientific approach to achieving clear sung Italian diction, the method also guides the performer through expressive choices that can be made.

Over the past decade, through my work as an Italian language coach, I've been fortunate to be able to put into practice and observe the benefits of the Melofonetica Method in a range of settings. The method proves effective for singers of diverse nationalities, language backgrounds and levels, from those at an early stage in their studies through to those preparing lead roles for the world's biggest opera houses.

Along the way, it has been invaluable for me to discuss and refine my approach with skilled singing teachers, opera coaches and leading conductors, and I am truly grateful for the opportunities I have had to do so. Highlights include collaborating with Sir John Eliot Gardiner on the award-winning Monteverdi 450 project in 2017, and with Sir Mark Elder and Carlo Rizzi on critically acclaimed recordings with Opera Rara since 2018. Hearing the results of the Melofonetica Method with professional singers and orchestras, and achieving recognition from critics for the quality of the text, has been truly rewarding.

Observation and feedback have consistently shown that the benefits of the Melofonetica Method extend beyond diction. With skilful use of sung Italian text, vocal quality improves, technical challenges are often resolved, musical interpretation of the score is enhanced, and performers find a new sense of empowerment. Singers and other music professionals also report that the method's approach to the structure of sung language is transferable and beneficial to singing in other languages.

I hope that the Melofonetica Method will give you a valuable new perspective on the sung Italian language. Perhaps it may also inspire similar melophonetic studies in other languages. Ultimately, I hope that the method will enable all performers and their audiences to enjoy to the fullest the beauty of Italian, a language built to be sung.

Matteo Dalle Fratte

ACKNOWLEDGEMENTS

I'm deeply grateful for the opportunities I've had to discuss sung Italian with so many knowledgeable and talented people during the years leading up to the publication of this book. I'm sorry if I have omitted to mention any of you individually below. My sincere thanks to:

- The UK educational establishments where I've had the privilege of teaching and sharing views with students and colleagues including the Royal College of Music, Guildhall School of Music & Drama (GSMD), Royal Conservatoire of Scotland, Royal Welsh College of Music & Drama, Cardiff University, University of Hull, Morley College, Oxenfoord International, National Opera Studio and the Royal Opera House Jette Parker Artist Programme. Particular thanks to GSMD for supporting the early stage of my research with a two-year research fellowship.
- The opera companies where I've had the invaluable opportunity to work as an Italian language coach, including the Royal Opera House, Sir John Eliot Gardiner's Monteverdi Choir & Orchestras, Opera Rara, Hallé Choir, Grange Park Opera, The English Concert, The Mozartists, Opera North, Welsh National Opera, the Grange Festival and Nevill Holt Opera.
- Professor Luciano Canepari for generously sharing with me his wisdom and expertise in Italian phonetics and *italiano neutro*.
- All those who have supported or guided my work in a range of ways: Melissa Addey, Paolo Badoer, Anna Laura Bellina, Gaetano Borgo, Adone Brandalise, Alessandra Brunati, Gabriele Dalle Fratte, Sir Mark Elder, Andrea Ferrari, Sir John Eliot Gardiner, Helena Gaunt, Jane Ginsborg, Giuliana Guidolin, Austin Gunn, Jennifer Heslop, Philip Hobbs, Scott Johnson, Ursula Jones, Panáretos Kyriatzidis, Pamela Lidiard, Malcolm Martineau OBE, Bruce and Jill McGuire,

Florent Mourier, Astrid Monten, Raffaello Monterosso, Maurizio Muraro, Leo Nucci, Ian Page, Roger Parker, Samuele Pellizzari, James Platt, Jo Ramadan, Mark Shanahan, Alessandro Timossi, Alice Turner, Anna Maria Vacchelli, Tann vom Hove and Philip White.

- All those who so generously gave their time and expertise to provide feedback on the draft manuscript of this book, including Nicholas Ansdell-Evans, Philippa Boyle, Finnegan Downie Dear, Emily Garland, Madeleine Holmes, Richard Strivens and Laura Woolthuis.
- The editors and compilers of this book, whose contributions have been invaluable throughout the complexity of this work: Jamila Jones, Julie Aherne, Peter Ford, Henrietta Bredin, Hazel Bird and Kim Birchall.
- My accomplished Melofonetica colleagues and coaches, Julie Aherne, Peter Ford, Alessandra Fasolo and Bernard Tan for their unwavering support and commitment to the method.
- All those who have participated so actively and enthusiastically in Melofonetica courses, and my classes and coaching sessions.
- The singers who bring the music examples in this book to life: Jonathan Kennedy, Shengzhi Ren, Rachel Roper and Lizzie Ryder.

I would also like to thank all of the publishing houses and authors that have given me their permission to reproduce material in this book. Similarly, my sincere thanks to all those who have kindly agreed to let me use their testimonial quotes and reviews.

And, last but not least, a heartfelt thanks to my family for their support and patience throughout this extraordinary, and sometimes exhausting, journey to the publication of this method. My gratitude, in particular, to my wife Jamila for her dedication, guidance and contribution to every aspect, and to my son, Raffaello, for bringing us so much joy during the final years of this work.

INTRODUCTION

The ability to sing well in Italian is central to an opera singer's skillset, but it can often be difficult to know exactly what to focus on to improve clarity and expression in sung Italian.

The Melofonetica Method is a transformative approach to lyric diction that demystifies the science and art of singing well in Italian. The method presents a pragmatic approach to vowels and reveals the fundamental role that long and short consonants play in delivering clear, resonant and idiomatic sung Italian in a performance space.

Based on over a decade of research and coaching, and with proven results on acclaimed productions and recordings, the Melofonetica Method helps singers of all levels and language backgrounds to:
- Rapidly achieve clearer, more expressive, more idiomatic Italian diction
- Enhance vocal quality and breath support
- Recognise the intrinsic rhythms that characterise Italian style
- Refine musical and dramatic interpretation
- Strengthen collaboration with accompanists, conductor and director
- Feel more self-assured and confident performing Italian repertoire

For coaches, the method supports a structured approach to teaching and learning, and provides new tools to define, communicate and benchmark the quality of sung Italian.

For accompanists, conductors and directors, the method puts a new lens on Italian text in music and drama, and enhances the creative partnership with singers.

The method is applicable to all Italian opera and classical repertoire, including arias, songs, recitatives and ensembles, by all composers throughout the centuries.

About this book

The prologue to this book is intended to contextualise the study of sung Italian. It explores how standard Italian, as we know it today, was carefully curated by poets to be beautiful to hear, particularly in sung form. The power of this language to stir the emotions, not only through meaning but also through the sounds and rhythms of words, led to the birth of opera as an art form. A deeper understanding and appreciation of this heritage informs and inspires our quest for clear and expressive Italian diction today.

The practical guide that follows presents all the principles of the Melofonetica Method, incorporating research and views from the fields of linguistics, phonetics, musicology, performance practice and vocal science.

Chapter 1 focuses on consonants, the phonetic backbone of the Italian language; Chapter 2 provides practical guidance on vowels; and Chapter 3 is dedicated to expressive tools. The concepts presented in each chapter are supported by 180+ notation examples, 120 vocalising exercises, 4 transcribed arias and access to 340+ audio recordings.

Terminology

While working through the book, it will be helpful to consult the glossary at the end, which provides explanations of phonetic, melophonetic and other technical terms used. Phonetic terminology is based on the rules of *italiano neutro* as set out in *La buona pronuncia italiana del terzo millennio* (Canepari and Giovannelli 2012). Several new melophonetic terms have also been created as part of the Melofonetica Method.

Descriptions relating to the place and manner of articulation of phonemes do not include diagrams of the vocal apparatus; singers are instead encouraged to explore these concepts in practice, together with their vocal coach.

Musical terms are referred to firstly with British terminology, with the equivalent American term given in brackets, as shown in the table that follows.

British	American	
Bar	Measure	
Bar line	Measure line	
Minim	Half note (1/2)	𝅗𝅥
Crotchet	Quarter note (1/4)	♩
Quaver	Eighth note (1/8)	♪
Semiquaver	Sixteenth note (1/16)	𝅘𝅥𝅯
Demisemiquaver	Thirty-second note (1/32)	𝅘𝅥𝅰

The Italian melophonetic alphabet and guide to pronunciation

Appendix A, 'The Italian melophonetic alphabet and notes on pronunciation', provides detailed guidance regarding the pronunciation of each Italian phoneme. Some readers may find it useful to read that section first.

Music examples

Music examples, including extracts from well-known operas, are included throughout Chapters 1, 2 and 3. Four complete arias are also included in Appendix D. The extracts from operas and arias are reproduced with the kind permission of the publishers indicated alongside each figure and full details of the editions used are provided in the Bibliography. Note that some *appoggiature* have been added by the author.

Melophonetic transcription

A system of melophonetic transcription completes the method and is used to concisely communicate the clear and expressive articulation of Italian lyrics. This is based on the symbols used in the International Phonetic Alphabet (International Phonetic Association 2020), the *can*IPA Natural Phonetics framework (Canepari 2009) and the elements created as part of the Melofonetica Method.

Throughout Chapters 1, 2 and 3, boxes entitled 'In melophonetic transcription' provide the symbols and information corresponding to each key aspect of the method. All the elements of melophonetic transcription are summarised together in Appendix B, 'Guide to melophonetic transcription'.

Note that in all transcriptions provided throughout this book, the five sung Italian archi-vowels are represented simply with the five symbols [a], [e], [i], [o] and [u], without differentiation of open, intermediate and closed sounds. For further information, see Chapter 2, 'Vowels'.

Melophonetic notation

Melophonetic notation is used in many music examples to show the precise placement, length and pitch (where applicable) of sung Italian vowels and consonants in music.

Audio recordings

To gain a complete understanding of each topic, the reader is strongly encouraged to listen to the audio recordings that are available online at **melofonetica.com/online-learning**. These accompany the notation examples, the vocalising exercises and the melophonetic transcriptions of arias, and are indicated with the headphones symbol (🎧). For any problems accessing the recordings, contact **info@melofonetica.com**.

Vocalising exercises

Vocalising exercises with corresponding melophonetic transcriptions are provided at the end of each chapter. The singer may practise each exercise by progressing semitone by semitone from the low to the medium and high registers, or vice versa. The singer may also explore the use of different tempi, together with other melodic variations and/or rhythms if desired. Accompanying audio recordings for all exercises are available online at **melofonetica.com/online-learning**.

Getting started quickly

The information in Chapters 1, 2 and 3 has been structured so as to provide an in-depth, layer-by-layer understanding of the building blocks of clear and expressive sung Italian. The reader is therefore advised to work through this content in sequential order. The summaries at the end of each chapter give an overview of all of the key concepts covered.

For readers who wish to start applying the Melofonetica Method quickly to any piece of Italian repertoire, Appendix C: 'How to prepare Italian text: a quick guide' summarises the key practical steps to take to improve diction and expression, and provides cross-references to the detailed information in the relevant chapters.

PROLOGUE

Italian, a language built to be sung

> *La continuità che lega la lingua di Dante, Petrarca e Boccaccio all'italiano moderno [...] è evidente ancor oggi [...] perché il nucleo primo di quella lingua, ossia le sue componenti fonomorfologiche, sono rimaste in buona parte le stesse.*
>
> [The continuity that connects the language of Dante, Petrarch and Boccaccio with modern Italian [...] is still evident today [...] because the core of that language, in other words its phono-morphological components, for the most part has remained the same.]
>
> — PAOLA MANNI (2003: 63)

Italian in its earliest form: the Sicilian School of poets in the thirteenth century

In the thirteenth century, and indeed for many centuries thereafter, Latin was the official written and spoken language of courts and universities in the Italian peninsula. However, different dialects or vernacular languages (*lingue volgari*) were widespread and were the real spoken languages used for everyday communication. These were the languages that were the vehicle for the recital of poetry – a popular form of entertainment during the many centuries when most people were unable to read or write.

As attempts were made to transcribe poetry, it became clear that the vernacular languages needed some refinement in order to distil them into one consistent, beautiful and noble language for use in art.

The most notable laboratory for this work took place from *c.* 1220 at the Sicilian court of Frederick II, the half-Norman, half-German King of Sicily and Holy Roman Emperor. King Frederick was himself a poet as well as a polyglot, and he gathered around him the best poets from Sicily and the mainland, together known as the 'Sicilian School'. These poets sought to combine the most beautiful sounds from the vernacular languages to be enjoyed in the art of poetry recital. At this point, the aim was not to create a common language as such, but rather to define a language that would be the most aurally pleasing version possible for artistic expression (Migliorini 2019: 168).

Sicily was a highly multicultural place at that time, being an economic hotspot in the middle of the Mediterranean with a thriving exchange of goods, culture and languages. The poets of the Sicilian School could therefore draw not only on the dialects spoken in Sicily but also on other languages, including Latin and Provençal (Migliorini 2019: 174). The poets crafted a language whose written form was dictated by the spoken form, and protected as such. This was unlike the path that would be taken by other languages such as English or French, where the spoken form continued to evolve while the official written form remained fixed.

A major outcome of the Sicilian poets' work was the invention of the sonnet form. The word sonnet, *sonetto* in Italian, means 'little song', and the sonnet was indeed a form of poetry intended to be sung, rather than read. We can understand the concept of 'sung' in this context as recited with a simple melody or chant (Zuliani 2011: 129).

The Sicilian school of poetry came to an end after the death of King Frederick II in 1250, but the experiments that had begun in Sicily continued to have a strong influence on poetic language. The aspiration to perfect the language for artistic expression spread throughout the peninsula, in particular to the flourishing Tuscan and Bolognese middle classes (Migliorini 2019: 178).

Here were the roots of the concept of the Italian language as a *lingua d'arte*, a language for art, rather than a *lingua dell'uso*, a language for practical, everyday use.

The refinement of Italian by Tuscan poets in the fourteenth century

Sicilian poetry was much appreciated in Tuscany where it had become fashionable among the emerging poets of the thirteenth century, who began to imitate its style and sounds, with some Tuscan adaptations (Migliorini 2019: 177–79).

The process of defining the most beautiful form of the new literary Italian continued into the fourteenth century, reaching a peak of stylistic perfection particularly in the works of the great Tuscan poets Dante Alighieri, Francesco Petrarca [Petrarch] and Giovanni Boccaccio. Proposing a new official language for poetic expression was a challenge for these artists, at a time when Latin was still the universal language of literature. However, in his Latin treatise *De vulgari eloquentia* [On eloquence in the vernacular], Dante aimed to promote the vernacular refined by the poets in order to start circulating a new and respected language that could be used in art – and understood by everybody. He described this as a 'dolce stil novo' [sweet new style] (*Commedia*: *Purgatorio*, Canto XXIV, Line 57), a language that was easy on the ear, comprising words and inflections, both ancient and modern, drawn from Italian dialects and other languages. Dante did not favour any one dialect in particular; in fact he pointed out that no individual dialect was as illustrious and beautiful to hear as the new literary form of Italian – not even Tuscan, the dialect of his own region (*De vulgari eloquentia*, Book 1, Chapters 10–16).

Dante's most acclaimed work, *Commedia* [The (Divine) Comedy] enshrined his ideas and became a bible of this new language for the entire peninsula. In each *cantica* [canticle], named *Inferno* [Hell], *Purgatorio* [Purgatory] and *Paradiso* [Paradise], Dante makes distinct choices of language for theatrical effect, using words whose phonetic elements are also evocative of their meaning. In doing so, he demonstrates the riches and potential of this new literary Italian as a language ideally suited to performance.

The sung language as a supreme form of expression

There is significant evidence that from the thirteenth century, Italian poetry was crafted to be conveyed in sung form, and that only in this way could the words reach their true expressive potential.

In *Parlar Cantando: The Practice of Reciting Verses in Italy from 1300 to 1600*, Elena Abramov-van Rijk points out that the fourteenth-century poet Gidino di Sommacampagna was seemingly the first to use the term *parlar cantando* [to speak in song] to describe the sung recitation of poetry. As she remarks, 'the first thing that comes to mind is the world of early opera. The unexpected presence and use of this expression two centuries earlier than the beginning of opera is striking' (2009: 26).[2]

Indeed, the concept of 'dressing' a poem with music was important for the performance of poetry. Abramov-van Rijk notes various examples of poets at the time, including Dante, who described their work as 'nude' until it was given a musical component by the performer. This 'allows us to assume the existence of an approach to the art of poetry that was very similar to that of the classical world of the past, that is, poetry that normally was expected to include a musical component' (2009: 61–62).[3]

There are various indications of the value that Dante placed on the sung recital of his poetry. In *De vulgari eloquentia*, Dante's discussions on the form of poetry known as the *cantio* or *canzone* indicate that he composed such verses with their sung form in mind. Nino Pirrotta believes that Dante 'aveva in mente, non soltanto possibile ma desiderabile, la concreta presenza di una melodia' [had in mind, as something not only possible but desirable, the concrete presence of a melody] (1966: 11). Raffaello Monterosso also notes Dante's conclusion that the perfect example of the *canzone* is one that is written with such a skilful choice of words that it is perfectly ready to be embellished by music (see Baldelli

---

2. Used with permission of Peter Lang Group AG, from *Parlar Cantando: The Practice of Reciting Verses in Italy from 1300 to 1600*, Elena Abramov-van Rijk, 2009; permission conveyed through Copyright Clearance Center, Inc.

3. See note 2 above.

and Monterosso 1970).[4] In *Commedia*, when Dante arrives in Purgatory he sees an old singer friend of his, Casella, and asks him for the solace he so often found in sung performance of poetry. When Casella breaks so sweetly into 'Amor che ne la mente mi ragiona' [Love, that reasons with me within my mind], the first line of one of Dante's *canzoni* in *Convivio* (Book 3, Canzone II, Line 1), all those listening are enthralled and Dante says that he still carries the sweetness of this song inside him (*Purgatorio*, Canto II, Lines 76–120). It seems that in song, Dante's words had found their most powerful and memorable form of expression.

Conveying the words of poetry in song not only enhanced the listener's enjoyment but also meant that the poets' work would communicate stories and emotions with greater impact and projection, and thus be more likely to become known and successful. Abramov-van Rijk points out that the sonnet 'Se Lippo amico se' tu che mi leggi' [If it is you reading this, my friend Lippo], sent by Dante to his performer friend, clearly shows that 'the purpose of "dressing" a poem was to enhance its recognition', adding that 'this was the specific task of *prolatores*, or performers of poetic compositions' (2009: 34).[5]

In the second half of the fourteenth century, the poetry of Petrarch took the refinement of the language further. Petrarch spent his entire working life conducting lengthy and detailed explorations of the sounds of words and distilling an exquisite style of verbal music perfectly suited to singing. His collection of poems, *Canzoniere*, became an example and model for future Italian poets. It was made up predominantly of sonnets but also included other types of poetry with a musical structure, including *canzoni* and *ballate*. Foscolo mentions a telling comment that Petrarch left in Latin alongside one of his sonnets that reads, 'I must make these

---

4. Used with kind permission of Enciclopedia Italiana Treccani. Any reproduction and/or use of this material that is not strictly for personal and private purposes is forbidden. Onward transmission online, or in any other form, is strictly forbidden.

5. Used with permission of Peter Lang Group AG, from *Parlar Cantando: The Practice of Reciting Verses in Italy from 1300 to 1600*, Elena Abramov-van Rijk, 2009; permission conveyed through Copyright Clearance Center, Inc.

two verses over again, singing them' (1823: 57). It seems that for Petrarch, too, the poetic potential of these lines could only be truly fulfilled in song.

Reciting poetry in song is also a recurrent feature in Giovanni Boccaccio's *The Decameron*. The collection of novellas comprises one hundred tales told over the course of ten days by ten friends who have fled Florence for a countryside villa to escape the plague. The tales include *canzoni* and other frequent references to song and dance, and each day of storytelling is concluded with a *ballata*.

The art of reciting poetry with a simple monodic vocal line continued to flourish in the fifteenth century, but there is little written evidence of the melodies that were used. Meanwhile, in polyphonic music, a form of composition known as the *frottola* had become popular, which often included a dominant (soprano) line alongside supporting parts. This is considered to be the forerunner to the madrigal and may provide some evidence of the types of melodies in use in monody.

Bembo and *la questione della lingua* in the sixteenth century

By the sixteenth century, the official languages of other countries around Europe were consolidating and beginning to supersede Latin. Castilian had become the official language of Spain in the late fifteenth century, while in Germany, Early New High German asserted itself over Latin, particularly with Martin Luther's translation of the Bible in 1522. In France, Parisian French was adopted as the official administrative language in 1539. In England, the advent of the printing press and Shakespeare's influence on the language helped to establish Early Modern English as the universal language of everyday use.

Italy, however, remained politically divided and it was the poets and writers who decided to tackle *la questione della lingua* [the language question] by seeking unification through the use of one literary language across the peninsula. A key figure in this discussion was the Venetian scholar Pietro Bembo, who worked on codifying and standardising the language of Dante, Petrarch and Boccaccio.

Bembo published his influential linguistic study *Prose della volgar lingua* [Writings on the vernacular language] in 1525. In this, he stated the case for an ideal language and promoted the refined and beautiful literary version that, having already begun its dissemination throughout the cultural centres of Italy, now had the potential to unite the entire Italian peninsula.

Niccolò Macchiavelli was a leading opponent of Bembo's views, believing instead that contemporary Tuscan would be a more suitable basis for a unifying language. However, Bembo's recommendations prevailed and, unlike elsewhere in Europe where linguists were looking to modernise, many of Italy's literati looked to the past to find the best model for a new official language (Migliorini 2019: 317).

In his examination of the language of the great poets of the thirteenth and fourteenth centuries, Bembo elevated the role of the sound and rhythm of words, i.e. their phonetic properties, in conveying meaning and eliciting an emotional response in the listener. Dean T. Mace discusses this work and the influence it may also have had upon musical composition in Italy from the sixteenth century onwards:

> Bembo was not interested in the word as a name but as an 'affective' sound [...] in this way [he] began a radical transformation in the theory of the function of sound and rhythm in poetic language. This transformation had enormous consequences in *cinquecento* Italian poetry, extending beyond the borders of language into music itself [...] [and] may have determined the direction taken by Italian music in the 16th century. For it was in Italian music, first in the madrigal (and later in the experiments leading to the opera), that sound stopped being mainly a mellifluous accompaniment to words [...] and sought to be significant in the manner of affective word sound. (1969: 69–70)[6]

Indeed, the beautiful sounds of *volgare illustre* [the illustrious vernacular language], as described by Dante in *De vulgari eloquentia* – and now showcased also in the works of the great sixteenth-century poets including

---

6. Dean T. Mace, 'Pietro Bembo and the Literary Origins of the Italian Madrigal', *Musical Quarterly*, 1969, 55, 1, 65–86, DOI: 10.1093/mq/lv.1.65. Reprinted by permission of Oxford University Press.

Giovanni Battista Guarini, Giambattista Marino, Jacopo Sannazzaro and Torquato Tasso – were undoubtedly a great source of inspiration for the early opera librettists and composers.

The birth of opera in the seventeenth century and the importance of clear diction

Towards the end of the sixteenth century, the development of musical composition was greatly influenced by discussions that took place in the circle known as the Camerata de' Bardi in Florence. Giovanni Bardi, Count of Vernio, was a wealthy composer, writer and scientist with wide-ranging cultural interests. He gathered other musicians, intellectuals, philosophers and poets around him to discuss the future of the art forms they loved, especially music and drama.

One topic in particular that drew the attention of the Camerata was text in music. The group's members were concerned that, when madrigals were sung in polyphony, with counterpoint and inventive harmonies (the form of composition known as the *prima pratica* [first practice]), it was difficult to hear the words. The poetry of Petrarch, in particular, was enormously popular at the time and many composers set his sonnets to music, but so often those words, which were so loved, could not be heard clearly when they were sung.

On the first page of his preface to *Le nuove musiche* [The new music] (1601/2), Giulio Caccini describes the importance the members of the Camerata placed on the clear and accurate delivery of text:

> Posso dire d'havere appreso più da i loro dotti ragionari, che in più di trent'anni non ho fatto nel contrappunto, imperò che questi intendentissimi gentilhuomini mi hanno sempre confortato, e con chiarissime ragioni convinto, à non pregiare quella sorte di musica, che non lasciando bene intendere le parole, guasta il concetto, e il verso, ora allungando, e ora scorciando le sillabe per accomodarsi al contrappunto, laceramento della Poesìa.
>
> [I can say that I gained more from their learned discussions than I did in thirty years of studying counterpoint. These insightful gentlemen always encouraged

me, and convinced me with the clearest of reasons, not to value the kind of music that, in preventing the words from being well understood, ruins the sense and form of the verse, elongating and shortening syllables here and there in order to fit the counterpoint, and turning the poetry to shreds.]

Caccini goes on to highlight the views expressed by Plato in *The Republic* that music is made up of words, rhythm and harmony, but rhythm and harmony must follow and adapt themselves to the words (Book III, 400d). This is so that music, Caccini says, may 'penetrare nell'altrui intelletto, e fare quei mirabili effetti' [penetrate the minds of listeners and create its marvellous effects] (1601/2).

The revival of Classical traditions was a fundamental characteristic of the Italian Renaissance period during the fifteenth and sixteenth centuries. Inspired by ancient Greek theatre and music, the Camerata had encouraged composers to prioritise storytelling. This laid the foundation for a new movement in composition known as the *seconda pratica* [second practice]. The aim to express the words to best effect meant that composers, including Caccini and Claudio Monteverdi, began to break the strict rules of counterpoint and harmony. It also resulted in the development of the monodic art form of *recitar cantando*, which involved one voice recounting a story through singing, accompanied simply by *basso continuo*. Here was the birth of early Italian opera.

Monteverdi's polyphonic madrigal compositions, which allowed flexibility in counterpoint, melody and harmony where the text required it, were strongly criticised by Giovanni Maria Artusi, theorist and composer (1600: 39–40). In a declaration at the end of a collection of his brother's songs, Giulio Cesare Monteverdi, brother of Claudio, later addressed Artusi's criticism: 'dice mio fratello, che non fa le sue cose a caso; atteso che la sua intenzione è stata [...] di far che l'oratione sia padrona del armonia e non serva' [my brother says that he does not compose without regard for [harmonic] rules, his intention was [...] to make the words the governor of the harmony rather than its servant] (1607). Like Caccini, Giulio Cesare Monteverdi also goes on to make reference to Plato's views on the important role of text in stirring the emotions.

The ultimate purpose of combining a beautiful language with musical harmony was to reflect the human condition through a theatrical experience, provoking joy, sadness, amusement, and all other emotions. The concept of *muovere gli affetti*, the stirring of the emotions through the power of words in music, became a manifesto for those involved in creating and performing early opera. Caccini reports the success of this new art form in the preface to *Le nuove musiche* (1601/2), stating that never before the new madrigals of the time had he heard a solo voice, accompanied simply by a string instrument, that had 'tanta forza di muovere l'affetto dell'animo' [such a power to stir the soul's emotions].

Claudio Monteverdi's concern with this aim is revealed in a letter dated 9 December 1616 to Alessandro Striggio, the librettist for *Le nozze di Tetide* [The marriage of Thetis], in which he requests that the winds be made real characters with spoken lines, explaining: 'Come, caro Signore, potrò io imitare il parlar de' venti, se non parlano?! E come potrò io con il mezzo loro movere li affetti?' [How, dear Sir, will I be able to imitate the speech of the winds if they do not speak?! And how will I be able, through their characters, to stir the emotions?] (1994: 49).

Almost a century after Monteverdi, the singer and composer Pier Francesco Tosi published his influential treatise on singing in Italian, *Opinioni de' cantori antichi, e moderni, o sieno Osservazioni sopra il canto figurato* [Opinions of ancient and modern singers; or, Observations on *canto figurato*], in which he advises:

> Corretta la pronunzia proccuri, che profferisca le medesime parole in maniera, che senza affettazione alcuna sieno così distintamente intese, che non se ne perda sillaba, poiché se non si sentono, chi canta priva gli ascoltanti d'una gran parte di quel diletto, che il canto riceve dalla loro forza: se non si sentono, quel cantore esclude la verità dall'artificio: e se finalmente non si sentono non si distingue la voce umana da quella d'un cornetto, o d'un haut-bois.

> [Once the singer has mastered correct pronunciation, he should make the words distinctly understood so that, without affectation, no syllable is lost, since if the words are not heard, the singer deprives listeners of a great part of that delight that is conveyed through the power of the words, the true essence of the art is lost and there is no difference between the human voice and that of a cornett or oboe.] (1723: 35)

Similarly, the celebrated librettist Pietro Metastasio set out his concerns regarding singers' attention to text in a letter dated August 1755, sent to Francesco d'Argenvillières:

> I cantori d'oggidì si sono dimenticati affatto, che l'obbligo loro è d'imitar la favella degli uomini col numero, e con l'armonia: anzi credono allora esser valent'uomini quanto più si dilungano dalla natura umana. I loro archetipi sono i rosignuoli, i grilli, e le cicale; non le persone, e gli affetti loro. Quando han suonata con la gola la loro sinfonìa, credono aver adempiti tutti i doveri dell'arte. Quindi lo spettatore ha sempre il cuore in perfettissima calma, e non aspetta dagli Attori, che la sua grattatina d'orecchie. Per ottener questo fine non v'è bisogno di buoni drammi; anzi il mio voto sarebbe, che si bandissero affatto dal nostro Teatro non solo tutte le parole, ma l'alfabeto intiero, alla riserva d'un paio di vocali.
>
> [Singers of today have completely forgotten that their duty is to convey words, together with rhythm and harmony, in fact they believe themselves to be more skilled the more they digress from human nature. They aspire to imitate the sounds of nightingales, crickets and cicadas instead of real people and emotions. When their symphony of vocalisation is over, they believe they have fulfilled all the obligations of this art. Thus, audiences remain with a perfectly unmoved heart and expect nothing more than a little tickling to the ears. To this end, there is no need for good libretti, in fact I'd say we may as well ban from our Theatre not only all the words, but the entire alphabet, in favour of a couple of vowels.] (1792: 37)

Later, in the nineteenth century, Giuseppe Verdi was similarly fervent about the importance of diction. Roger Freitas notes that:

> Of all the virtues a singer might possess, clear enunciation was easily one of the most important to Verdi. The evidence for the composer's position is overwhelming, as virtually every time he wrote about singers he mentioned the issue. [...] For Verdi, clarity of diction outweighs virtually all other qualities in a singer. (2002: 239)[7]

The fundamental role of text and diction remained clear: opera could only fulfil its purpose through effective delivery of the words.

---

7. Roger Freitas, 'Towards a Verdian Ideal of Singing: Emancipation from Modern Orthodoxy', *Journal of the Royal Musical Association*, 127, 2, 226–57, reproduced with permission.

The quest to define standard Italian in the nineteenth and twentieth centuries

When Italy became a unified nation in 1861, the question of an official language arose again. While the literary language had been used increasingly in poetry and prose since the sixteenth century, spoken communication was still conducted in regional and local dialects. At this point, the discussion therefore centred on how to define and spread a standard national language that would be for common (civil) use, spoken as well as written.

The prominent Italian poet and novelist Alessandro Manzoni proposed the model of contemporary Florentine, believing it more practical to take a real everyday spoken form of the language as a model rather than, in his view, an antiquated literary language. His idea was approved of by many, but was also strongly opposed by others, in particular Graziadio Isaia Ascoli, an eminent Italian linguist and scholar. Ascoli believed that it was preferable to support the continued dissemination of the unifying literary language, allowing this to naturally assimilate influences from Italy's polycentric culture (see Ascoli 1873). This is indeed closer to how Italian continued to develop over the years that followed.

Through schooling and mass-media in particular, the standardisation of Italian continued. But, while standard Italian today is, for the most part, the same as thirteenth-century Italian (Migliorini 2019: 281), linguistic differences remain throughout Italy, 'evidence of the heritage of many centuries of political division and cultural diversity' (A. Tosi 2001: 3). Most Italians nowadays speak standard Italian with a regional accent and the incorporation of regional or local terminology, while many still use their local or regional dialect for everyday communication.

The study of *italiano neutro* and Italian phonetics into the twenty-first century

The aim to define one neutral version of the spoken Italian language, i.e. one that is free of discernible regional or local accents, is a scientific approach to standardising Italian pronunciation. This work has continued into the twenty-first century, particularly to guide those who use their voice professionally, including presenters, actors and singers.

A leading expert in the field of Italian phonetics is Luciano Canepari, Professor of Phonetics and Phonology at the University of Venice and author of a number of key publications on the rules of Italian diction, including the *Dizionario di pronuncia italiana: Il DiPI* [Dictionary of Italian pronunciation: The DiPI] (2009) and *La buona pronuncia italiana del terzo millennio* [Good Italian pronunciation for the third millennium] (2012), co-authored by Barbara Giovannelli.

Canepari and Giovannelli (2012: 24–29) have defined *italiano neutro* [neutral, standard Italian] according to the phonological structure of Italian as it is spoken in the 'phono-linguistic centre' of Italy. This refers to specific provinces of the regions of Tuscany, Umbria, Le Marche, Lazio and Abruzzo, where the language remains closest to its Latin phonetic roots and therefore has 'una funzione mediatrice' [a mediatory function] (Migliorini 2019: 57). However, as Canepari and Giovannelli point out, even in the central regions of Italy, there are still influences from local dialects on phonetics and intonation, and it should not be assumed that every aspect of pronunciation in these regions can automatically be considered 'good' (2012: 27).

Italiano neutro acknowledges and encompasses acceptable phonetic variants, particularly for those elements of the language that were not defined in the written language by the poets. These include open and closed *e* and *o* vowels, and the voicing of *s* and *z*. Given the variability that still exists for these aspects, 'norme ferree non esistono, dato che a volte, sono più le eccezioni delle regole' [there cannot be cast iron rules since there are sometimes more exceptions than rules] (Canepari and Giovannelli 2012: 67).

From phonetics to melophonetics

'Melophonetics' is a new term coined with this research to define the study and transcription of sounds in *sung* language. The Melofonetica Method, presented here, examines Italian melophonetics in the context of opera and classical singing. This approach is based on the phonetics of spoken *italiano neutro* but incorporates the modifications and rules that are necessary for sung Italian to be delivered clearly and expressively in a performance space. These include:

- The classification of all consonants as either short or long
- Guidance on recognising and articulating each type of consonant
- The metrical representation of consonant length in notation
- The concept of five 'archi-vowels' rather than nine vocoids
- A system of vowel prioritisation for groups of vowels (which also resolves the use of the approximant consonants *i* [j] and *u* [w])
- The unvoicing of voiced *s* [z] and *z* [dz]
- The articulation of long *v* and *f* as occlu-constrictive (stop) consonants
- The introduction of expressive tools including 'melo-gemination' (the lengthening of a short consonant at the beginning of a syllable to add emphasis)

While some aspects of spoken Italian are transcended in singing, others are magnified – in particular, the backbone of long and short consonants that gives the sung language its distinctive idiomatic sound, musicality and style.

This book fully investigates the melophonetic properties of Italian in operatic singing, exploring the science behind the art that continues to move and inspire audiences around the world.

CHAPTER 1

Consonants

> **LEARNING OUTCOMES**
>
> *By the end of this chapter, you should be able to:*
> 1. Describe the concept of consonant length in Italian
> 2. Identify short consonants, long consonants and groups of consonants in sung Italian
> 3. Correctly articulate short and long consonants
> 4. Place consonants correctly in notation
> 5. Classify long consonants into three categories of sound
> 6. Use coarticulation where necessary
> 7. Identify the three musical effects in sung Italian
> 8. Describe the technical benefits of long consonants
> 9. Experience the benefits of vocalising with text

Consonants make up the majority of phonemes (units of sound) in the Italian language. They are either short or long. The ability to correctly and distinctly articulate short and long consonants is fundamental to clear Italian diction – and, as will be explored later, to resonant and expressive sung Italian.

1.1 The distinctive duration of consonants

È necessario che [...] l'allievo faccia particolare attenzione di non impiegare doppie consonanti ove occorrono le semplici, e viceversa.

[The student must pay particular attention to avoiding the use of double consonants where single consonants occur, and vice versa.]

— Francesco Lamperti (1864: 13)

Consonant length can directly determine the meaning of a word in Italian. This is known as 'distinctive duration' and is an important characteristic inherited from Latin.

In Latin, both vowels and consonants have distinctive duration. Unlike most other modern European languages, Italian has retained only the distinctive length of consonants. There are therefore numerous examples of words where consonant length changes meaning in Italian. For example, there is quite a difference between saying 'Conosco la nona di Beethoven' (*nona* with short *n*), which means 'I know Beethoven's ninth symphony', and 'Conosco la nonna di Beethoven' (*nonna* with long *n*), which means 'I know Beethoven's grandmother'!

1.2 Short vs. long consonants

In Italian, a short consonant is so fleeting that it creates almost no interruption between the preceding and subsequent sounds. It is useful to think of a short consonant as no more than a very quick 'tap'. Examples of short consonants in Italian include:
- *m* in *come* [ˈkoː me]
- *t* in *seta* [ˈseː ta]

A long consonant, on the other hand, is known as a 'geminated' consonant in phonetics. The term gemination comes from the Latin *gemini* and means 'twinning' or 'doubling'. In practice, a geminated consonant in spoken or sung Italian often has a greater duration than the combined length of two short consonants. Examples of long consonants in Italian include:
- *ll* in *bello* [ˈbelː lo]
- *ss* in *posso* [ˈposː so]
- *tt* in *atto* [ˈatː to]

It is important to note that there are also a number of consonants in Italian that are written as single consonants but pronounced as long consonants when spoken or sung, as will be explained fully in Section 1.6, 'Identifying long consonants'.

1.3 The onset, hold and release of consonants

To understand the concept of consonant length in singing, it is helpful to consider every consonant as having both an onset and a release. Onset denotes the point at which a consonant starts, either immediately after a preceding sound or following an in-breath. The release means the final part of the consonant, which releases either into the phoneme that follows or the silence at the end of a line.

The onset and release of short consonants occur consecutively and, due to the speed of their enunciation, are perceived as one single event. For a short consonant to be correctly articulated, there should be no audible holding of its sound. The preceding vowel will always be long and sustained.

Long consonants have both an earlier onset than short consonants, and a hold between their onset and release that identifies them as long. The onset of a long consonant will always shorten the preceding vowel. The length of the hold will depend on note duration, but, in slower tempi, the full length of a long consonant can be up to approximately five times the length of a short consonant.

The concepts of onset, hold and release are explained for each type of consonant in the following sections and illustrated with notated examples that show how consonants and vowels share space in sung Italian. The intention is not to concern the singer with achieving mathematical perfection in the production of long and short consonants, but rather to facilitate an understanding of the relative proportions of length for each. With practice, these proportions become embedded into aural and muscle memory and, in time, become intuitive and spontaneous.

1.4 Identifying short consonants

Single consonants within a word

In Italian, a single consonant that is intervocalic (between two vowels) and within a word is always short, for example:
- *c* in *eco* [ˈeː ko]
- *m* in *amo* [ˈaː mo]

The only exception to this is *z*, which is always pronounced as a long consonant when it is between two vowels (see 'Self-gemination' in Section 1.6).

Single consonants at the beginning of a word

A short consonant can occur at the beginning of a word where it is preceded by a word that ends with a vowel and followed by a vowel, for example:
- *p* in *di pace* [diː ˈpaː t͡ʃe]
- *v* in *i vati* [iː ˈvaː ti]

However, single consonants at the beginning of words may be lengthened in certain circumstances – as explained in '"Hidden" long consonants' in Section 1.6; Section 3.1, 'The *attacco del suono*'; and Section 3.2, 'Melo-gemination: the lengthening of short consonants for emphasis'.

Single consonants at the end of a word

In Italian, barring a few exceptions, the only consonants that occur at the end of words are:
- *l*, e.g. in *ciel*
- *m*, e.g. in *andiam*
- *n*, e.g. in *sen*
- *r*, e.g. in *cor*

Where a single *l*, *m*, *n* or *r* ends a word and is followed by a vowel at the beginning of the next word, the consonant is always short. The same applies where the word ending with a consonant also ends the line or is followed by an in-breath. For example, in a line ending with the words *un amor*, the *n*, *m* and *r* are all short.

If the singer wishes to finish the line more dramatically, the short consonant at the end may be slightly lengthened, but it should not be as long as a long consonant.

In some instances, vowel elision (omission) may be applied where a word ends with a vowel and the next word starts with a vowel (see 'Vowel elision' in Section 2.4). The elision of the first of the two vowels will result in the first word ending with a consonant; however, the length of this consonant is unaffected by the elision. For example, in *poc'anzi*, the *c* remains short, as it would be in *poco*.

Exceptions

1. The first exception occurs where a euphonic *d* is added to the preposition *a* [at/to] and the conjunctions *e* [and] and *o* [or] where they precede a word starting with a vowel. This results in *ad*, *ed* and *od* respectively, which are easier to articulate and clearer before the vowel that follows. The euphonic *d* is often present in sung Italian text and the addition of the *d* makes no difference to meaning. The *d* is usually short but can sometimes be lengthened for expressive reasons – see 'Applying emphasis to a syllable beginning with a vowel' in Section 3.2.

2. In onomatopoeic or non-Italian words, consonants other than *l*, *m*, *n*, *r* or *d* can occur at the end of a word. In these cases, the final consonant is always long where it precedes a word that begins with a vowel (see 'Post-gemination' in Section 1.6). Examples include:
    - Long *c* [k] in *tic irregolare* [ˈtikː kirː reː goː ˈlaː re]
    - Long *s* in *Amneris ai vezzi* [amː ˈneː ɾis sai̯ ˈvetsː tsi]

Short consonants within groups of consonants

Where two or more consonants occur consecutively, either within a word or across two words, these form what is defined in the Melofonetica Method as a 'group of consonants' (sometimes referred to as a 'consonant cluster'). Examples includes *nt* in *canto* or *ltr* in *sul trono*. Consonants that occur in groups can be either short or long, depending on the combination they are in. To identify short and long consonants in groups, see Section 1.10, 'Groups of consonants'.

Full list of short consonants in sung Italian

Table 1 shows a full list of short consonants in Italian. They are each categorised with their type of phonation, i.e. voiced or unvoiced. Voiced means that the consonant is produced with vibration of the vocal folds, while unvoiced (voiceless) means the consonant is produced without vibration of the vocal folds.

The place and manner of articulation are provided for each consonant. Place of articulation refers to the place in the mouth or vocal tract where an obstruction is created by one of the articulators (lips, teeth, gums, tongue, hard palate, soft palate or glottis) to produce the sound. Manner of articulation describes the way that the air is diverted or constricted as it flows out of the vocal tract.

For detailed guidance regarding the pronunciation of each consonant, see Appendix A, 'The Italian melophonetic alphabet and notes on pronunciation'. For full explanations of phonetic terminology, refer to the glossary at the end of this book, and for more information on the symbols used in the transcriptions, see Appendix B, 'Guide to melophonetic transcription'.

Table 1. Short consonants in sung Italian.

Consonant	Voiced	Unvoiced	Place and manner of articulation
b	Short b as in cibo [ˈtʃiː bo]		Bilabial occlusive
c		Short c [tʃ] as in baci [ˈbaː tʃi]	Post-alveolar occlu-constrictive
		Short c [k] as in foco [ˈfoː ko]	Velar occlusive
d	Short d as in vado [ˈvaː do]		Denti-alveolar occlusive
f		Short f as in afa [ˈaː fa]	Labio-dental constrictive
g	Short g [g] as in vaga [ˈvaː ga]		Velar occlusive
	Short g [dʒ] as in regi [ˈreː dʒi]		Post-alveolar occlu-constrictive
gl*	Short gl [ʎ] as in gli [ˈʎi]		Palatal lateral
gn*	Short gn [ɲ] as in gnocchi [ˈɲokː ki]		Palatal nasal
l**	Short l as in solo [ˈsoː lo]		Alveolar lateral
m**	Short m as in freme [ˈfreː me]		Bilabial nasal
n**	Short n as in seno [ˈseː no]		Alveolar nasal

Consonant	Voiced	Unvoiced	Place and manner of articulation
p		Short *p* as in *capo* [ˈkaː po]	Bilabial occlusive
q		Short *q* as in *equo* [ˈeː kuo̯]	Velar occlusive
r	Short *r* [ɾ] as in *ara* [ˈaː ɾa]		Alveolar vibrant (tap)
s	Short *s* as in *casa* [ˈkaː za]***	Short *s* as in *risuona* [ɾiː ˈsuo̯ː na]	Denti-alveolar grooved constrictive
sc*		Short *sc* [ʃ] as in *scena* [ˈʃeː na]	Post-alveolar grooved constrictive
t		Short *t* as in *fato* [ˈfaː to]	Denti-alveolar occlusive
v	Short *v* as in *devi* [ˈdeː vi]		Labio-dental constrictive
z*	Short *z* as in *zitti* [ˈdzit ti]****	Short *z* as in *zeffiro* [ˈtsefː fiː ɾo]	Denti-alveolar occlu-constrictive

*Note that *gl* [ʎ], *gn* [ɲ], *sc* [ʃ] and *z* [dz/ts] are always long where they occur between vowels, and can only be short in groups of consonants and sometimes at the beginning of a line – see Section 1.10, 'Groups of consonants', and Section 3.1, 'The *attacco del suono*'.

**Allophones (phonetic variants) exist for the consonants *l*, *m* and *n* where these directly precede other specific consonants. See Section 1.11, 'Coarticulation of consonants', and Appendix A, 'The Italian melophonetic alphabet and notes on pronunciation'.

***See Note 8, '*s* as unvoiced [s] or voiced [z]' in Appendix A.

****See Note 12, '*z* as unvoiced [ts] or voiced [dz]' in Appendix A.

1.5 Short consonants in notation

All short consonants, voiced or unvoiced, are so brief that their onset and release occur consecutively at the beginning of the note, and are always as short as possible, regardless of note duration. In the examples that follow in Figures 1 to 4, each short consonant is therefore represented as a demi-semiquaver (thirty-second note).

> IN MELOFONETIC TRANSCRIPTION
>
> A short consonant is represented with a single symbol, denoting both its onset and release. Where a short consonant is preceded by a vowel, the vowel is always long and therefore denoted with a chroneme [ː], which indicates a long sound.

🎧 Figure 1. Short voiced *m* in *amo*.

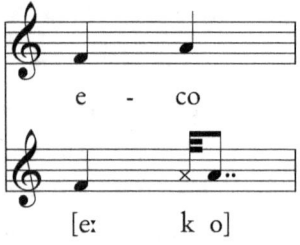

🎧 Figure 2. Short unvoiced *c* [k] in *eco*. Note the difference between this and *ecco* in Figure 24 in Section 1.9.

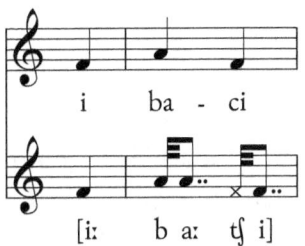

🎧 Figure 3. Short voiced *b* and unvoiced *c* [tʃ] in *i baci*.

🎧 Figure 4. Short voiced *n* in *un*; short voiced *n* and *r* [ɾ] in *onor*.

Note that music examples showing rhythmic variants are not provided here for short consonants, since their onset and release will always be as short as possible. This is unlike long consonants, where the length of the hold is proportionate to note duration.

1.6 Identifying long consonants

The simplest long consonant sounds to identify in Italian are written double consonants, but there are also a number of 'hidden' long consonants, i.e. those that are written as single consonants but are lengthened (geminated) when pronounced.

Written double consonants

Examples of written double consonants occurring within a word include:
- *mm* in *mamma* [ˈmam: ma]
- *ss* in *passo* [ˈpas: so]
- *tt* in *tutto* [ˈtut: to]

Written double consonants can also occur across two words, for example:
- *ll* in *al lato* [al: ˈla: to]
- *rr* in *mar rosso* [mar: ˈros: so]

'Hidden' long consonants

The following are all written as single consonants but are lengthened when pronounced:
- Self-geminated consonants
- Co-geminated consonants
- Post-geminated consonants
- Consonants that are geminated when they form part of a group of consonants – see 'Gemination in groups of consonants' in Section 1.10

There are also other consonants that can be lengthened for expressive reasons – see Section 3.1, '*The attacco del suono*', Section 3.2, 'Melo-gemination: the lengthening of short consonants for emphasis' and Section 3.5, 'The incorporation of rests and punctuation into diction'.

Self-gemination

In Italian, there are a few consonant sounds that are always long, or 'self-geminated', when they occur between two vowels:
- *gl* is pronounced as long [ʎ], e.g. in *figlio* [ˈfiʎː ʎo]
- *gn* is pronounced as long [ɲ], e.g. in *signor* [siɲː ˈɲoɾ]
- *sc* is pronounced as long [ʃ], e.g. in *esci* [ˈeʃː ʃi]
- *z* is pronounced as long [ts] or [dz], e.g. in *grazie* [ˈgratsː tsi̯e] or *la Zerlina* [ladzː dzerː ˈliː na] – see also Note 12, '*z* as unvoiced [ts] or voiced [dz]' in Appendix A

Co-gemination

To 'co-geminate' means to 'geminate together'. In Italian, there are certain words, in particular monosyllabic words, that end with a vowel and activate the gemination of the short consonant at the beginning of the following word, creating a long consonant. This is also known as *raddoppiamento* or *rafforzamento (fono)sintattico*, or phrasal doubling. For example, *ma dove* is pronounced [madː ˈdoː ve] because *ma* is an activator of co-gemination and lengthens the short *d* at the beginning of *dove*.

The rule of co-gemination comes from Latin and can be illustrated by looking at the Latin words *ad casam* [at home]. In *ad casam*, the group of two consonants *dc* bridges the two words. At some point in spoken Latin, the *d* would have been assimilated into the *c* to make it easier to pronounce, because in written Italian we now have *a casa*, written with just a single *c*. However, in spoken standard Italian, the length of the two consonants *dc* has been maintained and these words are instead pronounced with a long *c* [k], i.e. [akː ˈkaː sa]. The single *c* is long in correct Italian diction because the *a* activates the co-gemination of the *c*.

The preposition *a* is always an activator of co-gemination and therefore always lengthens a short consonant occurring at the beginning of the following word, for example:
- *a ballare* is pronounced [abː balː ˈlaː ɾe] with a long *b*
- *a me* is pronounced [amː ˈme] with a long *m*

Spoken co-gemination has also influenced the spelling of some words in Italian, for example:
- *della* (*de+la*) [ˈdelː la]
- *giammai* (*già+mai*) [dʒamː ˈmai̯]
- *treppiede* (*tre+piede*) [trepː ˈpi̯eː de]

There are many common monosyllabic words to look out for that activate co-gemination. A comprehensive list is provided under 'Activators of co-gemination and a-gemination' later in this section.

Additionally, polysyllabic words that end with a stress on the final syllable activate co-gemination, for example:
- *città*
- *così*
- *perché*
- *prenderò*

Co-gemination also applies to the first consonant in the following groups of two short consonants: *b/c/d/f/g/p/t/v* + *l/m/n/r/s* (see 'Groups of two consonants (1)' in Section 1.10), for example:
- *che clamore* is pronounced [kekː klaː ˈmoː re] with a long *c*
- *ma prima* is pronounced [mapː ˈpriː ma] with a long *p*

Post-gemination

In some words that end with a single consonant, this consonant becomes long when the following word begins with a vowel. This is called 'post-gemination', and can be thought of as a co-gemination that occurs at the end rather than at the beginning of a word.

Post-gemination only occurs at the end of onomatopoeic words or non-Italian words. For example:
- *crac impressionante* is pronounced [ˈkrakː kimː presː si̯oː ˈnanː te]
- *Ford è un bue* is pronounced [ˈfordː de̯umː ˈbu̯e]
- *Radames attende* is pronounced [raː daː ˈmesː satː ˈtenː de]
- *ron assordante* is pronounced [ˈronː nasː sorː ˈdanː te]

A-gemination

There are certain monosyllabic words ending with a vowel, including articles, pronouns and prepositions, that work in the opposite way to co-gemination and do not allow the consonant that follows to be lengthened. This is called 'a-gemination' and is also a rule inherited from Latin. Common monosyllabic words that activate a-gemination include *di*, *gli* and *la*. For example:
- *di luna* is pronounced with a short *l* [di: ˈlu: na]
- *gli dico* is pronounced with a short *d* [ʎi: ˈdi: ko]
- *la voce* is pronounced with a short *v* [la: ˈvo: tʃe]

A comprehensive list of activators of a-gemination is provided under 'Activators of co-gemination and a-gemination' later in this section.

De-gemination

'De-gemination' means the optional shortening of a long consonant (to a short consonant) for expressive reasons only. This will be discussed further in 'Exceptions' to the *attacco del suono* in Section 3.1, 'How to apply melo-gemination' in Section 3.2 and 'Identifying, creating and enhancing the Michelangelo effect' in Section 3.6. De-gemination can only be applied to:
- Co-geminated consonants
- Geminated consonants in groups of consonants (see 'Gemination in groups of consonants' in Section 1.10)
- The written double *l* in an articulated preposition, i.e. a single word that combines a preposition and a definite article, such as *allo*, *dell'* or *nella*

Activators of co-gemination and a-gemination

The following list provides common monosyllabic words that activate co-gemination (denoted by *) or a-gemination (denoted by °). In a few instances, either co-gemination or a-gemination is acceptable; the choice made will be determined by the desired expressive effect.

Words given below that end with a group of vowels become activators of a-gemination only when they are pronounced as shown in square brackets (see Section 2.4, 'Groups of vowels and vowel prioritisation').

This information is reproduced with the kind permission of Luciano Canepari and Zanichelli, from *Dizionario di pronuncia italiana*: *Il DiPI* [Dictionary of Italian pronunciation: The DiPI], 2009, also available online at dipionline.it.

a *
ah °/*
ahi °
beh °/*
blu *
ce ° (adverb or pronoun)
che *
ché *
chi *
ci ° (adverb or pronoun)
ciò *
co' ° (short form of *coi*)
cui ° [ku̯i]
da °/*
dà *
de *
de' ° (short form of *dei*)
deh °/*
di °
di' °/*

dì *
diè *
dio ° [di̯o]
do * (verb or noun)
due ° [du̯e]
e *
è *
fa * (verb or noun)
fé *
fe' *
fia ° [fi̯a]
fra *
fu *
fui ° [fu̯i]
già *
giù *
gli ° (article or pronoun)
glie °
ha *
ho *

CONSONANTS

i°
io° [io̦]
la° (article or pronoun)
là*
le° (article or pronoun)
li° (pronoun)
lì*
lo° (article or pronoun)
lui° [lui̦]
ma*
mah °/*
me°
mi° (pronoun)
mia° [mia̦]
mie° [mie̦]
mio° [mio̦]
ne° (adverb or pronoun)
ne* (preposition)
né*
no*
o* (conjunction)
o °/* (exclamation)
oh °/*
piè*
più*
po' °/*
può*
qua*
qui*
re*
sa*
se* (conjunction)
se° (pronoun)
se' ° (short form of sei)

sé*
si° (pronoun)
sì* (affirmative or adverb)
sia° [sia̦]
so*
sta*
sta' °/* (short form of stai)
sta° (short form of questa)
ste° (short form of queste)
sti° (short form of questi)
sto° (short form of questo)
sto*
su*
sua° [sua̦]
sue° [sue̦]
sui° [sui̦]
suo° [suo̦]
te° (pronoun)
tè*
ti°
tra*
tre*
tu*
tua° [tua̦]
tue° [tue̦]
tuo° [tuo̦]
uh °/*
va*
va' °/* (short form of vai)
ve°
vi°
via° [via̦]
vo */° (short form of vado)
vo' °/* (short form of voglio)

1.7 Long sung consonant categories

In the Melofonetica Method, three overarching categories of sound are used to classify long consonants in sung Italian:
- Sibilant (grooved constrictive consonants)
- Sonorant (nasal, lateral and vibrant consonants)
- Stop (occlusive and occlu-constrictive consonants)

Given their speed of enunciation, short consonants are not labelled as sibilant, sonorant or stop, but are simply classified as voiced or unvoiced. It is in the description of long consonants that the categories of sibilant, sonorant and stop are useful, since the nature of each long consonant sound is sustained and clearly audible.

The sections that follow provide more information on each category of long consonant. For explanations of the phonetic terminology used, see the glossary at the end of this book. See also Appendix A, 'The Italian melophonetic alphabet and notes on pronunciation', and Appendix B, 'Guide to melophonetic transcription'.

Sibilant consonants

Sibilant consonants have a continuous unvoiced (hissing) sound and, in Italian, have one manner of articulation: grooved constrictive. Their place of articulation is either denti-alveolar or post-alveolar:
- Long *s*, denti-alveolar grooved constrictive [s] as in *rosso* [ˈros: so]
- Long *sc*, post-alveolar grooved constrictive [ʃ] as in *uscite* [uʃ: ˈʃi: te]

Sonorant consonants

Sonorant consonants have a continuous voiced (pitchable) sound and, in Italian, have three manners of articulation: nasal, lateral or vibrant. Within each of these, there are three different places of articulation, depending on the consonant that is being produced: alveolar, bilabial or palatal:

Nasal

- Long *gn*, palatal [ɲ] as in *segno* [ˈseɲː ɲo]
- Long *m*, bilabial [m] as in *gemma* [ˈdʒemː ma]
- Long *n*, alveolar [n] as in *penna* [ˈpenː na]

Lateral

- Long *gl*, palatal [ʎ] as in *figlio* [ˈfiʎː ʎo]
- Long *l*, alveolar [l] as in *bella* [ˈbelː la]

Vibrant (trill)

- Long *r*, alveolar [r] as in *ferro* [ˈferː ro]

Note that allophones (phonetic variants) exist for the consonants *l*, *m* and *n* when these directly precede other specific consonants. See Section 1.11, 'Coarticulation of consonants' and Appendix A, 'The Italian melophonetic alphabet and notes on pronunciation'.

Stop consonants

The onset of a stop consonant occurs when the consonant is positioned with an instant closure at its place of articulation but instead of an immediate release of sound, there is a silence (hold) before the air pressure is released with the final sound, allowing listeners to identify the consonant.

Stop consonants have two manners of articulation: occlusive or occlu-constrictive. They have six places of articulation, which depend on the consonant that is being produced: bilabial, denti-alveolar, labio-dental, palatal, post-alveolar or velar. All of these consonants can be released as either voiced or unvoiced sounds, as shown in Table 2.

Table 2. Stop consonants in sung Italian.

Consonant	Voiced release	Unvoiced release	Place and manner of articulation
b, p	Long *b* as in *gabbo* [ˈgab: bo]	Long *p* as in *mappa* [ˈmap: pa]	Bilabial occlusive
d, t	Long *d* as in *freddo* [ˈfred: do]	Long *t* as in *petto* [ˈpet: to]	Denti-alveolar occlusive
c, g, q	Long *g* as in *reggo* [ˈreg: go]	Long *c* as in *bocca* [ˈbok: ka] Long *q* as in *soqquadro* [sok: ˈku̯a: dro]	Velar occlusive
c, g	Long *g* as in *raggi* [ˈradʒ: dʒi]	Long *c* as in *facce* [ˈfatʃ: tʃe]	Post-alveolar occlu-constrictive
f, v*	Long *v* as in *ovvero* [ov: ˈve: ro]	Long *f* as in *buffo* [ˈbuf: fo]	Labio-dental occlu-constrictive
z**	Long *z* as in *mezzo* [ˈmedz: dzo]	Long *z* as in *pazzo* [ˈpats: tso]	Denti-alveolar occlu-constrictive

*See Note 3, 'Long *f* and *v* as stop consonants', in Appendix A.
**See Note 12, '*z* as unvoiced [ts] or voiced [dz]' in Appendix A.

Additionally, there is the long glottal occlusive consonant [ʔ], which can be articulated immediately before a vowel at the beginning of a word or syllable for clarity and/or emphasis. See Section 3.1, 'The *attacco del suono*', Section 3.2, 'Melo-gemination: the lengthening of short consonants for emphasis', and Section 3.5, 'The incorporation of rests and punctuation into diction'.

1.8 Length, not strength

It is important that singers differentiate long consonants from short consonants through the use of *length*, not strength. Attempting to emphasise long consonants by increasing their volume or over-engaging the breath support not only compromises their quality but also jeopardises breath management and can result in jaw tension. When long consonants are correctly articulated, with steady and sustained length, the vocal apparatus naturally engages in the correct way.

Stop consonants need particular attention in this regard. Since there is already an adequate build-up of air pressure created by their very nature, there is no need to add greater force to their release. Doing so can result in an accompanying burst of aspiration, similar to an [h]. This is noticeable particularly with the long consonants *c*, *p*, *q* and *t*. Aspiration jeopardises idiomatic diction and causes a drop in subglottal pressure that compromises breath support and the quality of the vowel that follows.

Length is applied to all stop consonants simply by lengthening the silent hold before their release. When long stop consonants are correctly articulated, they help the singer to maintain the breath support and expand and prepare the pharyngeal space for the subsequent production of a healthy, resonant vowel – see Section 1.13, 'The technical benefits of long consonants'.

In contrast to stop consonants, long sonorant and sibilant consonants are characterised by their continuous flow of sound. It is important for the singer not to apply too much air pressure to these consonants as this can interrupt their smooth, sustained quality and jeopardise breath management. This is particularly noticeable in the articulation of the long sibilant *s* when the articulators are not positioned correctly and the channel for the outward airflow is too narrow, which can result in a 'squeezed', higher-frequency, intermittent sound. To make a correct Italian long *s*, there should be a large groove in the tongue to enable a stable, balanced outflow of air and a sustaining of the long sound. See Note 9, 'Long Italian *s*', in Appendix A and Section 1.13, 'The technical benefits of long consonants'.

1.9 Long consonants in notation

To demonstrate the placement of long consonants between vowels in notation, they are initially explained and illustrated occurring across two crotchets (quarter notes). The length of a long consonant's hold is proportionate to note duration, as shown in the rhythmic variants provided.

> **IN MELOPHONETIC TRANSCRIPTION**
>
> A long consonant between vowels is placed across two consecutive syllables and is represented with two symbols. The first symbol is placed at the end of the first syllable and is followed by a chroneme; these represent the onset and hold of the consonant. The second symbol is placed at the beginning of the second syllable and represents the release.

Sibilant consonants

Sibilant consonants are unvoiced. The onset and hold of a sibilant consonant are together a quaver (eighth note) of unpitched continuous sound that belongs to the first note. This shortens the preceding vowel sound accordingly. The release of the consonant belongs to the second note and is as short as possible, shown here as a demisemiquaver (thirty-second note) of unpitched sound. Together, the onset, hold and release of a sibilant consonant merge to form one long 'hissing' sound that bridges the two notes. The placement of a sibilant consonant across two crotchets is shown in Figure 5, with rhythmic variants illustrated in Figures 6 to 13.

🎧 Figure 5. Long sibilant *s* in *esso*.

Rhythmic variants

🎧 Figure 6

🎧 Figure 7

🎧 Figure 8

🎧 Figure 9

🎧 Figure 10

🎧 Figure 11

🎧 Figure 12

🎧 Figure 13

Note that Figures 11 to 13 show melismatic passages with notes of short duration ('melisma' means the singing of one syllable across two or more notes, usually of different pitch). In these, the onset and hold of the long consonant occur as soon as the pitch of the final note is reached. A short slide on the preceding vowel is shown in the melophonetic notation; this is fundamental in order to hear the last note of the melisma before the placement of the consonant. In melismatic passages with notes of longer duration, the final part of the vowel and the onset and hold of the long consonant share the final note, as in Figure 5.

Sonorant consonants

Sonorant consonants are voiced. The onset and hold of a sonorant consonant are together a quaver (eighth note) of continuous pitched sound that belongs to the first note. This shortens the preceding vowel sound accordingly. The release of the consonant belongs to the second note and is as short as possible, shown here as a demisemiquaver (thirty-second note).

Where the sonorant consonant occurs across two notes of the same pitch, it is obviously one continuous sound without a slide. Between two different pitches there must be a moment of transition from the hold on one note to the release on the next. This is a very quick, instinctive slide (shown here as a demisemiquaver). Note that where a *portamento* slide is applied on the preceding vowel, the sonorant consonant will instead be pitched fully on the second note (see Figure 180 in Section 3.9).

The placement of a sonorant consonant across two crotchets is shown in Figure 14, with rhythmic variants illustrated in Figures 15 to 22.

🎧 Figure 14. Long sonorant *n* in *anno*.

Consonants

Rhythmic variants

🎧 Figure 15

🎧 Figure 16

🎧 Figure 17

🎧 Figure 18

🎧 Figure 19

🎧 Figure 20

🎧 Figure 21

🎧 Figure 22

For Figures 20 to 22, see the note for Figures 11 to 13 in 'Sibilant consonants' regarding the placement of long consonants in melismatic passages.

Stop consonants

The onset and silent hold of a stop consonant are together a quaver rest (eighth rest) in length. These belong to the first note and shorten the preceding vowel sound accordingly. The release is either voiced or unvoiced, belongs to the second note and is as short as possible, shown here as a demisemiquaver (thirty-second note). The placement of a stop consonant across two crotchets is shown in Figures 23 and 24, and rhythmic variants are illustrated in Figures 25 to 32.

🎧 Figure 23. Long stop *b* (voiced release) in *ebbe*. Note that pitching of the sound should only be heard on the release on note two.

🎧 Figure 24. Long stop *c* [k] (unvoiced release) in *ecco*.

Rhythmic variants

🎧 Figure 25

🎧 Figure 26

🎧 Figure 27

🎧 Figure 28

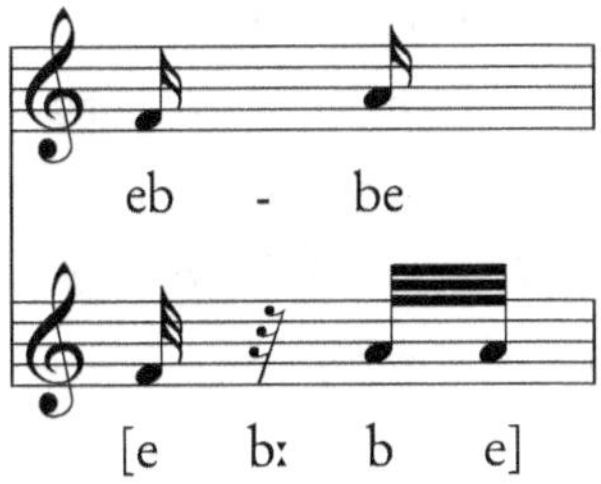

🎧 Figure 29

🎧 Figure 30

🎧 Figure 31

🎧 Figure 32

For Figures 30 to 32, see the note for Figures 11 to 13 in 'Sibilant consonants' regarding the placement of long consonants in melismatic passages.

1.10 Groups of consonants

The term 'group of consonants' is used in the Melofonetica Method to define two, three or four consonants that occur consecutively, either within a word or across two words. This is sometimes referred to as a 'consonant cluster'. Examples include:
- *pr* in *aprite*
- *spl* in *splende*
- *rstr* in *per strada*

Gemination in groups of consonants

In all groups of consonants (apart from some groups of two), one of the consonants is always geminated (long) in spoken or sung Italian, while the others remain short. In singing, the long consonant in a group can easily be identified in the score: groups of consonants containing a long consonant always occur across two notes (two syllables) and the long consonant will always be the last consonant belonging to the first note (first syllable). This guideline applies in almost all instances unless expressive emphasis is applied within the group of consonants – see Section 3.2, 'Melo-gemination: the lengthening of short consonants for emphasis'.

The only anomaly occurs with *s*. Where *s* is geminated in a group of consonants, its placement in the division of syllables traditionally used in scores can be misleading as it is incongruent with the phonic syllable (the way that the syllable is pronounced). The long *s* should always be articulated at the end of the first syllable, as is the case with all other instances of long consonants in groups. For example:
- *esca* is written as *e-sca* in scores but is sung as [ˈesː ka], as shown in Figure 38
- *è strano* is written as *è-stra-no* in scores but is sung as [esː ˈtraː no]

Where *s* is geminated in a group of consonants and also occurs at the beginning of a line, the *s* is placed before the first note, as shown in Figure 39.

Groups of consonants in notation

To demonstrate the placement of groups of consonants in notation, they are explained and illustrated here occurring across two crotchets (quarter notes). The length of the hold of each long consonant is proportionate to note duration, as shown in the rhythmic variants in Section 1.9. Note that the following does not apply if melo-gemination is used within the group of consonants – see Section 3.2, 'Melo-gemination: the lengthening of short consonants for emphasis'.

In all groups of consonants containing a long consonant, apart from the second category of groups of two consonants, the long consonant will have its onset, hold and release entirely within the first note. Unless there are any other preceding short consonants to share the space, the full length of the long consonant is a quaver (eighth note). Where short consonants occur before the long consonant, they will therefore share some of the quaver space on the first note. Where short consonants occur after the long consonant, they are placed on the second note.

Groups of two consonants (I)

b/c/d/f/g/p/t/v + l/m/n/r/s

Both consonants remain short (unless the first is a written double or co-geminated – see 'Groups of two consonants (II)'), for example:
- *gr* in *agro* [ˈaː ɡɾo]
- *pr* in *apri* [ˈaː pɾi]

Across two crotchets, both short consonants belong to the second note and are each represented in Figures 33 and 34 as a demisemiquaver (thirty-second note):

🎧 Figure 33. Short *g* [g] and short *r* [ɾ] in *agro*.

🎧 Figure 34. Short *p* and short *r* [ɾ] in *apri*.

GROUPS OF TWO CONSONANTS (II)

Written double or co-geminated *b/c/d/f/g/p/t/v* + *l/m/n/r/s*

The first consonant is long while the second consonant remains short, for example:
- *bbr* in *ebbro* [ˈebː bro]
- *tr* in *e tre* [ˈetː tre]

Across two crotchets, the onset and silent hold of the first (long stop) consonant are together a quaver rest in length and belong to the first note. The release of the first consonant occurs at the beginning of the second note, followed by the second (short) consonant, each represented in Figures 35 and 36 as a demisemiquaver.

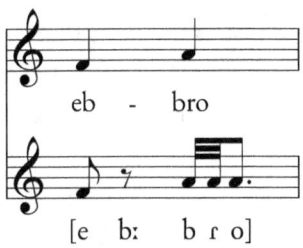

🎧 Figure 35. Long *b* and short *r* [ɾ] in *ebbro*.

🎧 Figure 36. Long *t* and short *r* [ɾ] in *e tre*.

Groups of two consonants (III)

l/m/n/r/s + any other consonant*

The first consonant is long while the second consonant remains short, for example:
- *lm* in *alma* ['al: ma]
- *lt* in *il tuo* [il̯: 'tu̯o]
- *rn* in *per noi* [per: 'nọi]
- *rp* in *arpa* ['ar: pa]
- *rsc* in *per scena* [per: 'ʃe: na]
- *sc* in *esca* ['es: ka]
- *st* in *stelle* [s: 'tel: le]

Across two crotchets, the onset, hold and release of the first (long sonorant or sibilant) consonant are together a quaver in length and belong to the first note. The second (short) consonant occurs at the beginning of the second note and is represented in Figures 37 to 39 as a demisemiquaver.

*Note that *gl* [ʎ], *gn* [ɲ] and *sc* [ʃ] are also considered 'any other consonant' here since they are each one distinct consonant sound (contoid).

IN MELOPHONETIC TRANSCRIPTION

For this group, and all that follow, the long consonant does not cross two syllables, so it is represented with a single symbol followed by a chroneme, to show its onset, hold and release all occurring on the first note (or all occurring before the first note in the case of long *s* at the beginning of a line – see Figure 39). Note that this applies only where no melo-gemination (expressive emphasis) is used within the group of consonants. The use of melo-gemination means that a different consonant in the group will be lengthened – see 'How to apply melo-gemination' in Section 3.2.

🎧 Figure 37. Long *l* and short *m* in *alma*.

🎧 Figure 38. Long *s* and short *c* [k] in *esca*. The onset, hold and release of the long *s* all occur on the first note. Note the division of syllables and the placement of the *s* in melophonetic transcription.

As previously mentioned, where *s* is the long consonant in a group of consonants at the beginning of a line, the *s* is placed before the first note, as shown in Figure 39.

🎧 Figure 39. Long *s* and short *t* in *stelle*. The onset, hold and release of the long *s* all occur before the first note.

GROUPS OF THREE CONSONANTS (I)

l/m/n/r/s   +   *b/c/d/f/g/p/t/v*   +   *l/m/n/r/s*

The first consonant is long while the following two consonants remain short, for example:
- *lpl* in *al placido* [al: ˈpla: tʃi: do]
- *mbr* in *ombra* [ˈom: bɾa]
- *str* in *astro* [ˈas: tɾo]

Across two crotchets, the onset, hold and release of the first (long sonorant or sibilant) consonant are together a quaver in length and belong to the first note (or occur before the first note in the case of long *s* at the beginning of a line, as shown in Figure 39). Both the second and third (short) consonants belong to the second note and are each represented in Figures 40 and 41 as a demisemiquaver.

🎧 Figure 40. Long *m*, short *b* and short *r* [ɾ] in *ombra*.

🎧 Figure 41. Long *s*, short *t* and short *r* [ɾ] in *astro*.

Groups of three consonants (ii)

l/m/n/r + *s* + any other consonant

The *s* (second consonant) is long while the first and third consonants remain short, for example:
- *lst* in *il star* [il̞s: 'taɾ]
- *rsm* in *per smania* [peɾs: 'ma: ni̞a]

Across two crotchets, the first (short) consonant occurs on the first note; this is represented in Figure 42 as a demisemiquaver. It is followed, also on the first note, by the onset, hold and release of the long *s*, which together are a quaver in length. The third (short) consonant occurs at the beginning of the second note and is represented here as a demisemiquaver.

🎧 Figure 42. Short *l* [l̞], long *s* and short *t* in *il star*.

GROUPS OF FOUR CONSONANTS

l/m/n/r + *s* + *b/c/d/f/g/p/t/v* + *l/m/n/r/s*

The *s* (second consonant) is long while the other three consonants remain short, for example:

- *nstr* in *un stral* [uṉsː ˈtɾal]
- *rstr* in *per strada* [peɾsː ˈtɾaː da]

Across two crotchets, the first (short) consonant occurs on the first note and is represented in Figure 43 as a demisemiquaver. This is followed, also on the first note, by the onset, hold and release of the long *s*, which together are a quaver in length. Both the third and fourth (short) consonants belong to the second note and are each represented here as a demisemiquaver.

🎧 Figure 43. Short *n* [ṉ], long *s*, short *t* and short *r* [ɾ] in *un stral*.

1.11 Coarticulation of consonants

Coarticulation is a phenomenon that exists in all languages whereby the articulation of specific phonemes changes due to the nature of preceding or subsequent phonemes.

In the pronunciation of Italian consonants, coarticulation occurs in some groups, where two consonants are articulated consecutively and the first assumes the place of articulation of the second. This process is also known as 'assimilation'. This type of coarticulation facilitates a smoother transition between the two consonants and avoids the creation of an evanescent vowel – a brief sound that is sometimes described as a 'ghost vowel' or 'shadow vowel'. In sung Italian, coarticulation not only makes diction aesthetically more fluid and elegant but also prevents the creation of extra syllables that interfere with metrics and rhythm.

In Italian, coarticulation applies when *l*, *m* or *n* are followed by other specific consonants. For example, *n* is usually an alveolar consonant, but where it is followed by *b*, *m* or *p*, all bilabial consonants, its place of articulation becomes bilabial, i.e. it becomes an *m*. This occurs, for example, in:

- *Don Pasquale* [dom: pas: ˈkua̯: le]
- *un ballo* [um: ˈbal: lo]
- *non mi dir* [nom: mi: ˈdir]

The different ways in which the consonants *l*, *m* and *n* are articulated, depending on the consonant that follows, are phonetic variants known as 'allophones'; these do not change the meaning of a word.

Coarticulated sounds often occur spontaneously, without conscious effort from the speaker or singer, and are naturally understood as part of the normal idiomatic flow of language. In fact, in Italian, a number of coarticulations are also reflected in the written language, for example, *bempensante* (instead of *benpensante*) or *pampepato* (instead of *panpepato*).

As Barbara Kühnert and Francis Nolan point out, 'it would be misleading to think of coarticulation in speech as if it were an imperfection in the way language is realized' (1999: 9).[8] Indeed, they explain that coarticulation is not only the result of 'the continuously flowing activity of the vocal mechanism, which is ill-suited to abrupt changes of configuration', research shows that it is also 'quite possible that coarticulation is favoured for perceptual reasons' since it helps the listener to identify the chain of phonemes being produced more quickly (1999: 29).[9]

Coarticulated consonants in sung Italian

A list of consonants that are coarticulated in sung Italian is provided in Table 3. This includes all combinations of coarticulated consonants in spoken *italiano neutro*, as outlined by Canepari and Giovannelli (2012: 58, 65), in addition to those that are recommended for singers in the Melofonetica Method. These combinations are explored in further detail in the numbered sections that follow the table.

There is an additional category of coarticulation in Italian that relates to the type of phonation. In spoken Italian, where *s* is followed by *b, d, g, l, m, n, r* or *v* (all voiced consonants), it becomes voiced [z]. However, in sung Italian, it is advisable to articulate *s* as unvoiced [s] in all groups of consonants. See Note 8, '*s* as unvoiced [s] or voiced [z]', in Appendix A.

---

8. Barbara Kühnert and Francis Nolan, 'The Origin of Coarticulation', in *Coarticulation: Theory, Data and Techniques*, ed. by William J. Hardcastle and Nigel Hewlett, © Cambridge University Press 1999. Reproduced with permission of Cambridge University Press through PLSclear.

9. See note 8 above.

Table 3. Coarticulated consonants in sung Italian.

		Followed by	Becomes
1.	*l*	*c* as [tʃ]/*g* as [dʒ]/*sc* as [ʃ]	Post-alveolar [l̠]
2.	*l*	*d*/*s*/*t*/*z*	Denti-alveolar [l̪]
3.	*l*	*gl* as [ʎ]/*gn*	Palatal [ʎ]
4.	*m*	*l*/*n*/*r*	Alveolar [n]
5.	*m*/*n*	*c* as [tʃ]/*g* as [dʒ]/*sc* as [ʃ]	Post-alveolar [n̠]
6.	*m*/*n*	*c* as [k]/*g* as [g]/*q*	Velar [ŋ]
7.	*m*/*n*	*d*/*s*/*t*/*z*	Denti-alveolar [n̪]
8.	*m*/*n*	*gl* as [ʎ]/*gn*	Palatal [ɲ]
9.	*m*/*n*	*f*/*v*	Labio-dental [ɱ]
10.	*n*	*b*/*m*/*p*	Bilabial [m]

1. When *l* is followed by *c* as [tʃ], *g* as [dʒ] or *sc* as [ʃ], it becomes post-alveolar [l̠], for example in:
   - *dolce dir* [dol̠ː tʃeː ˈdir]
   - *nel giardin* [nel̠ː dʒarː ˈdin]
   - *mal sciablar* [mal̠ː ʃaː ˈblar]

   See Figures 44 to 46.

🎧 Figure 44. In *dolce dir*, *l* before *c* [tʃ] becomes post-alveolar [l̠].

nel   giar - din
[neɭ: dʒar: din]

🎧 Figure 45. In *nel giardin*, *l* before *g* [dʒ] becomes post-alveolar [ɭ].

mal   scia - blar
[maɭ: ʃa: blaɾ]

🎧 Figure 46. In *mal sciablar*, *l* before *sc* [ʃ] becomes post-alveolar [ɭ].

2. When *l* is followed by *d*, *s*, *t* or *z*, it becomes denti-alveolar [l̪], for example in:
   - *tal dolor* [tal̪: do: 'loɾ]
   - *al signor* [al̪: siɲ: 'ɲoɾ]
   - *saltellar* [sal̪: tel: 'laɾ]
   - *balza su* [bal̪: tsa: 'su]

See Figures 47 to 50.

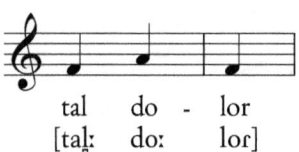

tal   do -   lor
[tal̪: do: loɾ]

🎧 Figure 47. In *tal dolor*, *l* before *d* becomes denti-alveolar [l̪].

al   si -   gnor
[al̪:   siɲ: ɲoɾ]

🎧 Figure 48. In *al signor*, *l* before *s* becomes denti-alveolar [l̪].

🎧 Figure 49. In *saltellar*, *l* before *t* becomes denti-alveolar [l̪].

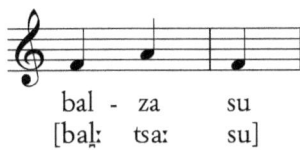

🎧 Figure 50. In *balza su*, *l* before *z* becomes denti-alveolar [l̪].

3. When *l* is followed by *gl* as [ʎ] or *gn*, it becomes palatal [ʎ], for example in:
   - *sol gli dà* [soʎ: ʎi: ˈda]
   - *quel gnaular* [kueʎ: ɲau: ˈlar]
   See Figures 51 and 52.

🎧 Figure 51. In *sol gli dà*, *l* before *gl* [ʎ] becomes palatal [ʎ].

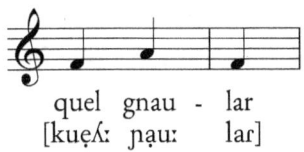

🎧 Figure 52. In *quel gnaular*, *l* before *gn* becomes palatal [ʎ].

4. When *m* is followed by *l*, *n* or *r*, it becomes alveolar [n], for example in:
   - *stiam laggiù* [sː ti̯an̠ː ladʒː 'dʒu]
   - *siam noi sol* [si̯an̠ː no̯iː 'sol]
   - *diam ragion* [di̯an̠ː ɾaː 'dʒon]

   See Figures 53 to 55.

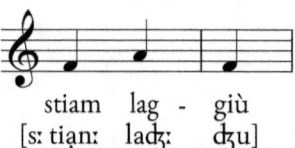

🎧 Figure 53. In *stiam laggiù*, *m* before *l* becomes alveolar [n].

🎧 Figure 54. In *siam noi sol*, *m* before *n* becomes alveolar [n].

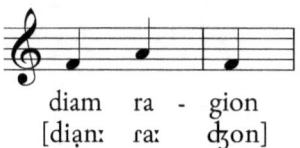

🎧 Figure 55. In *diam ragion*, *m* before *r* becomes alveolar [n].

5. When *m* or *n* are followed by *c* as [tʃ], *g* as [dʒ] or *sc* as [ʃ], they become post-alveolar [ɲ], for example in:
   - *siam giovial* [si̯aɲː dʒoː 'vi̯al]
   - *vincerò* [viɲː tʃeː 'ɾo]
   - *non sciupar* [noɲː ʃuː 'paɾ]

   See Figures 56 to 58.

🎧 Figure 56. In *siam giovial*, *m* before *g* [dʒ] becomes post-alveolar [ɲ].

🎧 Figure 57. In *vincerò*, *n* before *c* [tʃ] becomes post-alveolar [ɲ].

🎧 Figure 58. In *non sciupar*, *n* before *sc* [ʃ] becomes post-alveolar [ɲ].

6. When *m* or *n* are followed by *c* as [k], *g* as [g] or *q*, they become velar [ŋ], for example in:
   - *stiam così* [sː tiaŋː koː ˈsi]
   - *siam quassù* [siaŋː kuasː ˈsu]
   - *ringraziar* [ɾiŋː gɾatsː ˈtsiaɾ]

   See Figures 59 to 61.

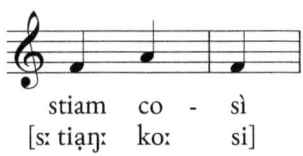

🎧 Figure 59. In *stiam così*, *m* before *c* [k] becomes velar [ŋ].

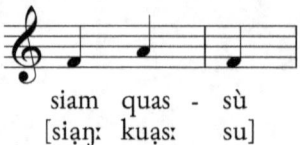

siam quas - sù
[siaŋ: kuas: su]

🎧 Figure 60. In *siam quassù*, *m* before *q* becomes velar [ŋ].

rin - gra - ziar
[riŋ: grats: tsiar]

🎧 Figure 61. In *ringraziar*, *n* before *g* [ɡ] becomes velar [ŋ].

7. When *m* or *n* are followed by *d*, *s*, *t* or *z*, they become denti-alveolar [n̪], for example in:
   - *stiam di là* [s: tian̪: di: ˈla]
   - *consolar* [kon̪: so: ˈlar]
   - *non tardar* [non̪: tar: ˈdar]
   - *siam zuccon* [sian̪: tsuk: kon]

See Figures 62 to 65.

stiam di là
[s: tian̪: di: la]

🎧 Figure 62. In *stiam di là*, *m* before *d* becomes denti-alveolar [n̪].

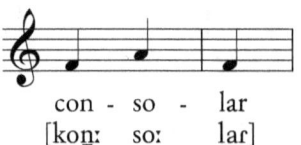

con - so - lar
[kon̪: so: lar]

🎧 Figure 63. In *consolar*, *n* before *s* becomes denti-alveolar [n̪].

🎧 Figure 64. In *non tardar*, n before t becomes denti-alveolar [n̪].

🎧 Figure 65. In *siam zuccon*, m before z becomes denti-alveolar [n̪].

8. When *m* or *n* are followed by *gl* as [ʎ] or *gn*, they become palatal [ɲ], for example in:
   - *vediam gnu* [veː diaɲː 'ɲu]
   - *son gl'attor* [soɲː ʎatː 'toɾ]

See Figures 66 and 67.

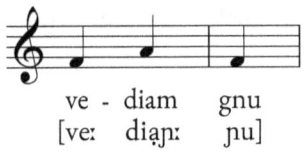

🎧 Figure 66. In *vediam gnu*, m before gn becomes palatal [ɲ].

🎧 Figure 67. In *son gl'attor*, n before gl becomes palatal [ɲ].

9. When *m* or *n* are followed by *f* or *v*, they become labio-dental [ɱ], for example in:
   - *abbiam fé* [ab: biaɱ: ˈfe]
   - *invitar* [iɱ: vi: ˈtaɾ]

   See Figures 68 and 69.

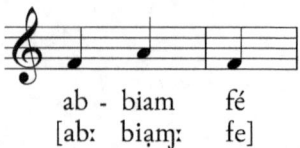

🎧 Figure 68. In *abbiam fé*, *m* before *f* becomes labio-dental [ɱ].

🎧 Figure 69. In *invitar*, *n* before *v* becomes labio-dental [ɱ].

10. When *n* is followed by *b*, *m* or *p*, it becomes bilabial [m], for example in:
    - *un balen* [um: ba: ˈlen]
    - *non mi dir* [nom: mi: ˈdiɾ]
    - *han pietà* [am: piɛ: ˈta]

    See Figures 70 to 72.

🎧 Figure 70. In *un balen*, *n* before *b* becomes bilabial [m].

🎧 Figure 71. In *non mi dir*, *n* before *m* becomes bilabial [m].

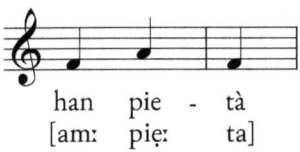

🎧 Figure 72. In *han pietà*, *n* before *p* becomes bilabial [m].

1.12 The three musical effects in sung Italian

The Italian language has an innate musical rhythm due to its sequences of long and short consonants and, specifically, the different ways in which consonants bridge vowels across syllables and notes. Listening closely to the phonetic patterns of sung Italian, it is possible to identify three different musical effects: *tenuto*, *staccato* and *martellato*.

Tenuto effect

Where two vowels are bridged by either a short consonant or a group of two short consonants, the first vowel occupies the full duration of the assigned note value. The short consonant, or group of two short consonants, is then articulated rapidly at the beginning of the following note. This articulation is so brief that there seems to be almost no interruption between the two vowels, creating an effect of *tenuto*, meaning 'held'. This effect also occurs where there are two or more consecutive vowels across two notes. The *tenuto* effect in the context of a line is shown in Figure 73.

Ferrando

U - n'au ra a - mo - ro - sa
[ʔː ʔuː nạːu raː moː roː sa]

From Mozart, *Così fan tutte*, Bärenreiter (2006: 158)

🎧 Figure 73. The *tenuto* effect, indicated with [–].

Staccato effect

A *staccato* effect is created where a vowel is followed either by a stop consonant or by a group of consonants containing a stop consonant. The *staccato* effect of stop consonants gives sung Italian an energised rhythm and serves as a contrast to the smoothness of the *tenuto* effect. The *staccato* effect in the context of a line is shown in Figure 74.

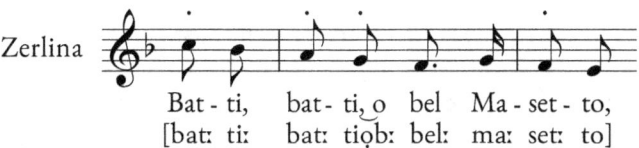

Bat - ti, bat - ti, o bel Ma - set - to,
[batː tiː batː tiọbː belː maː setː to]

From Mozart, *Don Giovanni*, Bärenreiter (2005: 155)

🎧 Figure 74. The *staccato* effect, indicated with [·].

Martellato effect

Martellato literally means 'hammered'. If we were to imitate the resonant sound of a hammer, we might use a sound such as 'bang' or 'tang'. These sounds end with a long sonorant (nasal) 'ng' that, being naturally quieter than the preceding oral vowel, creates a sudden *diminuendo*, similar to the reverberation of a hammer's blow. A similar effect is created with the natural *diminuendo* that occurs when a vowel is followed by any long sonorant or sibilant consonant. The *martellato* effect in the context of a line is shown in Figure 75.

Ah sì, ben mio; col - l'es - se - re
[asː siː bemː mjoː kolː lesː seː r̬e]

From Verdi, *Il trovatore*, University of Chicago Press and Ricordi (2002: 251)

🎧 Figure 75. The *martellato* effect, indicated with [∧].

Tenuto, staccato and *martellato* in sequence

Together, the three musical effects present in Italian text give the sung language its rich, varied texture and create contrast and interest in the musical line, as shown in Figure 76.

From Puccini, *La rondine*, Sonzogno (1917: 21)

🎧 Figure 76. The three musical effects in sequence.

The example in Figure 76 is a sequential repetition of a two-bar (two-measure) phrase, with no rhythmic variation. Each phrase begins with an identical *martellato* effect, created by the double *l* in *folle*. The second part of the first phrase contains only short consonants and is therefore rendered *tenuto*. The second part of the second phrase contains stop consonants at corresponding positions and is therefore rendered *staccato*.

In choosing these specific words and their precise metrical placements, the librettist has created a sense of development and growing intensity between *Folle amore!* [crazy love], and *Folle ebbrezza!* [crazy intoxication]. In keeping the two phrases rhythmically identical, Puccini has allowed the singer the opportunity to show this dramatic escalation through the contrasting effects inherent in the text.

1.13 The technical benefits of long consonants

Many singers and singing teachers view consonants as their enemies; however, given our understanding of the anatomy and physiology of articulation synchronized with good abdominal support, it is obvious that they can also be the singer's friend.

— Ron Morris and Janice L. Chapman (2017: 135)

Over the centuries, various methods of singing in Italian have made clear that there is a direct link between good diction and good singing technique. Good diction is integral to the much desired 'Italianate' way of singing, since good sung Italian diction requires the singing apparatus to behave in a way that is conducive to operatic singing.

Short and long consonants form the backbone of sung Italian and it is long consonants in particular that, when well articulated, bring a range of technical benefits. The value of correctly articulated long consonants has also been recognised in other sung languages, particularly German. For example, Margo Garrett, eminent collaborative pianist and educator, highlights the work of Martin Isepp, accompanist, conductor and vocal coach, with singers in German repertoire. She describes singers' revelation at how much the use of long consonants 'helps them enunciate, aids breath length, and magically makes for more lyric and colorful vowels, without ever discussing vowels at all' (2018a: 82).

Similarly, Richard Miller observes that 'consonants need not be considered unwelcome intruders that impede good vocalization' and that 'singers have long recognized the value of prefacing vowels with some specific consonant that improves subsequent timbre' (1986: 79).

Indeed, my extensive observation, combined with feedback from singers and coaches, has consistently shown that the correct production of long consonants in sung Italian improves the quality of ensuing vowels. When a singer correctly produces a long consonant, they find that the subsequent vowel is better supported, easier to produce and more comfortable, particularly in challenging passages with top notes. Listeners also notice a better projected, better pitched and more resonant vowel.

While scientific studies to explore these benefits in more detail would be worthwhile, vocal science already demonstrates a range of ways in which consonants are beneficial to singing technique, as discussed in the sections that follow.

Activation of the breath support

Consonants can be a powerful tool in enabling the singer to effectively activate their breath support: 'when a consonant is supported, the following vowel will also be "on the body"' (Morris and Chapman 2017: 135).

The long Italian sibilant consonants [s] and [ʃ] allow the singer to check that the abdominal muscles are engaged and that the air is flowing. Janice Chapman and Ron Morris describe a sequence of simplified Accent Method exercises that use fricative (constrictive) consonants, including [s] and [ʃ], that 'lead quickly into the location and recognition of abdominal support centers' (2017: 51).

Similarly, long sonorant consonants build awareness of breath support. A key sonorant consonant in sung Italian is the long rolled *r*. Miller observes that 'there is a marked sensation in the anterolateral abdominal wall during the execution of the prolonged tongue blade trill, as is also the case with nasal continuants' (1986: 94). This 'alerts the singer to sturdy appoggio engagement [...] [and] can spur good breath management' (2004: 98).[10] The production of long nasal consonants also creates 'heightened "support" sensations experienced in the torso, which are the result of total or partial closure of the mouth' (1986: 89).

Stop consonants are created by the complete occlusion of the airflow from the place of articulation. Research has shown that in the produc-

---

10. Richard Miller, *Solutions for Singers: Tools for Performers and Teachers*, Copyright © 2004 by Oxford University Press, Inc. Reproduced with permission of Oxford Publishing Limited through PLSclear.

tion of both voiced and unvoiced stop consonants, the respiratory system generates constant subglottal pressure (Löfqvist 1975). It can be assumed that this build-up of air pressure serves to activate the muscles involved in breath support. Indeed, my work with singers shows that when long stop consonants are correctly articulated in sung Italian, with length rather than strength, the quality of subsequent vowels is improved and singers experience a sensation of stronger, more engaged breath support and dynamism in the line.

Optimisation of the tongue position and pharyngeal space

The correct articulation of the continuous sequence of long and short consonants in Italian demands such control that the singer's back tongue (the rear area on the upper surface of the tongue, between the centre and root) must be in a high resting position in order to stay active. Morris and Chapman comment: 'The ideal for classical singing should be to acquire an Italianate position for the tongue. Studies have shown that the Italian language uses a higher back tongue resting position, which facilitates the speed and flexibility of the organ itself' (2017: 116). When non-Italian speakers practise good Italian diction, they will often notice the work that is demanded of the tongue.

In addition to its role in articulation, the Italianate setting of the tongue is conducive to operatic singing because it avoids constriction of the pharyngeal space. This helps singers to achieve the so-called 'loft resonance' which is 'created by re-laxing and enlarging the pharynx, and lifting the soft palate' (McCoy 2019: 5). Stop consonants are particularly helpful in this regard as the soft palate must lift in order to block the nasal passage, thus expanding and preparing the pharyngeal space to resonate well on the vowel that follows.

There are also various long consonants in Italian that help to reduce tongue root tension. The long rolled *r*, a sonorant trill, creates freedom in both the pharynx and tongue muscle and is described by Miller as 'one of the most important of all technical devices for inducing looseness of the tongue at both its frontal and its hyoidal extremities' (1986: 93). He explains: 'in order for the flapping motion of the tongue blade to take place, no tension may exist within the muscle bundles that make up the body of the tongue'. Miller also notes that vocalising exercises with the long nasal consonant *m* can help to eliminate tension in the tongue and soft palate (1986: 81).

Location of the best formant frequencies for operatic sound

The larger pharyngeal space encouraged by consonant production in Italian optimises the resonance space for operatic singing. The larger the resonating space, the lower the formant frequencies (the peaks of acoustic energy that give each resonant sound its characteristic quality). This is desirable for opera singers because the formant frequencies that characterise rich operatic sound have been found to be, on average, lower than those in other types of singing (Björkner 2008).

The long nasal consonants *gn*, *m* and *n* and the long lateral consonants *gl* and *l*, in particular, help the singer to find the low formant frequencies needed for the best quality of operatic sound. Indeed, Miller points out that:

> The main route of vocal pedagogy to which most professional singers of international stature adhere is based on resonance precepts of the historic Italian School as articulated in the second half of the nineteenth century and the early decades of the twentieth century. Nasal continuants play a major role in those concepts. (1986: 89)

The reason for this is that nasal consonants resonate through the nose instead of the mouth. The distance from the vocal folds to the nostrils is longer than that from the vocal folds to the lips, so nasal sounds benefit from a longer resonating tract than oral sounds. Similarly, lateral consonants are created by the tongue forming two curved pipes on each side of the mouth, so these consonants also have a longer resonating space than oral vowels. Resonating through a longer pipe means that frequencies are lowered when these consonants are produced (Johnson 2012: 136).[11]

An additional benefit of nasal and lateral consonants relates to the fact that the soft tissues involved in the production of these sounds, throughout the nasal cavities and under the tongue, are spongier than the hard palate and teeth. This environment allows for the absorption of vibrational energy, known as sound-damping (Johnson 2012: 186–87).[12] This has a similar effect to singing in a sound-damped studio, giving the singer a greater awareness of their own sensation of resonance, and helping them better control their sound. Exercises with *gn* [ɲ] are of particular benefit in this regard, as Miller explains:

> The ultimate location of high 'head sensation' is often experienced with the phoneme [ɲ], pinpointing a feeling of 'resonance' squarely in the center of the masque, or behind the nose, the eyes, or in some related area of the face, depending on subjective responses of the singer. (1986: 86)

Furthermore, the long grooved constrictive consonant *s* in Italian is articulated with a larger groove in the tongue than the English *s* (see Note 9, 'Long Italian *s*', in Appendix A). The Italian articulation creates more resonating space for the outward airstream and thus lower formant frequencies. Similarly, the long grooved constrictive consonant *sc* [ʃ], which is produced with a sublingual cavity and protrusion of the lips, adds length to the vocal tract, also helping to lower frequencies (Johnson 2012: 164–65).[13]

---

11. Used with permission of John Wiley & Sons - Books, from *Acoustic and Auditory Phonetics*, Keith Johnson, 3rd edn, 2012; permission conveyed through Copyright Clearance Center, Inc.
12. See note 11 above.
13. See note 11 above.

1.14 Vocalising with text

Pel Cantante vorrei: [...] esercizi di voce e parola con pronunzia chiara e perfetta.

[For singers, I would like: [...] vocal exercises using text, delivered with clear and perfect pronunciation.]

— Giuseppe Verdi in a letter to Senator Piroli, 20 February 1871, with his recommendations to the Italian government for improving teaching and learning in conservatoires (Verdi, Cesari, and Luzio 1913: 250)

Vocalising with Italian text is the most effective way to improve both diction and technique in sung Italian. Rather than exercises based solely on single phonemes, it is through singing complete words and lines, with all phonetic elements in context, that the singer gains a full awareness of how consonants affect vowels, how airflow is managed appropriately across different phonemes, and how the correct production of long consonants in particular benefits the production of ensuing vowels.

The pianist Martin Néron discusses the shortcomings, for students of lyric diction, of attempting to learn the pronunciation of a language through the imitation of sounds in isolation and out of context. He highlights the views on language learning of phonetician George Straka, who 'maintained that repeating an elongated and reinforced vowel sound was the most inaccurate way to teach a foreign sound system' since the articulatory apparatus behaves in a different way; 'the isolated vowel is deprived of a proper phonetic context [...] and therefore is difficult to render as it would naturally occur within a word' (Néron 2018: 175).

The use of vocalising exercises based on Italian words and phrases enables the singer to fully grasp the sequencing of long and short consonants and, over time, to build the correct proportions of consonant length into the aural and muscle memory. With the consistent practice of exercises such as those provided in this book, clear, idiomatic sung Italian diction becomes intuitive and spontaneous.

CHAPTER SUMMARY

▶ Consonants make up the majority of phonemes in the Italian language. They are either short or long, and their length can directly determine the meaning of a word ('distinctive duration'). The correct articulation of long and short consonants is fundamental to clear Italian diction – and also to resonant and expressive sung Italian.

▶ Long consonants are known as 'geminated' consonants in phonetics. The term 'gemination' comes from the Latin word *gemini* and means 'twinning' or 'doubling'. In practice, a long consonant in sung Italian can be up to five times longer than a short consonant.

▶ Short consonants are so brief that their onset and release are perceived as a single event. For a short consonant to be correctly articulated, there should be no audible holding of its sound.

▶ It is important that long consonants are differentiated from short consonants through the use of length, not strength: long consonants have an earlier onset than short consonants and an audible hold before their release.

▶ Across two consecutive notes, where a consonant occurs between vowels, a short consonant will always be as short as possible and belong entirely to the beginning of the second note, while a long consonant will have its onset and hold on the first note and its release at the beginning of the second note. The hold of a long consonant is proportionate to note duration.

▶ All single consonants that occur between vowels and within a word are short (except for *z*, which is always long). Short consonants can also occur at the beginning or end of words, and within groups of consonants (consonant clusters).

CHAPTER SUMMARY CONT.

▶ All written double consonants are long. There are also various types of 'hidden' long consonants that are written as single consonants but are lengthened when pronounced. These are: self-geminated, co-geminated, and post-geminated consonants, and consonants that are geminated when they form part of a group of consonants. There are also other consonants that can be lengthened for expressive emphasis, as will be discussed in Chapter 3, 'Expression'.

▶ Long consonants are categorised in the Melofonetica Method as sibilant (a continuous unvoiced sound), sonorant (a continuous voiced sound) or stop (with a silent hold before an unvoiced or voiced release).

▶ Groups of consonants contain two, three or four consecutive consonants and can occur within a word or across two words. In almost all groups of consonants, one of the consonants is long when pronounced. The placement of groups of consonants in notation differs according to the number of consonants in the group and whether the group contains a long consonant or not.

▶ Coarticulation occurs in some groups of consonants, where two consonants are articulated consecutively and the first assumes the place of articulation of the second. This facilitates a smoother transition between consonants. Coarticulation makes diction more fluid, avoids the production of evanescent ('ghost') vowels and prevents the creation of extra syllables that interfere with metrics and rhythm.

▶ In Italian pronunciation, coarticulation applies when *l*, *m* or *n* are followed by other specific consonants. This results in allophones (phonetic variants) of *l*, *m* and *n*.

CHAPTER SUMMARY CONT.

▶ Long and short consonants in Italian – and, specifically, the different ways in which they bridge vowels across syllables and notes – create three contrasting musical effects in sung Italian: *tenuto*, *staccato* and *martellato*.

▶ When correctly articulated, long consonants provide a range of technical benefits to the singer and improve the quality of ensuing vowels. Vocal science demonstrates that long consonants can help the singer to activate the breath support, optimise tongue position and pharyngeal space, and locate the best formant frequencies for operatic sound.

▶ Vocalising with words and lines of text, rather than single sounds in isolation, is the most effective way to improve sung Italian diction. This approach enables the singer to fully grasp the sequencing of long and short consonants, to experience how consonants benefit vowel production and, over time, to build the correct proportions of consonant length into the aural and muscle memory.

Vocalising exercises

🎧 1. Short consonants

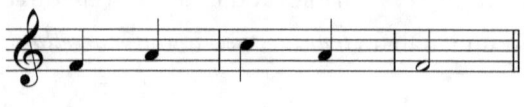

1. a - ma - bi - le
2. a - mo - ro - sa
3. or un' e - co
4. a - gi - ta - to cor
5. i pa - ci - fi - ci
6. ed i va - ghi

Transcriptions:
1. *amabile* [aː maː biː le]
2. *amorosa* [aː moː roː sa]
3. *or un eco* [oː ruː neː ko]
4. *agitato cor* [aː ɟiː taː toː kor]
5. *i pacifici* [iː paː tʃiː fiː tʃi]
6. *ed i vaghi* [eː diː vaː ɟi]

🎧 2. Sibilant consonants

1. ah s'u - scis - se
2. e - sci s'es - sa u - scì

Transcriptions:
1. *ah s'uscisse* [asː suʃː ʃisː se]
2. *esci s'essa uscì* [eʃː ʃisː sesː sa̯uʃː ʃi]

🎧 3. Sonorant consonants

1. am - ma - gliam - mo
2. a - gli‿a - gnel - li
3. o - gnun nar - rò

Transcriptions:
1. *ammagliammo* [am: maʎ: ʎam: mo]
2. *agli agnelli* [aʎ: ʎiaɲ: ɲel: li]
3. *ognun narrò* [oɲ: ɲun: nar: ro]

🎧 4. Stop consonants

1. e tu gab - bi
2. ah che dì fug - gì
3. o' che cep - po
4. e vez - zeg - gi

Transcriptions:
1. *e tu gabbi* [et: tug: gab: bi]
2. *ah che dì fuggì* [ak: ked: dif: fudʒ: dʒi]
3. *o' che ceppo* [ok: ketʃ: tʃep: po]
4. *e vezzeggi* [ev: vets: tsedʒ: dʒi]

🎧 5. Long consonants, various

1. a   pen - nel - lo
2. at - ter - ri   - sce
3. o - gni‿af - fet - to
4. as - sot - ti   - glia

Transcriptions:
1. *a pennello* [ap: pen: nel: lo]
2. *atterrisce* [at: ter: riʃ: ʃe]
3. *ogni affetto* ['oɲ: ɲi̯af: fet: to]
4. *assottiglia* [as: sot: tiʎ: ʎa]

6. Short vs. long consonants

1.	no	-	na,	non	-	na
2.	m'a	-	ma,	mam	-	ma
3.	pa	-	la,	pal	-	la
4.	ca	-	ro,	car	-	ro
5.	ca	-	sa,	cas	-	sa
6.	no	-	te,	not	-	te
7.	e	-	co,	ec	-	co
8.	tu	-	fo,	tuf	-	fo
9.	pa	-	pa,	pap	-	pa
10.	fa	-	ce,	fac	-	ce

Transcriptions:
1. *nona, nonna* [noː na: nonː na]
2. *m'ama, mamma* [maː ma: mamː ma]
3. *pala, palla* [paː la: palː la]
4. *caro, carro* [kaː ɾo: karː ro]
5. *casa, cassa* [kaː sa: kasː sa]
6. *note, notte* [noː te: notː te]
7. *eco, ecco* [eː ko: ekː ko]
8. *tufo, tuffo* [tuː fo: tufː fo]
9. *papa, pappa* [paː pa: papː pa]
10. *face, facce* [faː tʃe: fatʃː tʃe]

🎧 7. Improving the rolled *r*

This exercise is designed to help the singer to master or improve the rolled *r* in sung Italian. *Attra* [atː tra] is not a real word in Italian but a combination of phonemes that, when articulated correctly, facilitate the rolling of the *r*. The exercise can also be practised with other similar combinations of long *t* or *d* followed by *r*, with a long stop before the *r*, and using different vowels.

The stop *t* builds air pressure and triggers the flicking at the tip of the tongue. The place of articulation of the *t* (denti-alveolar) is already very close to that of the rolling *r* (alveolar), so the built-up air pressure goes directly to the correct area. The singer should make sure that the stop before the *r* is long and connected, that the tongue is relaxed, and that strong breath support and a steady airflow are maintained to enable the vibration to occur easily at the tongue tip.

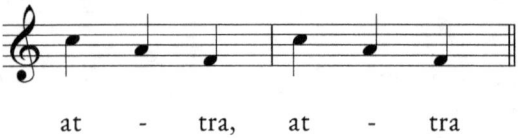

at - tra, at - tra

Transcription:
attra [atː traː atː tra]

🎧 8. Short and long consonants, various

1. ah   se   tu   m'a - mi
2. bel - l'A - ma - ril - li
3. o'   pu - pil - let - te
4. che fi - lo - so - fi - co
5. ma   non ar - re - sa
6. o - gnor ac - co - glie - re

Transcriptions:
1. *ah se tu m'ami* [aː seː tuː maː mi]
2. *bell'Amarilli* [belː laː maː ɾilː li]
3. *o' pupillette* [oː puː pilː letː te]
4. *che filosofico* [keː fiː loː soː fiː ko]
5. *ma non arresa* [maːn noː naɾː ɾeː sa]
6. *ognor accogliere* [oɲː ɲoː ɾakː koʎː ʎeː ɾe]

🎧 9. Groups of consonants

1.	al - ma	for	-	te
2.	a - vrà	pre	-	sto
3.	sol fra	l'om	-	bra
4.	con lor	stra	-	li
5.	or nel	pal	-	co
6.	cor sprez - za		-	sti

Transcriptions:
1. *alma forte* [alː maː forː te]
2. *avrà presto* [aː vrapː presː to]
3. *sol fra l'ombra* [solː fralː lomː bra]
4. *con lor strali* [konː lorsː traː li]
5. *or nel palco* [orː nelː palː ko]
6. *cor sprezzasti* [korsː pretsː tsasː ti]

🎧 10. Groups of consonants with coarticulation

1.	ful - gi - do	sal	-	ce	
2.	il	sol te'l	di	-	ce
3.	e	mal gli	par	-	la
4.	fac - ciam	no	-	to	
5.	an - gel	in	cie	-	lo
6.	un	cor	in - gra	-	to
7.	son	sen - z'in -	ten	-	ti
8.	ma	son gl'a -	mi	-	ci
9.	in - ver	in -	fo	-	ca
10.	con	man pon	bat - te - re		

Transcriptions:
1. *fulgido salce* [ful̪: ʤi: do: sal̪: ʧe]
2. *il sol te'l dice* [il̪: sol̪: tel̪: di: ʧe]
3. *e mal gli parla* [em: maʎ: ʎi: par: la]
4. *facciam noto* [faʧ: ʧan: no: to]
5. *angel in cielo* [aɲ: ʤe: liɲ: ʧe: lo]
6. *un cor ingrato* [uŋ: ko: ɾiŋ: gra: to]
7. *son senz'intenti* [son̪: sen̪: tsin̪: ten̪: ti]
8. *ma son gl'amici* [mas: soʎ: ʎa: mi: ʧi]
9. *inver infoca* [iŋ: ve: ɾiŋ: fo: ka]
10. *con man pon battere* [kom: mam: pom: bat: te: ɾe]

CHAPTER 2

Vowels

> **LEARNING OUTCOMES**
>
> *By the end of this chapter, you should be able to:*
>
> 1. Explain the concept of archi-vowels in sung Italian
> 2. Describe the roles of resonance, dynamics and timbre in vowel modification
> 3. Explain why the application of open and closed vowels is not necessary or beneficial in sung Italian
> 4. Identify and correctly articulate groups of vowels, applying the rules of vowel prioritisation as appropriate
> 5. Recognise diacritic *i* in groups of vowels
> 6. Determine where and how to apply vowel elision

This chapter explores the flexibility in sung Italian to colour vowels according to the requirements of resonance, dynamics and timbre. This allows singers to shape their interpretation through their own innate vocal nature, technique and musicianship. Comprehensive guidance is also provided on prioritisation in groups of vowels (two or more consecutive vowels occurring on the same note), including the use of vowel elision.

Vowel length is not discussed here since, as seen in Chapter 1, consonant length and note duration naturally determine the length of vowels (though note that the term 'long vowel' is occasionally used in Chapter 3 to identify a vowel that is not followed by a long consonant and is therefore sustained for the duration of a note).

2.1 The five archi-vowels

In spoken *italiano neutro*, there are nine vowel sounds (vocoids): *a* [a], *e* [ɛ] (open), *e* [ᴇ] (intermediate, i.e. a sound that is neither open nor closed), *e* [e] (closed), *i* [i], *o* [ɔ] (open), *o* [ʊ] (intermediate), *o* [o] (closed) and *u* [u]. In practice, there are many factors that modify spoken vowel sounds, including regional accent, expression, emphasis and speed of enunciation (Canepari and Giovannelli 2012: 50–52).

In sung language, vowel sounds have even greater flexibility. Scott McCoy points out that:

> Vowels morph from one to another as the scale ascends [...] regardless of how hard you try to maintain the purity of the vowel. [...] Whether they know it or not, all singers modify their vowels to one degree or another. Formant locations constantly are shifted during singing to optimize timbre and sound output. (2019: 94)

The Melofonetica Method recognises that for each of the five written Italian vowels, *a, e, i, o* and *u*, there is a wide spectrum of corresponding sung sounds (beyond the nine spoken vocoids) and that a sung Italian vowel can be anywhere within each range. These five spectra of vowel sounds are therefore referred to as 'archi-vowels'.

The five archi-vowels also comprise all vowels that carry accents in spelling, i.e. *à, è, é, ì, ò, ó* and *ù*. In certain words in spoken Italian, these accents serve to indicate a stressed syllable and, where relevant, the opening or closing of *e* or *o*, but these distinctions are transcended in sung Italian.

As will be seen in the sections that follow, the idea that open and closed *e* and *o* vowels, or specific timbres of *a, i* and *u*, are characteristic of good sung Italian diction, or result in an idiomatic Italian sound, is a misconception. Particularly in light of the fact that Italian retained from Latin the distinctive duration of consonants and lost the distinctive duration of vowels, good articulation in sung Italian relies upon the correct articulation of consonants while vowels may be shaped according to resonance, dynamics and timbre, without affecting the quality of diction or comprehension of words in context. This applies throughout all vocal registers and in all repertoire, whether arias, recitatives or ensembles.

Flexibility in vowel articulation

The vocograms in Figure 77 show, in a simplified form, the spectrum of sound for each of the five archi-vowels in sung Italian. These tables are based on Luciano Canepari's vocograms, which show the phonetic variants of all vowel sounds (2007: 115). The table on the left shows unrounded sounds, produced with relaxed lips. The table on the right shows rounded sounds, produced with protruded lips. The columns from left to right indicate the horizontal position of the tongue, from front through the centre to back. The rows from top to bottom indicate the vertical position of the tongue, from high to low.

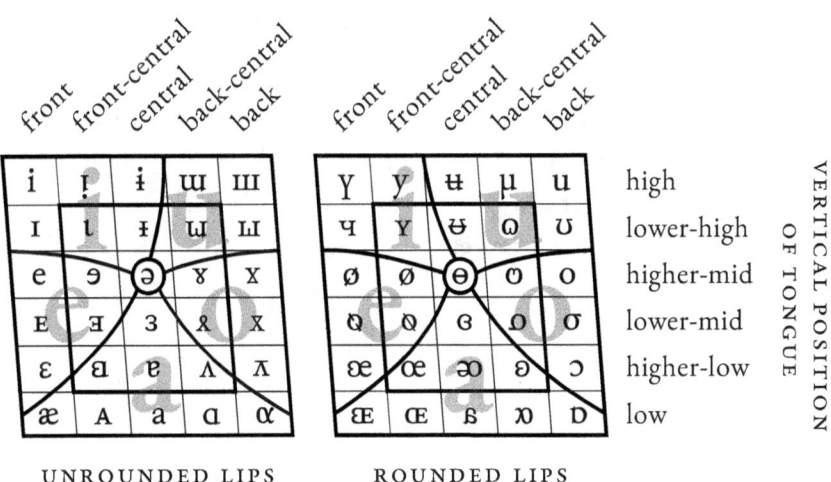

Figure 77. Vocograms showing the range of vowel variants within the five archi-vowels. Adapted with kind permission of Luciano Canepari and Lincom, from *Natural Phonetics & Tonetics: Articulatory, Auditory, & Functional*, 2007.

The vocoids around the outer edges of each table are quite distinct from one another and correspond to speech level in *italiano neutro* (the nine vowels of spoken Italian can be found here). Moving towards the centre of each table, there is increasing similarity in the sounds as they progress through the middle register and finally reach the uppermost notes of the high register, represented by the central vocoid, where all the sounds converge. The areas for each archi-vowel are labelled in large grey font and approximate boundaries between each are shown with a curved line. An inner grid is also marked, showing where sung vowels are more likely to occur.

The 60 vocoids shown in Figure 77 cannot fully represent all of the nuances that are possible within each phoneme. As Canepari explains, there are in fact 'somewhere from 500 to 1,000 possible vowel sounds' (2017: 124). Indeed, sung vowel sounds are modified by more than just tongue or lip position; movements of other articulators, such as the jaw or larynx, can also modify the sound (McCoy 2019: 84).

IN MELOPHONETIC TRANSCRIPTION

For practical purposes, the five sung Italian archi-vowels are represented simply with the five symbols [a], [e], [i], [o] and [u] – acknowledging that the individual singer will have an expansive target area for each sung Italian vowel.

2.2 Vowel modification

Resonance, dynamics and timbre are interdependent but, for simplicity, the roles that they play in shaping sung vowels are discussed individually in the sections that follow.

Resonance

Resonance is dependent on the unique nature of each singer's vocal apparatus. Singing technique then builds upon nature. There are different approaches, with some schools of thought favouring a dark sound and others prioritising brightness. This can be for aesthetic reasons, or due to traditional or modern methods of building the operatic voice.

Many studies have established that, for good resonance, a certain amount of vowel modification is needed, according to the register (low, middle or high). In *Coffin's Sounds of Singing* (2002), Berton Coffin sets out his 'Chromatic Vowel Chart for Voice Building and Tone Placing'. This shows the resonance tracking of vocoids, i.e. which vowel sounds produce the best resonance at each pitch. However, Ingo R. Titze observes that this process is not necessarily so linear given that, 'unlike in a woodwind or brass instrument, where the horn is long and steady in its geometry, the vocal tract in humans is relatively short and constantly changing due to articulation of phonemes' (2007: 199). There are also other variables involved; in his article 'Vowel Modification Revisited', John Nix notes that 'the amount of modification needed varies with the size of the voice, the "weight" of the voice, the duration of the note being considered, the dynamic level, and how the note in question is approached' (2004: 173).

Furthermore, the emotional and physical state of the singer will also impact vowel articulation. Vowel sounds will naturally differ from one performance to the next (García Jr. 1847: II. 2) and may even change during the day depending on how much the singer has warmed up (Nix 2004: 173).

Dynamics

Dynamics and dynamic variation, i.e. the use of *piano, forte, crescendo* and *diminuendo*, will naturally require an expansion or reduction in the spaces within the vocal apparatus. This affects the timbre of vowel sounds and how they are shaped (Appelman 1986: 221).[14]

Dynamic variation also plays a significant role in creating *chiaroscuro* timbral effects, as noted in the Tommaseo-Bellini dictionary definition of *chiaroscuro* (Rossi 1865: 1389 citing Galeazzi 1791: 202).

Timbre

> *Les timbres font si essentiellement partie du discours, ils sont la condition si vraie d'un sentiment sincère, qu'on ne saurait en négliger le choix sans tomber infailliblement dans le faux. Ce sont eux qui révèlent le sentiment intime que les paroles n'expriment pas toujours suffisamment.*
>
> [Timbres are such an important part of singing, and so necessary to convey sincere sentiment, that to neglect their choice would be infallibly wrong. It is timbres that reveal the intimate feelings that words do not always adequately express.]
>
> — Manuel García Jr. (1847: II. 54)

The choice of vowel timbre is a musical and theatrical decision to produce a specific tone that is appropriate to both character and drama. A dark sound can be warm, seductive or anxious; a bright sound can be aggressive, comic or joyful. A comic moment might require a nasal sound, or a breathy sound might be employed in a moment of suffering. These decisions can be explored in collaboration with director, coach and conductor, in line with the nature of the individual singer's voice and technique.

---

14. Used with permission of Indiana University Press, from *The Science of Vocal Pedagogy: Theory and Application*, Ralph Dudley Appleman, 1986; permission conveyed through Copyright Clearance Center, Inc.

2.3 Open and closed vowels

The punctilious singer or coach looking for consistency in this matter of the Italian e – o *vowels will be totally frustrated, as there is no consistency possible, and certainly no inflexible rules to be followed. Italian singers have used, do use, and <u>will</u> continue to use these* e – o *vowels to suit their VOCAL NEEDS, and not their VOCALIC (vowel) preferences.*

— Nico Castel (2000: xviii)[15]

Nico Castel's accurate observations, based on his extensive experience as a comprimario tenor and three decades of service as staff diction coach at the Metropolitan Opera in New York, are noted in the preface of all of his Italian libretto transcriptions. They are supported by what is now a vast body of recorded material, accumulated over more than a century.

It is evident that the spoken-language rules for open and closed vowels are not observed in the greatest performances of sung Italian. The following sections explore the reasons that this has been, and should continue to be, the case.

Comprehension

Variation in vowel length or timbre does not change meaning in Italian (barring the few exceptions discussed below) or jeopardise the comprehension of words in context.

While there are a few words in Italian whose meaning can change according to open or closed vowels (for example, *è/e* [ɛ/e], *o/ho* [ɔ/o], *pesca* [ˈpɛska/ˈpeska] and *volto* [ˈvɔltɔ/ˈvoltɔ]), in practice, regional accents override what is considered correct in *italiano neutro*, rendering these variations interchangeable. Furthermore, there are various examples of such words where both open and closed vowels are acceptable variants, as

---

15. Used with the permission of Leyerle Publications, www.leyerlepublications.com © Copyright 2000 Leyerle Publications.

seen in Canepari's *Dizionario di pronuncia italiana: Il DiPI* [Dictionary of Italian pronunciation: The DiPI] (2009). Examples include *lettera* [ˈlettɛra/ˈlɛttɛra], *fedele* [fɛˈdelɛ/fɛˈdɛlɛ], *nome* [ˈnomɛ/ˈnɔmɛ] and *proposta* [prɔˈposta/prɔˈpɔsta]. Ultimately, all of these words are naturally understood in context.

McCoy observes that it is consonants and context that 'often help text remain intelligible even at high fundamental frequencies' (2019: 95). Indeed, in sung Italian the most important elements for comprehension are consonant length and context. While modification of vowel sounds may present challenges in languages where the length and/or timbre of vowels are fundamental for delivering meaning, in Italian this is not the case and text comprehension is not affected when vowel sounds vary.

Variability according to ictus and neighbouring sounds

While dictionary definitions provide information on open and closed *e* and *o* vowels, these consider individual words in isolation. In *italiano neutro*, open and closed vowels only occur on the stressed syllable in a word and the remaining unaccented vowels are intermediate sounds. For example, in the words *donna*, *è* and *mobile*, the *Dizionario di pronuncia italiana* tells us that the *o* in both *donna* and *mobile* are open, as is the *è* (Canepari 2009: 223, 342, 227).

In the context of phrases, however, open and closed vowels are dependent on where the predominant rhythmical or metrical stress (ictus) of the sentence lies. When *la donna è mobile* is produced as a complete (spoken) phrase, the main ictus lies on the *o* in *mobile*. This therefore remains open while the *o* in *donna* and the *è* become unstressed syllables and thus intermediate sounds.

Furthermore, as discussed in Section 1.11, 'Coarticulation of consonants', in a chain of speech – and, by extension, a chain of sung text – consecutively produced sounds affect and alter one another. As Italian linguist Pier Marco Bertinetto (2010) points out, 'se infatti isoliamo una [a] entro una catena fonica, rischiamo di non riconoscerla; ma se la ricollochiamo nel contesto in cui è stata prodotta, non abbiamo dubbi circa la sua identità' [if we isolate an [a] in a speech chain, we may not recognise the sound, but putting this back into context, we have no doubts about its identity].[16]

So, while a dictionary is a valuable tool, its usefulness is limited because of the complexities created by variability in accordance with phrasal stresses and neighbouring sounds.

Subjectivity of vowel perception

Within all sung vowels, whether open or closed, there is a combination of both bright and dark sound, or *chiaroscuro*. 'Brightness in the sound provides brilliance and carrying power; darkness provides warmth and fullness' (McCoy 2019: 5). In a complex operatic sound, sometimes the listener is more aware of brightness, while at other times they may perceive more darkness in the sound. Particularly when singers perform in larger spaces, the bright or dark qualities of vowels may also be perceived differently according to the listener's position in the auditorium (Moore 1983: 7).

Furthermore, singers do not experience their own vowels exactly as their listeners do. Given that high-frequency sounds, or the brightness (*squillo*) of the operatic voice, travel more directionally than lower frequencies, 'singers do not hear the true strength of their "ring" (singer's formant), especially in poor acoustic environments' (McCoy 2019: 445).

In summary, the acoustics of a performance space affect how a singer perceives their own vowel qualities, and this does not necessarily represent how listeners will experience the very same performance.

---

16. Used with kind permission of Enciclopedia Italiana Treccani. Any reproduction and/or use of this material that is not strictly for personal and private purposes is forbidden. Onward transmission online, or in any other form, is strictly forbidden.

Phonological irrelevance in poetry

Opera libretti are poetry. Notably, within the very strict rules of Italian metrics – and despite having been greatly inspired by Provençal poetry in the eleventh and twelfth centuries, which strictly rhymed open vowels with open, and closed with closed – the poets who built the Italian language disregarded the difference between open and closed vowels in rhyme. Pietro G. Beltrami points out that this was in fact already the case in medieval Latin poetry (2011: 208).

In his examination of Italian metrics, W. Theodor Elwert notes the particular care that Italian poets, as far back as the ancient Sicilian School, have taken with the purity of rhyme, yet they still consider rhyme to be perfect when open *e* and *o* are rhymed with closed *e* and *o*. For example, it is entirely acceptable to rhyme *core* (with an open *o*) with *amore* (with a closed *o*). Elwert points out the extent of vowel variation across dialects, and even among variants of the Tuscan dialect itself, explaining that these differences are phonologically irrelevant in Italian poetry (1984: 80).

Achieving clear, idiomatic sung diction

> *Acoustically, a sung phoneme is not the same as a spoken phoneme. [...] All sung sounds are modifications of speech sounds.*
>
> — D. Ralph Appelman (1986: 221)[17]

As discussed in this section, the production and perception of sung vowel sounds are, at any point, affected by a substantial range of interacting factors. Observation shows that any attempt to forcibly open or close *e* and *o* vowels in sung Italian in accordance with the spoken language is of no benefit to clarity of communication or the production of an idiomatic Italian sound. The result instead is usually a sudden over-brightening

---

17. Used with permission of Indiana University Press, from *The Science of Vocal Pedagogy: Theory and Application*, Ralph Dudley Appleman, 1986; permission conveyed through Copyright Clearance Center, Inc.

or over-darkening of timbre, which can be musically unexpected and technically unhelpful.

By seeking to make vowels conform to the rules of spoken *italiano neutro*, the singer is more likely to overlook the correct sequencing of long and short consonants, the fundamental element for clear and idiomatic Italian diction. Instead, the singer is encouraged to enjoy the freedom of colour and expression afforded to them within the five sung Italian archi-vowels.

2.4 Groups of vowels and vowel prioritisation

The term 'group of vowels' is used in the Melofonetica Method to refer to two, three or (more rarely) four consecutive vowels occurring on the same note. These can be in the middle of a word or across two, or even three, words. Examples include:

- *ai* in *mai*
- *eo* in *sempre onor*
- *iua* in *non più andrai*
- *iaea* in *l'aria è ancor*

The following system of vowel prioritisation has been created to identify which vowel in a group should take the majority of the note's duration.

Priority vowels should be audibly longer than other vowels in the group. Vowels that are not prioritised should be very short; these are therefore represented in the notation examples that follow as a demisemiquaver (thirty-second note) each. The priority vowel takes the remainder of the note value, excluding any space required for the consonants that follow. Where groups of vowels occur on notes of short duration and/or in faster tempi, prioritisation becomes obsolete since all vowels are sung rapidly.

In sung Italian, unless the group of vowels contains a stressed vowel, as discussed later in 'Exceptions: stressed vowels', all vowels (including those that are accented in written Italian) should be prioritised in the following order:

1. *a* 2. *e/o* 3. *i/u*

The vowels *e* and *o*, and *i* and *u*, share second and third places respectively. Where both *e* and *o*, or both *i* and *u*, occur in the same group, priority should be given to whichever of the two vowels occurs last. Likewise, if the same vowel appears more than once in the group, priority is given to whichever occurrence of the vowel comes last.

Note that in some groups of three vowels, and particularly in the rarely occurring groups of four vowels, the elision of one vowel is often advisable in order to render the syllable more fluid and idiomatic – see 'Vowel elision' later in this section.

The proportionate lengths given to vowels occurring on the same note are illustrated in Figure 78, while groups of vowels in different contexts are shown in Figures 79 to 86.

> IN MELOPHONETIC TRANSCRIPTION
>
> A dot is placed beneath the priority vowel in a group, for example [ai̯].

Figure 78. The proportionate lengths given to vowels occurring in different combinations within a crotchet (quarter note). For simplicity, these examples do not incorporate the placement of consonants. A group of four vowels is not shown here, since these groups are rare and vowel elision is usually advisable in such instances.

🎧 Figure 79. Priority on *a* in the group *ai* in *mai*.

🎧 Figure 80. Priority on *e* in the group *oe* in *vedo errar*.

🎧 Figure 81. Priority on *o* in the group *eo* in *sempre oprar*.

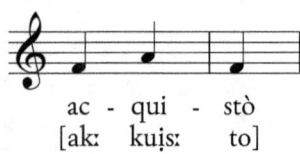

🎧 Figure 82. Priority on *u* in the group *iu* in *rifiutar*.

🎧 Figure 83. Priority on *i* in the group *ui* in *acquistò*.

🎧 Figure 84. Priority on *a* in the group *iua* in *più amar*.

🎧 Figure 85. Priority on *o* in the group *uoi* in *tuoi*.

🎧 Figure 86. Priority on *a* in the group *aei* in *pena ei*.

Exceptions: stressed vowels

There are some exceptions to the vowel prioritisation rules outlined in this section. These occur in words that contain two consecutive vowels, where one of the vowels takes priority because it is a stressed vowel. Exceptions only apply where the group of two vowels occurs entirely within one word and on a stressed beat or note of long duration (a full beat or more). In many instances, the composer will already have placed the vowels on separate notes, but, if not, it is important to be aware of where such exceptions may occur.

For example, in the word *mio*, the stress is on the *i*. If the group of vowels *io* occurs on a stressed beat or on a note of long duration, priority is given to the *i* instead of the *o*, as shown in Figures 87 and 88 respectively.

il   cor   mio
[il: kor: mi̯o]

🎧 Figure 87. Priority on *i* in the group *io* in *mio*, since this occurs on a stressed beat of the line.

il   mio   cor
[il: mi:o   kor]

🎧 Figure 88. Priority on *i* in the group *io* in *mio*, since this occurs on a note of long duration.

If, however, the group of vowels *io* occurs on an unstressed beat and this is also a note of short duration, priority is given instead to the *o* as per the rules of vowel prioritisation. This is shown in Figure 89.

il mio cor
[il: mio: koɾ]

🎧 Figure 89. Priority on *o* in the group *io* in *mio*, since this occurs on an unstressed beat that is also a note of short duration.

Table 4 provides a list of words that contain a stressed vowel in a group of two vowels, and therefore may not (depending on musical placement) follow the vowel prioritisation rules presented in this section. This list is not exhaustive and the singer is advised to consult a good Italian dictionary to identify other such words containing stressed vowels.

Table 4. Words that contain a stressed vowel in a group of two vowels.

Vowels	Examples
ae* [ae̩]	*attraente, maestro, paese, Raffaello, saetta*
ai [ai̩]	*Aida, aita*
ao [ao̩]	*baraonda, caotico, faraone*
au [au̩]	*balaustra, baule*
ea [e̩a]	*dea, Enea, idea, livrea, marea, rea*; verbs ending in *ea*, e.g. *crea, credea, dicea, volea*
ei [ei̩]	*inveire, reina*
eo [e̩o]	*babbeo, corteo, deo, ebreo, europeo, Galileo, imeneo, meteora, Orfeo, Perseo, plebeo, Pompeo, Romeo, torneo, trofeo*
ia [i̩a]	*allegria, arpia, balia, bramosia, bugia, cavalleria, cortesia, eresia, fantasia, fellonia, filisofia, follia, frenesia, gelosia, Lucia, magia, malia, malinconia, Maria, mia, nostalgia, osteria, pia, poesia, pria, profezia, ria, scia, simpatia, spia, via, zia*; verbs ending in *ia*, e.g. *fia, potria, sia*

Vowels		Examples
ie	[i̯e]	Plural forms of words ending in *ia*, e.g. *follie*
io	[i̯o]	*addio, brio, desio, Dio, etiope, fruscio, iddio, io, lavorio, mio, oblio, pendio, pio, rio, ronzio, trio, zio*
oa	[o̯a]	*oasi, boa*
oe	[o̯e]	*Cloe, eroe*
oi	[o̯i̯]	*moina, oboista*
ua	[u̯a]	*prua, sua, tua*
ue	[u̯e]	*bue, due, sue, tue*
ui	[u̯i]	*altrui, bui, colui, costui, cui, fui, lui, sui*
uo	[u̯o]	*duo, suo, tuo*

*Note that in the articulation of *ae*, the singer should avoid creating the approximant consonant *j*, i.e. this should not become [aje].

Mute *h*

Mute *h* is disregarded when it occurs within a group of vowels and does not affect vowel priority, as shown in Figures 90 and 91.

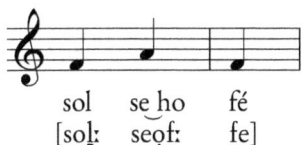

sol se ho fé
[soḷ: seo̯f: fe]

🎧 Figure 90. Priority on *o* in the group *eo* in *se ho*.

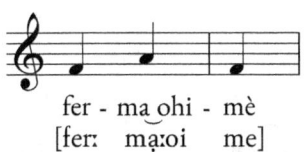

fer - ma ohi - mè
[fer: ma:oi me]

🎧 Figure 91. Priority on *a* in the group *aoi* in *ferma ohimè*.

Diacritic *i*

The letter *i* is sometimes a diacritic symbol, meaning it is not pronounced in its own right but instead signals a specific pronunciation of the preceding consonant. See Note 6, 'Diacritic *i*', in Appendix A.

Diacritic *i* can be found in the following combinations where they occur within a word (not across two words):

- *ci* + *a, e, o* or *u*, e.g. *cielo* ['tʃe: lo]
- *gi* + *a, e, o* or *u*, e.g. *gioco* ['dʒo: ko]
- *gli* + *a, e, o* or *u*, e.g. *soglia* ['soʎ: ʎa]
- *sci* + *a, e, o* or *u*, e.g. *usciamo* [uʃ: 'ʃa: mo]

When applying the rules of vowel prioritisation, diacritic *i* is disregarded, as shown in Figures 92 to 95.

nel   ba - ciar
[nel: ba: tʃar]

🎧 Figure 92. In *baciar*, the *i* is diacritic so this is pronounced [ba: 'tʃar] and no vowel prioritisation is needed.

col   gio - ir
[kol̬: dʒo: ir]

🎧 Figure 93. In *gioir*, the first *i* is diacritic so this is pronounced [dʒo: 'ir] and no vowel prioritisation is needed.

fi - glio è in   te
[fiʎ: ʎoe̯in: te]

🎧 Figure 94. In *figlio*, the second *i* is diacritic so this is pronounced ['fiʎ: ʎo]. In *figlio è in*, there are therefore three vowel sounds, *o*, *è* and *i*, and priority is given to the *è*.

la - scia in   mar
[laʃ: ʃaim: mar]

🎧 Figure 95. In *lascia*, the *i* is diacritic so this is pronounced [ˈlaʃ: ʃa]. In *lascia in*, there are therefore two vowel sounds, *a* and *i*, and priority is given to the *a*.

Note that in some words, the *i* is not diacritic, for example in *magia* [ma: dʒia] – see Note 6, 'Diacritic *i*', in Appendix A.

Double vowels

Where two identical vowels are adjacent and belong to one note, they merge to become one single vowel and should never be split with a glottal occlusive consonant [ʔ] or an in-breath. It does not matter if one vowel carries an accent – this applies in all circumstances (unless there is a deliberate pause for expressive reasons), as shown in Figures 96 to 98. In rarely occurring instances of three adjacent identical vowels that belong to one note, the same approach should also be applied.

mo - stra al - lor
[mos: traːl: loɾ]

🎧 Figure 96. The double *a* in *mostra allor* becomes one *a*.

no - me è   tal
[no: met: tal]

🎧 Figure 97. The *e* and *è* in *nome è* become one *e*. Note that distinct timbres do not need to be applied to distinguish *e* and *è*; see Section 2.1, 'The five archi-vowels'.

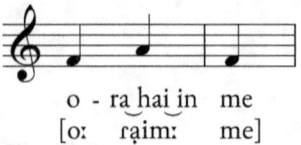

o - ra hai in me
[oː   ṛaimː   me]

🎧 Figure 98. In *ora hai in*, the *h* is mute, the double *a* becomes one *a* and the double *i* becomes one *i*. In *ora hai in*, there are therefore two vowel sounds, *a* and *i*, and priority is given to the *a*.

Punctuation within groups of vowels

Punctuation that occurs within groups of vowels on one note is usually disregarded and makes no difference to vowel prioritisation (unless there is a deliberate pause for expressive reasons), as shown in Figures 99 and 100.

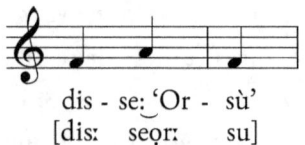

dis - seː 'Or - sù'
[disː   seọrː   su]

🎧 Figure 99. In *disse: 'Orsù'*, *eo* is a group of vowels; the colon and speech mark are disregarded and *o* takes priority.

cre - di, è a - mor
[kreː   dieạː   moɾ]

🎧 Figure 100. In *credi, è amor*, *ièa* is a group of vowels; the comma is disregarded and *a* takes priority.

Vowel elision

Where consecutive vowels occur on the same note but belong to different words, elision can be applied, which means omitting one of the vowels in order to make the phrase more fluid and idiomatic. This occurs frequently in spoken *italiano neutro* (Canepari and Giovannelli 2012: 82).

In many instances, vowel elision has become compulsory in both spoken and written Italian, for example in *l'amore* (instead of *lo amore*) or *c'ero* (instead of *ci ero*). Such occurrences in sung Italian will already be written in the score.

In other instances, vowel elision is optional and can be applied by the singer – as long as confusion is not created, particularly in slower tempi, regarding noun gender (masculine or feminine) or number (singular or plural). In faster tempi, there is more flexibility to use vowel elision, particularly where this facilitates space for the correct articulation of long consonants.

WHERE AND HOW TO APPLY VOWEL ELISION

Elision may be applied to the final vowel in any of the following:
1. The monosyllabic words *ci*, *di*, *gli*, *la*, *lo*, *mi*, *ne*, *si*, *ti* and *vi*. Examples are shown in Figures 101 and 102.

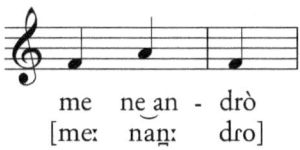

🎧 Figure 101. Elision applied to *e* in *ne*.

🎧 Figure 102. Elision applied to *i* in *si*.

2. The infinitive form of any verb, for example *dare*, *dire*, *essere* or *stare*. Examples are shown in Figures 103 and 104.

da - re al - men
[daː   ɾalː   men]

🎧 Figure 103. Elision applied to *e* in *dare*.

fa - re un   po'
[faː   ɾumː   po]

🎧 Figure 104. Elision applied to *e* in *fare*.

3. The commonly occurring words *alcuno*, *anche*, *ciascuno*, *come*, *grande*, *nessuno*, *quando*, *quanto*, *questo* and *senza*. Examples are shown in Figures 105 and 106.

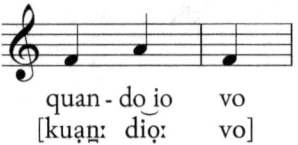

quan - do io   vo
[kuan̪ː   di̯oː   vo]

🎧 Figure 105. Elision applied to *o* in *quando*.

sen - za ur - lar
[sen̪ː   tsuɾː   laɾ]

🎧 Figure 106. Elision applied to *a* in *senza*.

Vowel elision is also preferable where a group of vowels contains the *i* in the article *il*. In this case, the *i* of *il* will always be the vowel that should be omitted. This occurs regularly in spoken Italian. An example in sung Italian is shown in Figure 107.

Figure 107. Elision applied to *i* in *splende il sol*.

In (rarely occurring) groups of four vowels, particularly in faster tempi, the use of vowel elision is often the most suitable and idiomatic way to articulate the line, as shown in Figure 108.

Figure 108. Elision applied to *a* in *aria*.

Groups of vowels in melismatic passages

Where a group of vowels is placed within a melisma (a syllable that spans two or more notes, usually of different pitch), the priority vowel should be placed on the first note, together with any preceding vowels, and it should take the majority of the melisma's duration. The placement of subsequent vowels is more flexible and subject to musical preference.

Approximant consonants [j] and [w]

In *italiano neutro*, where the vowels *i* and *u* directly precede another vowel, they are sometimes the 'approximant' consonant sounds [j] and [w]. The term 'approximant' describes a sound that is produced when two articulators come into close proximity but do not touch one another, creating only a slight obstruction to the airflow. For example:
- *i* in *piano* is [j] (palatal approximant)
- *u* in *uomo* is [w] (velar approximant with protrusion of lips)

Rarely, where *i* is the approximant [j], this can be found spelt with the letter *j* in scores, for example *jeri* instead of *ieri*.

There is no significant difference in the way the tongue articulates *i* as [i] or [j], or *u* as [u] or [w]; it is only speed of enunciation that creates approximant consonants. When we speak slowly or emphatically, approximant consonants are often vowels instead (Canepari and Giovannelli 2012: 63–64).

In sung Italian, approximant [j] and [w] only occur within groups of vowels on one note. The combinations of vowels within which *i* and *u* behave as approximant [j] and [w] are such that these are never given priority within the system of vowel prioritisation outlined in this section. This means that they are not given greater length than other vowels in a group and will automatically be articulated more rapidly as approximant consonants where appropriate. As long as the rules of vowel prioritisation are followed, there is nothing further that the singer needs to do. As such, approximant [j] and [w] are not marked in melophonetic transcription but are simply shown as the archi-vowels [i] and [u].

CHAPTER SUMMARY

▶ In spoken *italiano neutro*, there are nine vowel sounds: *a* [a], *e* [ɛ] (open), *e* [ɛ] (intermediate), *e* [e] (closed), *i* [i], *o* [ɔ] (open), *o* [ʊ] (intermediate), *o* [o] (closed) and *u* [u]. However, many factors modify spoken vowels, including regional accent, expression, emphasis and speed of enunciation (Canepari and Giovannelli 2012: 50–52). In sung Italian, vowel sounds have even greater flexibility.

▶ The Melofonetica Method recognises that for each of the five written Italian vowels, *a*, *e*, *i*, *o* and *u*, there is a wide spectrum of corresponding sung sounds (beyond the nine spoken vocoids) and that a sung Italian vowel can be anywhere within each range. These five spectra of vowel sounds are therefore referred to as 'archi-vowels'.

▶ The idea that open and closed *e* and *o* vowels, or specific timbres of *a*, *i* or *u*, are characteristic of good sung Italian diction is a misconception. Observation shows that any attempt to forcibly open or close *e* and *o* vowels in sung Italian in accordance with the spoken language is of no benefit to clarity of communication or the production of an idiomatic Italian sound.

▶ The choices that the singer makes within the five archi-vowels should be driven by the requirements of resonance, dynamics and the timbre that is appropriate to musical and dramatic content. Sung vowels need to be modified continuously by the singer in order to optimise these three factors.

▶ The term 'group of vowels' refers to two, three or (rarely) four consecutive vowels occurring on the same note, either in the middle of a word or across two or three words. The system of vowel prioritisation developed in the Melofonetica Method identifies which vowel in a group should take the majority of the note's duration, with vowels being prioritised in the following order: *a*, *e*/*o*, *i*/*u*. Exceptions occur in words

CHAPTER SUMMARY CONT.

that contain stressed vowels. Mute *h* and punctuation marks are disregarded when they occur within groups of vowels and do not affect vowel priority.

▶ The letter *i* is often a diacritic symbol in the following combinations where they occur within a word: *ci/gi/sci/gli* + *a*, *e*, *o* or *u*. In these instances, the *i* signals a different pronunciation of the preceding consonant and is disregarded in vowel prioritisation.

▶ Where two identical vowels are adjacent and belong to one note, they merge to become one single vowel.

▶ Where consecutive vowels occur on the same note but belong to different words, elision may be applied in some circumstances. This means omitting one of the vowels in order to make the phrase more fluid and idiomatic.

Vocalising exercises

🎧 Vowel prioritisation

1. giun - se al   mio   sen -   tier
2. sem - pre ai   prie - ghi or   vai
3. la   sua   fiam - ma in   cuor
4. sia   ch'io   pian - ga al - fin
5. mai   più i   suoi   pia -   cer
6. oh, il mio e - roe   qui   sia
7. dei   miei   gior - ni o -   mai
8. mer -   to o   no il   suo ar - dor
9. se il   suo a - mo -   re è   qui
10. l'a - ria è an - cor   nei   cuor

Transcriptions:
1. *giunse al mio sentier* [ʤuṇ: seal: mi̯o: seṇ: ti̯eɾ]
2. *sempre ai prieghi or vai* [sem: pre̯a:i pri̯e: gi̯oɾ: vai̯]
3. *la sua fiamma in cuor* [la: su̯a: fi̯am: ma̯iŋ: ku̯oɾ]
4. *sia ch'io pianga alfin* [si̯:a ki̯o: pi̯aŋ: gal: fin]
5. *mai più i suoi piacer* [ma̯i pi̯u:i su̯o:i pi̯a: ʧeɾ]
6. *oh, il mio eroe qui sia* [ol: mi̯oe̯: ɾoe: ku̯i̯s: si̯a]
7. *dei miei giorni omai* [de̯:i mi̯e:i ʤor: ni̯o: ma̯i]
8. *merto o no il suo ardor* [mer: ton: nol̩: su̯aɾ: doɾ]
9. *se il suo amore è qui* [sel̩: su̯a: mo: ɾek: ku̯i̯]
10. *l'aria è ancor nei cuor* [la: ɾi̯ea̯ŋ: kor: ne̯i: ku̯oɾ]

CHAPTER 3

Expression

> **LEARNING OUTCOMES**
>
> *By the end of this chapter, you should be able to:*
> 1. Begin each line with clear intention by applying the *attacco del suono*
> 2. Add emphasis to significant words using melo-gemination
> 3. Enhance expression through the use of the agogic accent
> 4. Incorporate rests and punctuation into diction
> 5. Recognise and highlight the 'Michelangelo effect', the melophonetic sequence at the heart of Italian style
> 6. Explain the concept of *notes inégales* as it applies to sung Italian
> 7. Discuss the concept of *canto legato* as referenced in eighteenth- and nineteenth-century Italian literature
> 8. Apply *portamento* appropriately
> 9. Describe the concepts of line and phrasing, and identify anchoring points in the text

The singer's sensitivity to text lifts his singing from mediocrity to inspired song; the words must not only be understood, they must become beloved.

— D. Ralph Appelman (1986: 191)[18]

The innate musicality in the Italian language has inspired poets and composers throughout the centuries. The meaning of the words and the rhythms of the librettist's carefully crafted text, both phonetic and metric, are the foundation of the composer's art. As meaning and sound in the language inspire and lead the work of librettist and composer, they also help to guide the singer in their creation of character and compelling drama. Through careful attention to diction, phrasing and expression, the singer 'emotionalizes and intensifies speech sounds, and he enables the listener to realize the meaning of the text' (Appelman 1986: 191).[19] The sections that follow discuss the key tools that help the singer to achieve this.

---

18. Used with permission of Indiana University Press, from *The Science of Vocal Pedagogy: Theory and Application*, Ralph Dudley Appleman, 1986; permission conveyed through Copyright Clearance Center, Inc.
19. See note 18 above.

3.1 The *attacco del suono*

La perfetta corrispondenza dell'azione col pensiero.

[The perfect connection of action and thought.]

— Gilda Dalla Rizza (cited in Dalle Fratte 2003: 338)

The *attacco del suono*, meaning the 'start of the sound', is a key element of expressive singing that has been mentioned in various methods and treatises over the centuries. When the singer begins each line with clear musical and dramatic intention, not only is it easier for the pianist or orchestra to follow that intention but there is also an immediate connection created with the audience.

In the Melofonetica Method, the *attacco del suono* is usually achieved by using a long consonant whenever the singer starts a new line or begins singing again after an in-breath.

Note that *attacco* here does not translate into English as 'attack' but simply means 'the start'. As discussed in Section 1.8, 'Length, not strength', the correct articulation of long consonants in sung Italian is achieved through applying length rather than force, and is independent from the use of dynamics. Whether the singer is singing *pianissimo* or *fortissimo*, the long consonant that creates the *attacco del suono* should still be applied in the same way.

How to apply the *attacco del suono*

The onset and hold of the *attacco del suono* are placed immediately following the in-breath, just before the first note, and the release occurs at the beginning of the first note. The proportional length of the hold is the same as that for any other long consonant between vowels and is adjusted according to tempo (see Section 1.9, 'Long consonants in notation') but can also be even longer to heighten suspense (see Section 3.3, 'The agogic accent').

The placement of the *attacco del suono* in notation is illustrated in Figures 109 to 111 with a long consonant placed between a crotchet rest (quarter rest) and a crotchet (quarter note).

Figure 109. *Attacco del suono* applied to the sibilant consonant *s* in *sì*.

Figure 110. *Attacco del suono* applied to the sonorant consonant *m* in *ma*.

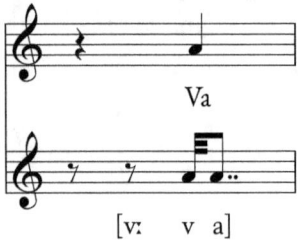

Figure 111. *Attacco del suono* applied to the stop consonant *v* in *va*.

The *attacco del suono* is applied in the same way to the first consonant in a group of two short consonants, as shown in Figure 112.

🎧 Figure 112. *Attacco del suono* applied to the group of two short consonants *tr* in *tra*.

Note that to correctly apply the *attacco del suono* to a word that begins with *s* followed by another consonant, it is always the second consonant that is lengthened, not the *s*, as shown in Figure 113. See 'How to apply melo-gemination' in Section 3.2 for further details.

🎧 Figure 113. *Attacco del suono* applied to the group of consonants *st* in *sto*.

Where the line starts with a vowel, the *attacco del suono* is applied by preceding the vowel with a long glottal occlusive consonant [ʔ], as shown in Figure 114.

🎧 Figure 114. *Attacco del suono* applied to the vowel *a* in *ah*.

Exceptions

1. An exception to the *attacco del suono* can occur where the first note is short in duration, for example, a semiquaver (sixteenth note) or less, or a crotchet (quarter note) or less in faster tempi, and is followed immediately by a long consonant that has its release on the second note. It is more comfortable in this case to use the long consonant that follows to set the intention of the line, as shown in Figures 115 and 116. However, if this long consonant is a co-geminated consonant, the singer can choose to de-geminate this in order to still apply the *attacco del suono* on the first note, both options are equally acceptable, as shown in Figure 117.

From Mozart, *Le nozze di Figaro*, Bärenreiter (2001: 341)

🎧 Figure 115. Double *f* in *Raffaello* sets the intention of the line rather than long *r*.

From Mozart, *Don Giovanni*, Bärenreiter (2005: 12)

🎧 Figure 116. Double *t* in *notte* sets the intention of the line rather than long *n*.

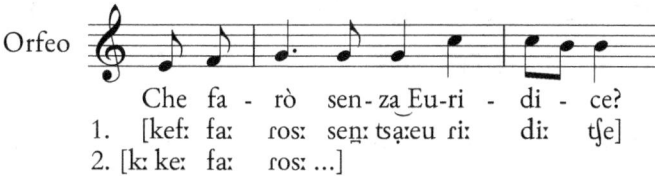

Che fa - rò sen- za Eu-ri - di - ce?
1. [kef: faː ɾɔs: sen: tsaːeu riː diː tʃe]
2. [kː keː faː ɾɔs: ...]

From Gluck, *Orfeo ed Euridice*, Vienna version of 1762, Bärenreiter (1962: 128)

🎧 Figure 117. In this example, the singer could choose to co-geminate the *f* in *farò* to set the intention of the line rather than lengthen the *c* [k] in *che*, or alternatively lengthen the *c* in *che* and de-geminate the *f* in *farò*.

In the same circumstances, where the line starts with a vowel, instead of applying a long glottal occlusive consonant [ʔ] before the vowel, it is preferable to use the long consonant that follows to set the intention of the line, as shown in Figure 118.

Ad - di - o,
[adː diː o]

From Puccini, *La bohème*, Ricordi (1961: 207)

🎧 Figure 118. The double *d* in *Addio* is used to set the intention of the line, rather than preceding the *a* with a long glottal occlusive consonant [ʔ].

2. Where the line starts with a vowel, instead of preceding the vowel with a long glottal occlusive consonant [ʔ], the singer may choose to begin with a breathy sound (*attacco aspirato*) for expressive reasons. This is achieved by preceding the vowel with the long glottal constrictive consonant [h].

3.2 Melo-gemination: the lengthening of short consonants for emphasis

Tous les mots énergiquement accentués ont de l'effet sur l'âme, parce qu'ils semblent dictés par une impression vive.

[All words that are emphasised with energy stir the soul, since they seem governed by intense feeling.]

— Manuel García Jr. (1847: II. 6)

In order to highlight a word or syllable (stressed or unstressed) that begins with a short consonant, in some instances it is possible to apply expressive emphasis by geminating the short consonant. For example, in *il padre*, the word *padre* may be emphasised by lengthening the *p* [ilp: pa: dɾe]. This type of emphatic stress is already present in idiomatic spoken Italian. In singing, it is a fundamental tool that singers often use instinctively to inject intensity at appropriate points in the text. In the Melofonetica Method, this expressive lengthening of short consonants is termed 'melo-gemination'.

Melo-gemination is similar to emphatic stress in other languages such as the lengthening of consonants in persuasive English (see Banzina 2016) or the *accent d'insistance* in sung French. Discussing the work of conductor, coach and pianist Pierre Vallet, Margo Garrett praises the transformative power of both the *accent d'insistance* in French singing and long German consonants, stating that:

> There is nothing more important to which a coach should aspire and labor than the thorough understanding of these two concepts and the identification in one's ears of the staggering powers they contain to aid a singer's ability, not just to be better understood, but to create a personal *defining* power over words. This power tells the listener not only what words *mean*, but what the singer *wants* the listener to believe about the meaning of words in the context of his or her wishes, interpretations, and desires. (2018b: 207)

Likewise, the use of melo-gemination – particularly in combination with the agogic accent, as will be seen in Section 3.3, 'The agogic accent' –

enables the singer to craft a more personal and convincing interpretation while guiding the listener to connect more profoundly with specific words and sentiments.

Where to apply melo-gemination

To identify where to apply melo-gemination, the singer firstly needs to have a good understanding of the meaning of the words in the piece and which words drive the drama. The first and/or subsequent syllables in these words are likely to have been highlighted musically by the composer through the expressive use of rhythm, melody, harmony, dynamics, tempo markings or other indications. These syllables will often be appropriate moments to lengthen short consonants through the use of melo-gemination.

Many composers, whether instinctively or consciously, appear to be drawn to the energy and accentuation of long consonants at significant points in each line – including those syllables where short consonants may be lengthened for expressive reasons. This is often evident where one or more of the following is used:
- A note of long duration
- A dotted rhythm or syncopation
- A tempo marking such as *rallentando*, *ritenuto*, *trattenuto*, *stentando* or *accelerando*
- A tonic accent created by an interval of a fourth or more (ascending or descending)
- A modulation (change in key) or dissonance
- A melisma, ornamentation or cadence
- A dynamic accent such as *forte*, *piano* or *pianissimo*
- An accent marking such as *marcato* or *sforzato*
- A rest

In contrast, there may instead be a noticeable absence of musical highlighting where significant words or lines occur. Such moments may be characterised by a simple melody and rhythm and/or the repetition of notes, often with a sparse accompaniment or no accompaniment at all.

It is particularly effective to apply melo-gemination to consonants that release on unstressed beats, in order to create the sequence of text described in the Melofonetica Method as the Michelangelo effect – see Section 3.6, 'The Michelangelo effect: the essence of Italian style'. Syllables that lend themselves well to the use of melo-gemination may also be appropriate points to simultaneously apply a suspensive agogic accent. This involves further lengthening a long phoneme in order to build suspense and intensify expressive effect, as will be seen in Section 3.3, 'The agogic accent'.

Note that the use of melo-gemination may or may not correspond to, and is independent of, the emphasis of stressed syllables in the spoken language – see Section 3.4, 'Stressed syllables'.

How to apply melo-gemination

Melo-gemination can be applied to some (not all) short consonants that occur at the beginning of a syllable. Melo-gemination should not be applied to single short consonants or groups of two short consonants that are within (rather than at the beginning of) a word; for example, it would be incorrect to melo-geminate the *m* in *amore* or the *d* in *vedrò*.

Melo-gemination may be applied to a short single consonant or the first consonant in a group of two short consonants at the beginning of a word, as shown in Figures 119 and 120 respectively.

From Donizetti, *L'elisir d'amore*, Ricordi (2005: 229–30)

🎧 Figure 119. Emphasis of *lagrima* [tear] through melo-gemination of *l*, triggered by the *marcato* marking (>).

Tu   fo - sti   tra - di - to:
[tuː   fosː   titː   traː   diː   to]

From Mozart, *La clemenza di Tito*, Bärenreiter (2001: 203)

🎧 Figure 120. Emphasis of *tradito* [betrayed] through melo-gemination of *t*, triggered by the dotted rhythm.

The singer may wish to apply melo-gemination to a short consonant that is part of a group where, ordinarily, the preceding consonant would be long (see 'Gemination in groups of consonants' in Section 1.10). In these instances, a 'switch' of gemination needs to occur whereby the consonant that would ordinarily be long is de-geminated (becomes short), making space for the melo-gemination to be applied instead to the consonant at the beginning of the syllable that follows. This switch of gemination also occurs naturally in expressive, idiomatic spoken Italian. Examples are shown in Figures 121 to 126.

🎧 Figure 121. Melo-gemination in the group *lm* in *alma*: *l* becomes short and *m* is melo-geminated.

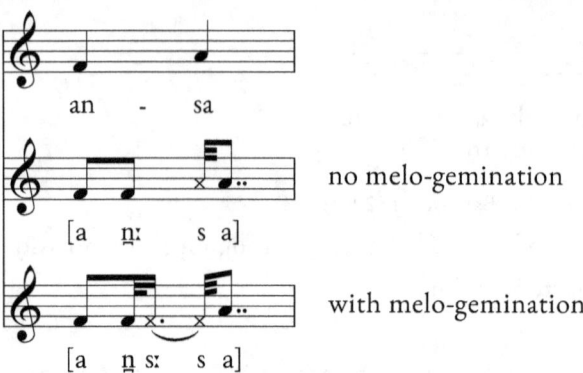

🎧 Figure 122. Melo-gemination in the group *ns* in *ansa*: *n* becomes short and *s* is melo-geminated.

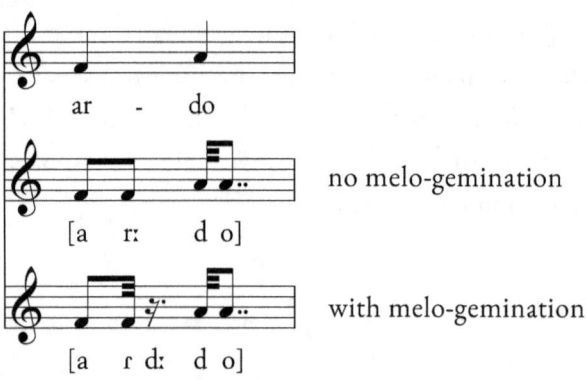

🎧 Figure 123. Melo-gemination in the group *rd* in *ardo*: *r* becomes short and *d* is melo-geminated.

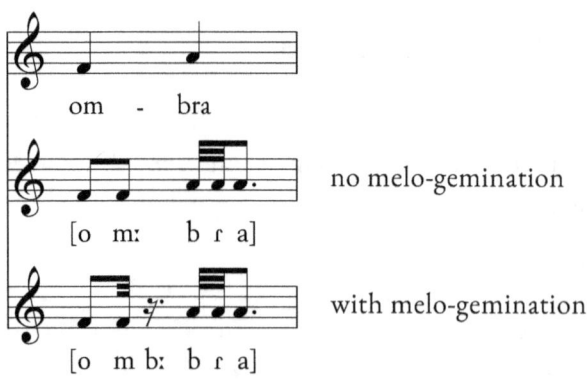

🎧 Figure 124. Melo-gemination in the group *mbr* in *ombra*: *m* becomes short, *b* is melo-geminated and *r* remains short.

From Mozart, *Don Giovanni*, Bärenreiter (2005: 345)

🎧 Figure 125. Emphasis of *vendicar* [to avenge] through melo-gemination of *d* in the group *nd*, triggered by the dotted rhythm: *n* becomes short and *d* is melo-geminated.

From Bellini, *I Capuleti e i Montecchi*, Ricordi (2003: 50–51)

🎧 Figure 126. Emphasis of *figlio* [son] through melo-gemination of *f* in the group *nf*, triggered by the tonic accent (descending perfect fourth): *n* becomes short and *f* is melo-geminated.

Note that, as mentioned in 'Gemination in groups of consonants' in Section 1.10, where *s* is ordinarily the long consonant in a group, its placement in the division of syllables traditionally used in Italian scores can be misleading as it is incongruent with the phonic syllable (the way that the syllable is pronounced). For example:

- *astro* is written as *a-stro* in scores but is pronounced ['as: tro]
- *la storia* is written as *la-sto-ria* in scores but is pronounced [las: 'to: ria]

The *s* should be aligned to the first syllable, while the consonant that follows begins the second syllable and is where melo-gemination should be applied. For example, applying melo-gemination correctly to *esca* would mean geminating the *c* (and de-geminating the *s*), resulting in ['esk: ka], as shown in Figure 127. Further examples are given in Figures 128 to 131.

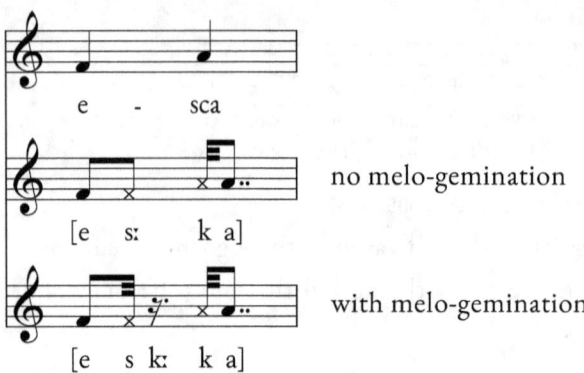

🎧 Figure 127. Melo-gemination in the group *sc* in *esca*: *s* becomes short and *c* is melo-geminated.

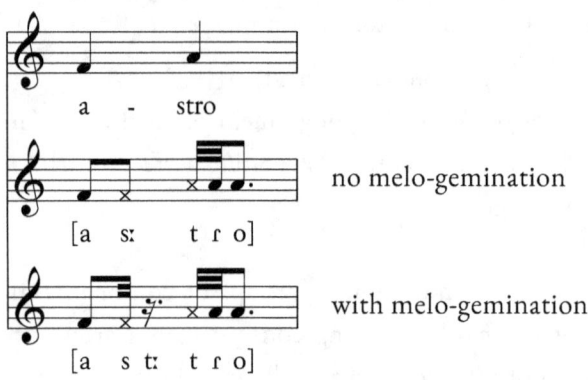

🎧 Figure 128. Melo-gemination in the group *str* in *astro*: *s* becomes short, *t* is melo-geminated and *r* remains short.

🎧 Figure 129. Melo-gemination in the group *lst* in *il star*: *l* remains short, *s* becomes short and *t* is melo-geminated.

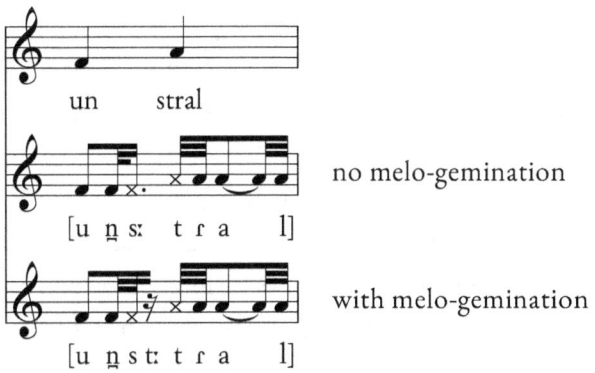

🎧 Figure 130. Melo-gemination in the group *nstr* in *un stral*: *n* and *r* remain short, *s* becomes short and *t* is melo-geminated.

From Bellini, *I puritani*, Naples version, Fondazione Claudio Monteverdi (2009: 277)

🎧 Figure 131. Emphasis of *speme* [hope] through melo-gemination of *p* in the group *sp*, triggered by the tonic accent (ascending major sixth): *s* becomes short and *p* is melo-geminated.

Applying melo-gemination where a-gemiination occurs

If the singer wishes to apply emphasis to the first short consonant of a word that follows an activator of a-gemination, i.e. the first consonant of the word in focus would ordinarily not be lengthened, melo-gemination may override the a-gemination in certain circumstances. This can apply where the composer has musically highlighted the syllable, as described previously in this section – see examples in Figures 132 and 133. It can also apply where the use of melo-gemination completes the sequence of text described as the Michelangelo effect – see Figure 168 in Section 3.6, 'The Michelangelo effect: the essence of Italian style'.

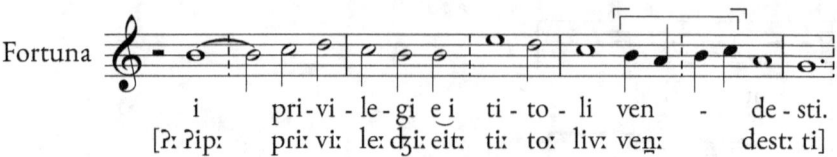

i pri - vi - le - gi e i ti - to - li ven - de - sti.
[ʔː ʔipː pri: viː leː dʒiː eitː tiː toː livː venː destː ti]

From Monteverdi, *L'incoronazione di Poppea*, Bärenreiter (2017: 3)

🎧 Figure 132. Emphasis of *privilegi* [privileges]: melo-gemination overrides the a-gemination of *p*, triggered by the note of long duration and syncopation; emphasis of *titoli* [titles]: melo-gemination overrides the a-gemination of *t*, triggered by the tonic accent (ascending perfect fourth).

La ca - lun-nia
[lː lakː kaː lunː nia]

From Rossini, *Il barbiere di Siviglia*, Ricordi (2014: 151)

🎧 Figure 133. Emphasis of *calunnia* [slander]: melo-gemination overrides the a-gemination of *c*, triggered by the note of long duration and dotted rhythm.

There are often instances where the composer has musically highlighted the activator of a-gemination rather than the word that follows. Where this is the case, melo-gemination can instead be applied to the first consonant of the activator. Activators of a-gemination are usually monosyllabic articles, prepositions or pronouns that are directly linked to the subsequent noun or verb, and as such their emphasis still serves to draw attention to the word that follows, as shown in Figure 134.

del Con - te la bel - la!
[delkː kontː telː laː belː la]

From Mozart, *Le nozze di Figaro*, Bärenreiter (2001: 58)

🎧 Figure 134. Emphasis of *la bella* [the beautiful one] through melo-gemination of the *l* in the article *la*, triggered by the dotted rhythm.

The first consonant of the activator of a-gemination may already be long due to co-gemination. In these circumstances, the singer *could* still apply additional emphasis to the word that follows through melo-gemination, but it is advisable to leave the emphasis on the activator, particularly where this falls on an unstressed beat, as shown in Figure 135.

From Puccini, *Turandot*, Ricordi (1926: 269)

🎧 Figure 135. Emphasis of *gel* [ice] already created through co-gemination of the *d* in the preposition *di* (*che* co-geminates with *di*).

Applying emphasis to a syllable beginning with a vowel

If the singer wishes to emphasise a syllable that begins with a vowel, this can only be done where the syllable occurs at the beginning of a word. If the word occurs at the beginning of a line, the guidance given in Section 3.1, 'The *attacco del suono*', should be followed. If the word occurs within a line, the vowel at the beginning of the syllable may be emphasised in the following ways, if applicable:

1. Where the preceding syllable ends with a vowel or a short consonant, a long glottal occlusive consonant [ʔ] may be applied prior to the vowel, as shown in Figure 136.

From Handel, *Rinaldo*, Bärenreiter (1998: 38)

🎧 Figure 136. Emphasis of *eventi* [events] through the use of a long glottal occlusive consonant [ʔ] before *e*.

If the vowel to be emphasised is followed immediately by a long consonant, it is only comfortable to use a long glottal occlusive consonant where the syllable occurs on a note of long duration.

2. Where the vowel is preceded by the euphonic *d* in *ad*, *ed* or *od*, melo-gemination of the *d* serves to emphasise the word that follows, as shown in Figure 137.

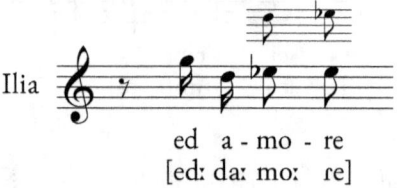

From Mozart, *Idomeneo*, Bärenreiter (2005: 15)

🎧 Figure 137. Emphasis of *amore* [love] through melo-gemination of the euphonic *d* in *ed*.

3.3 The agogic accent

In Italian, in addition to lengthening short consonants for emphasis (as discussed in the previous section), we may also increase the significance of a particular word or syllable through the use of volume, pitch or duration – or sometimes a combination of these. In music, these elements correspond to the dynamic, tonic and agogic accents respectively:

- A dynamic accent is created through a change in volume: *piano*, *forte*, *crescendo* or *diminuendo*. While this form of accent may often be notated, the singer is free to employ dynamics as an expressive tool.
- A tonic accent is created through the use of an interval that is significantly higher or lower in pitch. Tonic accents are most often notated by the composer, but they may also be added by the singer through the use of *appoggiatura* or other ornamentation.
- An agogic accent is created by extending or shortening the duration of a note. Agogic accents may be notated by the composer, but they may also be added by the singer for expressive emphasis.

Where the singer uses an agogic accent, this often results in *tempo rubato* (usually referred to simply as *rubato*). This literally means 'stolen time' and involves the singer creating slight variations in tempo and/or rhythm. Manuel García Jr. observes that *rubato* not only 'sert à rompre la monotonie des mouvements égaux' [breaks up the monotony of equal movements] but also 'favorise les élans de la passion' [helps the singer to express moments of particular passion] (1847: II. 24). Pierfrancesco Tosi even goes so far as to say that 'chi non sa rubare il tempo cantando, non sa comporre, né accompagnarsi, e resta privo del miglior gusto, e della maggiore intelligenza' [the singer who is unable to use *rubato* in their singing is capable neither of composing nor accompanying, and lacks the best taste and intelligence] (1723: 99)!

The skilled use of the agogic accent, particularly in combination with melo-gemination, strengthens the communicative power of text. Observation and feedback show that, when used together, these expressive tools can make the difference between a good and a great performance.

Three types of agogic accent

There are three ways that an agogic accent may be used to emphasise a note or syllable:

1. The first is notated in the metre of the music, where a specific note is given a longer or shorter duration than others in a line, for example a minim (half note) among crotchets (quarter notes) or a dotted rhythm. In these instances, the agogic accent is an integral part of the rhythm and does not result in *rubato*, as shown in Figure 138.

From Monteverdi, *Il ritorno d'Ulisse in patria*, Bärenreiter (2007: 1)

Figure 138. Dotted rhythm in the first instance of *tutto* [everything], note of long duration in the repetition of *tutto* and note of long duration in *turba* [disturbs].

2. The second use of the agogic accent occurs outside the metre of the music. In this case, either the composer or the singer lengthens or shortens a particular note that they would like to draw attention to, resulting in *rubato*. The composer achieves this through the use of tempo markings such as *rallentando* or a *fermata*, as shown in Figure 139, or occasionally *accelerando*. Emphasis is created by extending or shortening the vowel (or priority vowel) of the syllable in focus. To maintain correct diction in Italian, the singer simply needs to ensure that the subsequent consonant is still articulated with correct length.

From Puccini, *La fanciulla del West*, Ricordi (1963: 306)

Figure 139. *Fermata* and *tenuto* markings (here *tenuto* refers to a delay in the metre of the music) on the first syllable of *solo* [only].

3. The third use of the agogic accent involves the singer highlighting a syllable, not by lengthening the note that the syllable occurs on, but instead by further lengthening the *preceding long phoneme* (vowel or consonant). In the Melofonetica Method, this is termed the 'suspensive agogic accent' because it builds suspense on the approach to the syllable in focus. This type of agogic accent is used instinctively in the expressive articulation of text and often results in *rubato*.

Where to apply the suspensive agogic accent

The singer's use of the suspensive agogic accent may complement the composer's use of musical highlighting including dynamic, tonic or agogic accents, changes in harmony, or a noticeable absence of musical highlighting – as explained in 'Where to apply melo-gemination' in Section 3.2. Such moments may already have been identified as appropriate points to apply melo-gemination and the use of the suspensive agogic accent serves to further enhance expressive emphasis. The use of a suspensive agogic accent is particularly suitable during cadences and/or in combination with the second type of agogic accent described previously in this section. Note that the use of the suspensive agogic accent is not linked to the emphasis of stressed syllables in the spoken language – see Section 3.4, 'Stressed syllables'.

How to apply the suspensive agogic accent

The suspensive agogic accent is applied by further lengthening the long phoneme that precedes the syllable in focus. When additional length is applied to a long vowel (a vowel or priority vowel that is not followed by a long consonant), this will always involve delaying the vowel's release. When additional length is applied to a long consonant, this involves lengthening its hold and can be achieved in two ways. The onset of the long consonant may be anticipated, which further shortens the preceding vowel. Alternatively, or additionally, the release of the long consonant may be delayed. Examples of the use of the suspensive agogic accent in different contexts are given in Figures 140 to 142.

IN MELOPHONETIC TRANSCRIPTION

The suspensive agogic accent is indicated with a half chroneme [·], which is placed in one of the following positions:
- Before the chroneme already in place [·ː] where the hold of a long consonant is anticipated
- After the chroneme already in place [ː·] where the release of a long consonant or long vowel is delayed
- Before and after the chroneme already in place [·ː·] where the hold of a long consonant is both anticipated and delayed

The extent of anticipation and/or delay will depend on tempo, note duration and the amount of emphasis that the singer wishes to add.

Contessa
o mi la - scia al-men mo - rir.
[omː miː laʃː ʃaːl memˑː moːr rir]

From Mozart, *Le nozze di Figaro*, Bärenreiter (2001: 132)

🎧 Figure 140. Two suspensive agogic accents used to reinforce the cadence and emphasise *morir* [to die], applied by:
- Anticipating the onset of the long (coarticulated) *m*
- Delaying the release of the long *o*

Cavaradossi
(pensando)
E lu - ce - van le stel - le...
[elː luː tʃeː vanː lestˑː telˑː le]

From Puccini, *Tosca*, Ricordi (1995: 288)

🎧 Figure 141. Three suspensive agogic accents used to interpret the direction *pensando* [thinking] and to emphasise significant words in the line, which are not musically highlighted but are instead set to a repetition of notes and simple rhythm. These accents are applied by:
- Anticipating the onset of the long (co-geminated) *l* to emphasise *luce-van* [(they) were shining]

- Anticipating the onset of the long (melo-geminated) *t* and delaying its release to emphasise *stelle* [stars]
- Delaying the release of the long *l* to emphasise *stelle* [stars]

In terms of creating dramatic tension, the lengthening of the hold (silence) before the release of a stop consonant is particularly effective, as seen in Figure 141. Barthold Kuijken discusses the guidance given in instrumental treatises of the eighteenth century, which, interestingly, 'always cite good singers as the examples to be imitated' and advise in particular that 'good notes', i.e. the principal notes in a bar (measure), are 'preceded by a silence rather than being pushed into, or can even come late' (2013: 50–51).[20] In sung Italian, this effect – particularly noticeable in the expressive articulation of stop consonants – occurs just as frequently, if not more so, on unstressed beats, creating an impression of spontaneity and a swing-like quality not dissimilar to that heard in jazz music, as shown in Figure 142. See also Section 3.6, 'The Michelangelo effect: the essence of Italian style'.

From Leoncavallo, *Pagliacci*, Sonzogno (1981: 104)

🎧 Figure 142. Two suspensive agogic accents used to reinforce the *ritenuto* marking and emphasise *di me* [to me], applied by:
- Delaying the release of the long (co-geminated) *d* prior to the unstressed beat
- Lengthening the long *i*

---

20. Used with permission of Indiana University Press, from *The Notation Is Not the Music: Reflections on Early Music Practice and Performance*, Barthold Kuijken, 2013; permission conveyed through Copyright Clearance Center, Inc.

3.4 Stressed syllables

There is sometimes a misconception that singers need to add volume or length to stressed syllables in sung Italian, particularly through the use of longer consonants. While this can work in other languages, the correct lengths of long and short consonants must be preserved in sung Italian.

In spoken Italian, the primary stressed syllables (ictuses) in words or phrases are accentuated through a slight increase in volume, pitch and/or length. However, when text is transferred into notation, the parameters of music take over. The composer aligns the primary stressed syllables in each line to stressed beats to ensure that they maintain their accentuation, while other stressed syllables become irrelevant in the context of the prosody. There is nothing further that singers need to do to accentuate stressed syllables in sung Italian per se. Stressed syllables may be given enhanced emphasis purely for expressive reasons through the use of melo-gemination and/or the suspensive agogic accent, but these tools can equally be applied to highlight unstressed syllables.

IN MELOPHONETIC TRANSCRIPTION

Where melophonetic transcription is used in conjunction with musical notation, primary stressed syllables are not marked since they will already be aligned to stressed beats. Elsewhere, the symbol [ˈ] immediately precedes primary stressed syllables to indicate correct accentuation, for example [aː ˈmaː ɾe].

3.5 The incorporation of rests and punctuation into diction

Rests in notation can occur between lines, between words and within words. Sometimes rests coincide with punctuation marks and sometimes they do not. Rests and punctuation marks can be treated in different ways: it may be necessary to use them to take a breath, for technical or expressive reasons. However, to enhance connection through words and phrases, it is often effective to incorporate rests of short duration and punctuation into expressive sung Italian diction. The way this is achieved will depend on the nature of the phonemes on either side of the rest or punctuation mark, as described in the sections that follow.

Rests between lines and sections of lines

Most rests divide lines, or sections of lines, and help the listener to understand the intention of the phrase and how it is shaped. Where these rests are of short duration, the most common way to incorporate them into diction is through the melo-gemination of the consonant that follows the rest.

As discussed in Section 3.1, 'The *attacco del suono*', a long consonant has the energy to make a clear start, both musically and dramatically. The onset and hold of a melo-geminated consonant can function as, and take the duration of, a rest between syllables, while its release at the beginning of the following syllable marks the next section of the phrase with new intention. A suspensive agogic accent can also be applied to the hold of the melo-geminated consonant to further highlight the pause and the beginning of the next part of the phrase, and create a greater sense of tension in the rhythm. In this way, a rest can be transformed from a simple silence into an expressive tool that, while marking a distinction between the first and second sections of the phrase, still maintains connection throughout.

While the onset and silent hold of a long stop consonant clearly create the effect of a rest, as shown in Figures 143 and 144, the onset and hold of a long sibilant or sonorant consonant create the *impression* of a rest through the interruption of the preceding vowel and a sudden, natural *diminuendo* (*martellato* effect), as shown in Figures 145 and 146.

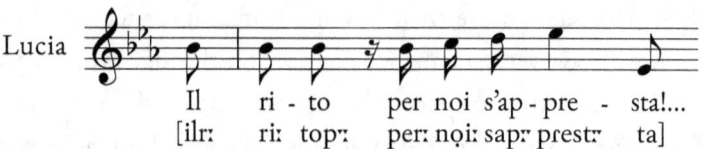

From Donizetti, *Lucia di Lammermoor*, Ricordi (2022: 258). Transposed version, found in contemporary vocal scores.

🎧 Figure 143. Rest created with the hold of the long (melo-geminated) *p* in *per*.

From Verdi, *La traviata*, Ricordi (2001: 116–17)

🎧 Figure 144. Rest (and intention of the colon and ellipsis) created with the hold of the long (melo-geminated) first *v* in *vivere*.

From Mozart, *Le nozze di Figaro*, Bärenreiter (2001: 150)

🎧 Figure 145. Impression of the rest created with the hold of the long (melo-geminated) *s* in *senza*.

Simone
No. Non è!
[nonː noː ne]

From Puccini, *Gianni Schicchi*, Ricordi (1987: 15)

🎧 Figure 146. Impression of the rest (and intention of the full stop) created with the hold of the long (melo-geminated) first *n* in *non*.

Where consonants immediately precede and follow the rest, they can be bridged to form a group of consonants. Melo-gemination can be applied here as it would normally be applied in a group of consonants (see 'How to apply melo-gemination' in Section 3.2), with the onset and hold of the melo-geminated consonant creating the effect of the rest, as shown in Figure 147. Note that the two consonants may also need to be coarticulated (see Section 1.11, 'Coarticulation of consonants').

Donna Anna

Que - sto è il fin   di   chi fa   mal,
[kː ku̯estː telfː   fi̯ndː diː kif fa   mal]

From Mozart, *Don Giovanni*, Bärenreiter (2005: 434)

🎧 Figure 147. Rest created with the hold of the long (melo-geminated) *d* in *di* (*n* and *d* become a group of consonants).

Where vowels immediately precede and follow the rest, the singer may instead lengthen the vowel (or priority vowel) on the note before the rest for the whole duration of the rest. Where possible, i.e. in slower tempi or where the note preceding the rest is of long duration, a *diminuendo* may also be applied on the vowel to lend the impression of a rest. For example, a quaver (eighth note) followed by a quaver rest (eighth note rest) may be interpreted as a crotchet (quarter note) with a *diminuendo* (♪ 𝄾 = ♩>). Alternatively, it is possible to create the rest through the hold of a long glottal occlusive consonant [ʔ], but this is used rarely for a more dramatic, *staccato* effect. Both options are shown in Figure 148.

Despina

Che vi-ta ma-le-det-ta   è il   far la ca-me-rie-ra!
1.[keː viː taː maːle: detː taː   elfː farː laː kaː meː rieː ra]
2.   [... taʔː ʔel: farː ...]

From Mozart, *Così fan tutte*, Bärenreiter (2006: 86)

🎧 Figure 148. Impression of a rest created by lengthening the final *a* in *maledetta*, or (more rarely) created with the hold of a long glottal occlusive consonant [ʔ]. If the latter option is used, it is less comfortable to melo-geminate the following *f* in *far*, so this is not shown in the melophonetic transcription.

Where the word preceding the rest ends with a short consonant and a vowel follows the rest, the vowel *before* the short consonant may instead take the length of the rest, with the onset and release of the short consonant placed instead on the note that follows. Where possible, i.e. in slower tempi or where the note preceding the rest is of long duration, a *diminuendo* may again be applied on the vowel to lend the impression of a rest. Care must be taken not to lengthen the short consonant.

Alternatively, it is possible to create the rest through the hold of a long glottal occlusive consonant [ʔ], but this is used rarely for a more dramatic, *staccato* effect. Both options are shown in Figure 149.

Virtù

        io   son,   io son la ve-ra sca - la
1. [ioː   soː   nioːsː sonː laː veːraskː kaː   la]
2.   [... sonʔː ʔioː sonː ...]

From Monteverdi, *L'incoronazione di Poppea*, Bärenreiter (2017: 4)

🎧 Figure 149. Impression of the rest (and intention of the comma) created by lengthening the *o* in *son* and optionally applying a *diminuendo*, or (more rarely) created with the hold of a long glottal occlusive consonant [ʔ]. If the latter option is used, it is less comfortable to melo-geminate the following *s* in *son*, so this is not shown in the melophonetic transcription.

Where the word preceding the rest ends with a consonant that can be post-geminated (see 'Post-gemination' in Section 1.6), the hold of this consonant can function as the rest, as shown in Figure 150.

From Verdi, *Falstaff*, Ricordi (1893: 54)

🎧 Figure 150. Rest (and intention of the exclamation mark) created with the hold of the long (post-geminated) *g* in *Meg*.

Rests between and within words

Rests can also occur between and within words for a particular musical or theatrical effect. Rather than interrupting each syllable, a skilful use of the text through the approach outlined previously in this section can create the impression of a hiatus between each syllable while also rendering such sequences more idiomatic and connected, as shown in Figures 151 and 152.

From Mozart, *Così fan tutte*, Bärenreiter (2006: 250)

🎧 Figure 151. Interpretation of rests:
- First rest created with the hold of the long (melo-geminated) *p* in *sospirando*
- Second rest created with the hold of the long (melo-geminated) *d* in *sospirando*
- Third rest created with the hold of the long (melo-geminated) *p* in *sospiretti*
- Fourth rest created with the hold of the long *t* in *sospiretti*

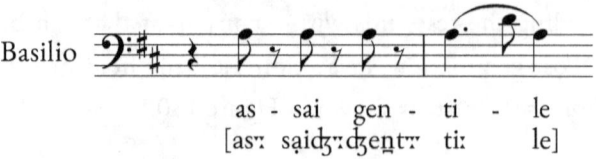

From Rossini, *Il barbiere di Siviglia*, Ricordi (2014: 151)

🎧 Figure 152. Interpretation of rests:
- Impression of the first rest created with the hold of the long *s* in *assai*
- Second rest created with the hold of the long (melo-geminated) *g* in *gentile*
- Third rest created with the hold of the long (melo-geminated) *t* in *gentile*

Where a short consonant between vowels precedes or follows the rest, or a group of two short consonants follows the rest, the vowel that precedes the rest may instead take the length of the rest, as shown in Figure 153. Where possible, i.e. in slower tempi or where the note preceding the rest is of long duration, a *diminuendo* may also be applied on the vowel to lend the impression of a rest. The onset and release of the short consonant, or group of two short consonants, is placed on the note that follows.

From Verdi, *Nabucodonosor*, University of Chicago Press and Ricordi (1996: 266–67)

🎧 Figure 153. Interpretation of rests in bar (measure) two:
- Impression of the first rest created by lengthening the *u* in *muta* and optionally applying a *diminuendo*
- Second rest created with the hold of the long (melo-geminated) *d* in *dal*
- Impression of the third rest created by lengthening the *a* in *salice* and optionally applying a *diminuendo*
- Impression of the fourth rest created by lengthening the *i* in *salice* and optionally applying a *diminuendo*

While the incorporation of rests into diction is not obligatory, in some instances it is the most intuitive way to interpret a line, as shown in Figures 154 and 155.

From Mozart, *Così fan tutte*, Bärenreiter (2006: 90)

🎧 Figure 154. Interpretation of rests:
- Impression of the first rest created by lengthening the *a* in *smanie*
- Second rest created with the hold of the long (melo-geminated) *p* in *implacabili*

From Verdi, *La traviata*, Ricordi (2001: 96)

🎧 Figure 155. Interpretation of rests:
- First rest created with the hold of the long (melo-geminated) *f* in *forse*
- Impression of the second rest created with the hold of the long (melo-geminated) *s* in *forse*
- Impression of the third rest created with the hold of the long (melo-geminated) *l* in *lui*

Punctuation

Where punctuation occurs without a rest, the singer may choose to breathe for technical or expressive reasons, but it is often effective to incorporate the intention of punctuation into diction by applying the same approach outlined previously in this section for rests. Examples are shown in Figures 156 to 158.

Sesto

Sve-glia-te - vi nel co-re, fu - rie d'u-n'al-ma of-fe- sa,
[sː veʎː ʎaː teː viː nelkː koː refː fuː ɾiɛː duː nalː maof. feː sa]

From Handel, *Giulio Cesare*, Bärenreiter (2005: 38)

🎧 Figure 156. Intention of the comma created with the hold of the long (melo-geminated) *f* in *furie*.

Marcello

Di - ca: quan-t'an - ni ha
[dː diː kakː kuaṇː tanː niː a]

From Puccini, *La bohème*, Ricordi (1961: 39)

🎧 Figure 157. Intention of the colon created with the hold of the long (melo-geminated) *q* in *quanti*.

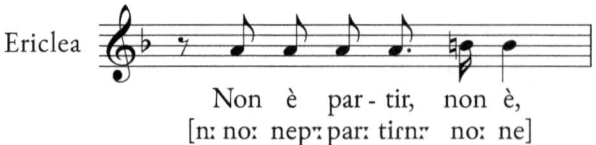

Ericlea

Non è par - tir, non è,
[nː noː nepː parː tiɾnː noː ne]

From Monteverdi, *Il ritorno d'Ulisse in patria*, Bärenreiter (2007: 16)

🎧 Figure 158. Intention of the comma created with the hold of the long (melo-geminated) *n* in *non* (*r* and *n* become a group of consonants).

Where the word preceding the punctuation mark ends with a short consonant and a vowel immediately follows, or where there are vowels immediately preceding and following the punctuation mark, it is likely that the composer will have used a tonic and/or agogic accent to denote the punctuation, in which case there is nothing further that the singer needs to do. The singer may choose to enhance the punctuation mark by applying a long glottal occlusive consonant [ʔ] before the vowel that follows the punctuation mark, but this is used rarely for a more dramatic, *staccato* effect. Both options are shown in Figures 159 and 160.

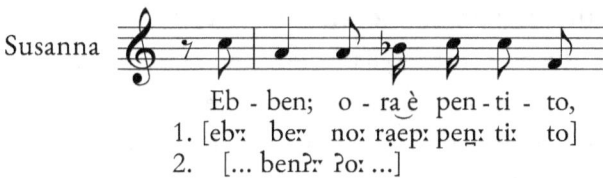

Eb - ben; o - ra è pen - ti - to,
1. [ebː beːr noː ra̯epː penː tiː to]
2. [... benʔːr ʔoː ...]

From Mozart, *Le nozze di Figaro*, Bärenreiter (2001: 34)

🎧 Figure 159. Semi-colon denoted by the composer through the use of an agogic accent (longer note value). The singer may choose to enhance this by applying a long glottal occlusive consonant [ʔ], as shown in option 2.

al ce - ner mi - o? A - stri ti - ran - ni!
1. [aɫ tʃːr tʃeːnermːr miː oː asː tritːr tiː ranː ni]
2.   [... oʔːr ʔasː ...]

From Handel, *Rodelinda*, Bärenreiter (2002: 39)

🎧 Figure 160. Question mark denoted by the composer through the use of two tonic accents (ascending augmented fourth and ascending minor third). The singer may choose to enhance this by applying a long glottal occlusive consonant [ʔ], as shown in option 2.

Where there is a punctuation mark between vowels on the same note, this is usually disregarded. See 'Punctuation within groups of vowels' in Section 2.4.

3.6 The Michelangelo effect: the essence of Italian style

The 'Michelangelo effect' is a term used in the Melofonetica Method to describe a particular sequence of text in music. This sequence occurs so often in sung Italian that it may be considered the defining melophonetic characteristic at the heart of 'Italian style' in vocal music.

The effect consists of a syllable that occurs on an unstressed beat and begins with the release of any long consonant, followed by a syllable that occurs on a stressed beat and begins with a short consonant or vowel. Note that in this definition, the term 'syllable' is used to mean a phonic syllable, i.e. the way that a syllable is pronounced rather than written in the score. The syncopation in the sequence is surprising and unpredictable: we hear an accented (emphasised) note where we are expecting an unaccented (unemphasised) note and vice versa. An example of the sequence is shown in Figure 161.

From Puccini, *Tosca*, Ricordi (1995: 242)

🎧 Figure 161. An example of the melophonetic sequence described as the Michelangelo effect: long *d* in *d'amore* (melo-gemination) accents the unstressed beat and is followed by long *a* crossing the bar line (measure line) and short *m*, which do not accent the stressed beat.

Drawing a parallel to the visual arts, the nature of this sequence brings to mind the blend of geometry and fluidity seen in Italian Renaissance art. The architecture and sculpture of Michelangelo Buonarroti, in particular, possess both an energy and an elegance that together create a captivating contrast, hence the labelling of this sequence as the 'Michelangelo effect'.

This pattern is evident in the spoken language but it is elevated and enhanced when set to music. The frequency with which the

Michelangelo effect occurs creates a distinctive and discernible style throughout Italian repertoire.

Firstly, the unstressed beat is emphasised by the momentum and drive of the long consonant. This is often a syllable that has been musically highlighted by the composer. As mentioned in Section 3.2, 'Melo-gemination: the lengthening of short consonants for emphasis', composers are often instinctively drawn to those points in the text where long consonants already exist or can be added for expressive reasons.

Secondly, the stressed beat that follows is not emphasised since its syllable begins with a short consonant, or no consonant at all, and is preceded by the continuity of a long vowel (*tenuto* effect) – or, in some instances, a long sibilant or sonorant consonant in a group. In many occurrences, the stressed beat is the first beat in a bar (measure), so when this is not accented by the text, the division of the bar line is disguised.

Identifying, creating and enhancing the Michelangelo effect

The Michelangelo effect can already occur through the correct articulation of long and short consonants, before any expressive emphasis is added, as shown in Figure 162.

From Mozart, *Le nozze di Figaro*, Bärenreiter (2001: 379)

🎧 Figure 162. Two Michelangelo effects created with:
- Long *s* in *soave* (co-gemination), which accents the unstressed beat, followed by long *o* crossing the bar line (measure line) and *a*, which do not accent the stressed beat
- Long *f* in *zeffiretto*, which accents the unstressed beat, followed by long *i* crossing the bar line and short *r*, which do not accent the stressed beat

The singer may also choose to trigger the Michelangelo effect through the use of melo-gemination (where appropriate), in order to create a long consonant that will accent the unstressed beat. Equally, the singer may opt to not apply melo-gemination or use de-gemination (see 'De-gemination' in Section 1.6) to create an unaccented stressed beat and thus complete the sequence. Examples that illustrate these scenarios are given in Figures 163 to 167.

Tonic and dynamic accents are independent of the structure of the Michelangelo effect, but their use complements the elements within it. Where there is no particular dynamic indication from the composer, an expressive and instinctive way to integrate dynamics (or micro-dynamics) into the Michelangelo effect is to use a *crescendo* towards the unstressed beat, changing suddenly to *piano* or *pianissimo* from the unstressed beat onwards. The opposite approach can also be effective, i.e. to lead from the *crescendo* into *forte* or *fortissimo* from the unstressed beat onwards. A similar approach can be taken with tempo, i.e. applying *accelerando* towards the unstressed beat and *ritenuto* from the unstressed beat onwards or vice versa. The sequence can also be enhanced by the use of the suspensive agogic accent on the approach to the unstressed and/or stressed beat, as shown in Figures 163–65, 167, 168 and 170.

From Bellini, *La sonnambula*, Ricordi (2010: 314)

🎧 Figure 163. Two Michelangelo effects created with:
- Long *c* in *credea* (melo-gemination), which accents the unstressed beat, followed by long *e* and short *d*, which do not accent the stressed beat
- Long *m* in *mirarti* (melo-gemination), which accents the unstressed beat, followed by long *i* crossing the bar line and short *r*, which do not accent the stressed beat

Donna Anna
Cru - de - le!   Ah   no, mio be - ne!
[kː kruː deː le] [ʔː ʔanː nomː mioːr beː ne]

From Mozart, *Don Giovanni*, Bärenreiter (2005: 372)

🎧 Figure 164. Two Michelangelo effects created with:
- Long *c* in *crudele* (*attacco del suono*), which accents the unstressed beat, followed by long *u* crossing the bar line (measure line) and short *d*, which do not accent the stressed beat
- Long *m* in *mio* (melo-gemination), which accents the unstressed beat, followed by long *o* (priority vowel) crossing the bar line and short *b* (a-gemination), which do not accent the stressed beat

Pinkerton
Be - via - mo ai no - vis - si - mi le - ga - mi,
[bː beː viaː moainːnoː visːː siː milːː leː gaː mi]

From Puccini, *Madama Butterfly*, Ricordi (1964: 110)

🎧 Figure 165. Four Michelangelo effects created with:
- Long *b* in *beviamo* (*attacco del suono*), which accents the unstressed beat, followed by long *e* crossing the bar line (measure line) and short *v*, which do not accent the stressed beat
- Long *n* in *novissimi* (melo-gemination), which accents the unstressed beat, followed by long *o* crossing the bar line and short *v*, which do not accent the stressed beat
- Long *s* in *novissimi*, which accents the unstressed beat, followed by long *i* and short *m*, which do not accent the stressed beat
- Long *l* in *legami* (melo-gemination), which accents the unstressed beat, followed by long *e* crossing the bar line and short *g*, which do not accent the stressed beat

Guglielmo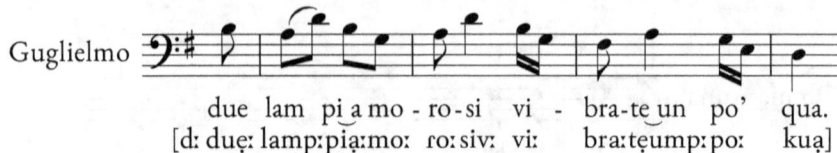

due lam pi a mo - ro - si vi - bra-te un po' qua.
[d: duẹ: lamp:piạ:mo: rọ:siv: vi: bra:tẹump:po: kuạ]

From Mozart, *Così fan tutte*, Bärenreiter (2006: 146)

🎧 Figure 166. Four Michelangelo effects created with:
- Long *d* in *due* (*attacco del suono*), which accents the unstressed beat, followed by long *e* (priority vowel) crossing the bar line (measure line) and short *l* in *lampi*, which do not accent the stressed beat
- Long *p* in *lampi* (melo-gemination), which accents the unstressed (weak) beat, followed by long *a* (priority vowel), long *o* crossing the bar line and short *r* in *amorosi*, which do not accent the stressed beat
- Long *v* in *vibrate* (melo-gemination), which accents the unstressed beat, followed by long *i* crossing the bar line and short *b*, which do not accent the stressed beat
- Long *p* in *po'* (melo-gemination), which accents the unstressed beat, followed by long *o* crossing the bar line and short *q* (a-gemination), which do not accent the stressed beat

The creation of the Michelangelo effect may be desirable where more than one Michelangelo effect is already present in a phrase and the singer wishes to maintain consistency of accentuation and rhythmic character throughout, as shown in Figure 167.

Cornelia
[n: no: nap: piu: ket: te: me: re]

From Handel, *Giulio Cesare*, Bärenreiter (2005: 288)

🎧 Figure 167. Three Michelangelo effects created with:
- Long *n* in *non* (*attacco del suono*), which accents the unstressed beat, followed by long *o* crossing the bar line (measure line) and short *n*, which do not accent the stressed beat
- Long *t* in *temere* (co-gemination), which accents the unstressed beat, followed by long *e* and short *m*, which do not accent the stressed beat
- Long *p* in *più* (co-gemination), which accents the unstressed beat, followed by long *u* and short *c* in *che* (de-gemination), which do not accent the stressed beat – de-gemination is suitable here in order to create the Michelangelo effect and maintain consistency in the phrase

Composers frequently copy rhythm and/or articulation to the vocal line, but in practice it is up to the singer to find the more intricate relationship between vocal line and accompaniment. The identification of the Michelangelo effect can help the singer to find a meeting point between the notation markings and the micro-rhythm of the text, as shown in Figure 168.

From Verdi, *La traviata*, University of Chicago Press and Ricordi (2001: 105)

🎧 Figure 168. Interpretation of *staccato* markings through the use of the Michelangelo effect:

- Long *d* in *diletti* (co-gemination) accents the unstressed beat, followed by long *i* crossing the bar line (measure line) and short *l*, which do not accent the stressed beat; the suspensive agogic accents applied to the hold of the long *d* and long *i* reinforce the composer's indication '*con effetto questo ripiglio*' [emphasise this reprise]
- Long *t* in *diletti* accents the unstressed beat, followed by long *i* and short *s* in *sempre* (no melo-gemination), which do not accent the stressed beat
- Long *p* in *sempre* (melo-gemination) accents the unstressed beat, followed by long *e* crossing the bar line and short *n* in *nuovi* (no melo-gemination), which do not accent the stressed beat
- Long *v* in *volare* accents the unstressed beat, followed by long *o* crossing the bar line and short *l*, which do not accent the stressed beat
- Long *p* in *pensier* (melo-gemination, overriding a-gemination) accents the unstressed beat, followed by long *n* crossing the bar line and short *s* (no melo-gemination), which do not accent the stressed beat

In Figure 168, the *staccato* markings in the vocal line are doubled by parts of the orchestra. However, the singer's use of the Michelangelo effect can result in an interesting contrast, with the long *d* in *diletti* and long *p* in *sempre* producing a *staccato* effect on the first in each pair of quavers (eighth notes), while the long *i* and long *e* on the quavers that follow result in a *tenuto* effect across the respective bar lines (measure lines).

Similarly, across the fourth bar line, the *staccato* in the orchestra parts can be mirrored in the vocal line with a long *p* in *pensier* while the long *n* creates a *tenuto* effect.

In the example in Figure 169, while the first three *staccato* quavers can be created with the hold of long stop consonants, the Michelangelo effect instead renders the fourth *staccato* as *tenuto*.

Mimì

quel cer - chiet - to d'or,
[kuel̯tʃː tʃerkː kiętː toː dor]

From Puccini, *La bohème*, Ricordi (1961: 208)

🎧 Figure 169. Interpretation of *staccato* markings through the use of the Michelangelo effect: long *t* in *cerchietto* accents the unstressed beat, followed by long *o* and short *d* in *d'or*, which create a *tenuto* effect and do not accent the stressed beat.

Care should be taken where *marcato* markings occur. Singers sometimes interpret all of these by adding length (and volume) to consonants, which can result in the incorrect articulation of short consonants. It is important to evaluate how accentuation can be added effectively without jeopardising diction. The correct use of melo-gemination, the agogic accent and the Michelangelo effect can all help singers to interpret *marcato* markings appropriately, as shown in Figure 170.

Giulietta

qual vit - ti - ma ca - der
[kː kualvː vitː tiː makː kaː der]

From Bellini, *I Capuleti e i Montecchi*, Ricordi (2003: 67)

🎧 Figure 170. Interpretation of *marcato* markings as follows:
- Long *v* (melo-gemination) in *vittima* interprets the first *marcato* marking, this can also be enhanced by an agogic accent
- The first Michelangelo effect begins with long *t* in *vittima*, enhanced by an agogic accent, interpreting the second *marcato* marking, this

is followed by long *i* and short *m*, which do not accent the third *marcato* marking but an agogic accent can be applied to interpret this

- The second Michelangelo effect begins with long *c* (melo-gemination) in *cader*, enhanced by an agogic accent, interpreting the fourth *marcato* marking; this is followed by long *a* and short *d*, which do not accent the fifth *marcato* marking but an agogic accent can be applied to interpret this

Case study: *Sì, mi chiamano Mimì*

In the opening line of the aria *Sì, mi chiamano Mimì* from Puccini's *La bohème*, there are four Michelangelo effects, as shown in Figure 171. Each begins with either a long *m* or a long *l* (sonorant consonants) accenting the unstressed beat, and observing all four creates a pleasing consistency of timbre and articulation throughout the phrase. This is the craftsmanship of the poet. The artistry of the composer is seen in the way that he has allowed space for each of these moments: firstly with a notated rest, subsequently through additional markings, and finally with two dotted rhythms. The interpreter's skill lies in recognising the rhythmic implications of these indicators and combining them with other musical elements to maximise expressive effect.

From Puccini, *La bohème*, Ricordi (1961: 69–70)

🎧 Figure 171. Four Michelangelo effects, each framing the bar line (measure line), discussed fully in the paragraphs that follow.

In Figure 171, the first Michelangelo effect begins with the long *m* in *mi*, this is either an *attacco del suono* (if a breath is desired after *Sì*) or a co-gemination reinforced by punctuation, sung through the rest – functionally a dotted rhythm. The short *c* in *chiamano* (a-gemination) completes the first Michelangelo effect.

The second Michelangelo effect also begins with a long *m* (melo-gemination) in *Mimì*. In the context of the drama, this is the moment that we first learn the name of the character, so the word is undoubtedly of importance. The composer has included both a *portamento* marking and a *crescendo* marking, as well as the significant intervallic move of a rising augmented fourth, to highlight this exact moment. To give the word its full expressive potential, the use of melo-gemination and thus the creation of the Michelangelo effect is ideal here. The short *m* following the bar line (measure line) in *Mimì* completes the second Michelangelo effect.

The third and fourth Michelangelo effects, long *m* in *mio* (melo-gemination triggered by the dotted rhythm) followed by short *n* in *nome* (a-gemination), and long *l* in *Lucia* (co-gemination) followed by short *c*, are indicated by the composer's choice of dotted rhythms and framed by significant intervallic choices, i.e. a falling diminished seventh and a repetition of the note, respectively.

A skilful use of the agogic accent and micro-dynamics complements the melophonetics of the Michelangelo effects in these lines, fulfilling their expressive potential.

The Michelangelo effect in ensembles

While the use of the Michelangelo effect serves to enhance the idiomatic quality of the language, its swing-like rhythm can also function purely for phonetic and musical effect. This is evident not only in arias and recitatives but also, particularly so, between vocal parts in ensemble pieces – whether homorhythmic (with the same rhythm across parts) or in counterpoint, as shown in Figures 172 and 173 respectively.

From Bellini, *I Capuleti e i Montecchi*, Ricordi (2003: 63–64).

🎧 Figure 172. Synchronisation of the Michelangelo effect across homorhythmic parts.

Romeo:
- Long *s* in both instances of *sì* (*attacco del suono* and co-gemination), followed by long *i* and short *c* in both instances of *costerà* (de-gemination); the commas that follow *sì* are disregarded in order to create the Michelangelo effect
- Long *t* in both instances of *costerà* (melo-gemination), followed by long *e* crossing the bar line (measure line) and short *r*

Tebaldo, Capellio and Coro:
- Long *f* in both instances of *fra* (*attacco del suono* and co-gemination), followed by long *a* and short *n* in both instances of *noi* (de-gemination)
- Long *p* in both instances of *potrà* (melo-gemination), followed by long *o* and short *t* and *r*

In the Monteverdi chorus excerpt shown in Figure 173, there is both synchronisation and counterpoint of the Michelangelo effect across the five vocal parts. This creates what John Eliot Gardiner describes (2018: 9) as the 'rhythmic frisson' that characterises so much of Monteverdi's composition.

From Monteverdi, *L'Orfeo*, Fondazione Claudio Monteverdi (2016: 42)

🎧 Figure 173. Synchronisation and counterpoint of the Michelangelo effect across parts:
- Long *t* in *apporti* (melo-gemination), followed by short *q* in *questi* (de-gemination)
- Long *t* in *questi* (melo-gemination) followed by short *m* in *amanti*
- Long *t* in *amanti* (melo-gemination) followed by short *d* in *i dì* (a-gemination)
- Long *s* (co-gemination) followed by short *r* in *sereni*

It is interesting to note the melophonetic similarities and differences across the four Michelangelo sequences in Figure 173. In the first three, the alliteration of long *t* within a group of consonants (*staccato* effect) accentuates the unstressed beat, while the final Michelangelo effect is softened with the use of a long *s* (*martellato* effect) on the word *sereni* [serene]. The transition through the timbres of the four long vowels that precede the stressed beats (*a*, *a*, *i* and *e*) also lends an overall effect of reduction and *diminuendo*.

Avoiding the creation of the Michelangelo effect

While non-accentuation of the stressed beat completes the Michelangelo effect and lends a spontaneous feel to a phrase, in some instances, the singer may opt to *avoid* the creation of the Michelangelo effect in favour of an accented stressed beat. This means that the release of a long consonant occurs instead on the stressed beat (whether through melo-gemination or the avoidance of de-gemination) and produces a more dramatic statement by reinforcing the accentuation of the musical ictus, as shown in Figures 174 and 175.

Bartolo

La   ven - det - ta,
[lː la(v)ː venddː detː ta]

From Mozart, *Le nozze di Figaro*, Bärenreiter (2001: 45)

🎧 Figure 174. Without the Michelangelo effect, a long *d* (melo-gemination) accents the stressed beat and highlights the word *vendetta* [revenge] more dramatically. The accentuation of the preceding unstressed beat is optional, i.e. the *v* may be long (melo-geminated) or remain short.

Amelia

From Verdi, *Simon Boccanegra*, Ricordi (2004: 85)

🎧 Figure 175. Without the Michelangelo effect, a long *l* (co-gemination) accents the stressed beat and highlights the word *luna* [moon] more dramatically. The accentuation of the preceding unstressed beat remains in place, since the *sc* in *unisce* must be long (self-gemination).

3.7 Notes inégales

A tempo del'affetto del animo, e non a quello de la mano.

[To the rhythm of the soul's emotions, and not that marked by the hand.]

— Claudio Monteverdi (1638: 54)

Monteverdi's instruction to the main character in *Lamento della ninfa* [The nymph's lament], to follow a rhythm that is led by the spontaneity of emotion rather than the regular, mechanical rhythm marked by the hand beating tempo, reminds the singer to find the most natural and instinctive way to express the text. This approach was fundamental to the new art form of opera, which strove to *muovere gli affetti*, i.e. to stir the emotions through the power of words in music. It was no doubt also a catalyst for the practice of *notes inégales* (literally meaning 'unequal notes') in instrumental music, which involves a freedom in the performance of smaller note values, inspired by vocal music.

During the seventeenth and eighteenth centuries in particular, instrumentalists strove to emulate the natural and expressive rhythm of the voice. Barthold Kuijken explains in *The Notation Is Not the Music: Reflections on Early Music Practice and Performance*:

> Instrumentalists were always required to take singers as their model, and indeed they will have needed to listen attentively to the singer in order to imitate or accompany well at appropriate places. In purely instrumental music, they will have applied a similar flexibility or have imagined a text under their notes. (2013: 41)[21]

Since singers knew which syllables in the text needed to be longer or shorter, composers frequently wrote equal notes in their vocal score while dotted notes were only shown in the part for the accompaniment (Kuijken 2013: 40).[22]

21. Used with permission of Indiana University Press, from *The Notation Is Not the Music: Reflections on Early Music Practice and Performance*, Barthold Kuijken, 2013; permission conveyed through Copyright Clearance Center, Inc.
22. See note 21 above.

In the instrumental world, the consequences of the desire to imitate the voice were far-reaching. Musicologist Anna Maria Vacchelli describes the revolution this sparked in the early seventeenth century, following the birth of opera: 'sopravvivono nell'uso pratico soltanto gli strumenti in grado di imitare le voci secondo il nuovo stile espressivo legato alla mozione degli affetti' [only those instruments capable of imitating the voice, in this new expressive style linked to the stirring of emotions, survived for practical use] (see Monteverdi 2014: 28).

In his examination of the notation of inequality, Kuijken describes the use of dotted notes as the 'closest approximation' but explains that inequality 'is normally less than dotted' (2013: 45).[23] He observes that in some scores there is over-dotting while in others there is under-dotting but ultimately 'the exact degree of inequality will depend on the specific text to be sung' (2013: 41).[24]

Inequality of rhythm is often evident in sung Italian, particularly across notes of smaller value, due to the sequencing of long and short consonants and the use of the agogic accent. This is at its most striking in the Michelangelo effect, where accentuated unstressed beats take precedence over stressed beats, as shown in Figure 176.

---

23. Used with permission of Indiana University Press, from *The Notation Is Not the Music: Reflections on Early Music Practice and Performance*, Barthold Kuijken, 2013; permission conveyed through Copyright Clearance Center, Inc.

24. See note 23 above.

From Mozart, *Don Giovanni*, Bärenreiter (2005: 196)

🎧 Figure 176. The Michelangelo effect created by the long *l* (melo-gemination) in *la*, which emphasises the unstressed beat, followed by the long *a* and short *l* at the beginning of *libertà*, which do not accent the stressed beat (*l* in *libertà* remains short since *la* is an activator of a-gemination). As a result of the Michelangelo effect and the suspensive agogic accent on the long *l* which creates *rubato*, there is an inequality in the two semiquavers (sixteenth notes), also hinted at by the dotted rhythm in the orchestral parts.

3.8 The colour palette of vowels

Chapter 2, 'Vowels', discusses the freedom that the sung Italian language gives singers to colour vowels in the way that is right for their voice and the expressive qualities they wish to deliver in each line.

As previously discussed, there is no one way to sing Italian vowels correctly, and the nature of vowel sounds is both a technical and an aesthetic choice. In balancing resonance, dynamics and timbre, singers may sing any of the range of sounds within each archi-vowel without compromising clarity of diction or delivery of meaning. Observation of the world's leading singers shows the confidence with which they use this freedom in Italian vowels to effectively portray character and emotion.

Vowel timbre is particularly important for expression. The singer's choice of timbre will be influenced by theatrical direction and the need to produce a sound that is appropriate to both character and drama, whether dark, bright, breathy, nasal or otherwise.

As a painter chooses to balance the colours and *chiaroscuro* of their painting, so singer, conductor and director can draw upon the colour palette of the five archi-vowels, and the many shades within them, to bring Italian repertoire to life.

3.9 *Canto legato* and *portamento di voce*

> *Ordinarily one would suppose that a larger proportion of obstruents in Italian would increase the number of occasions when voice is interrupted in fluent speaking and singing and, in consequence, reduce the 'smooth flow' of voice production. This, however, is not the impression received when listening to fluent Italian.*
>
> — Adrian Fourcin (2017: 266)

Despite the apparent fluidity of the sung language, Italian has fewer vowels and more obstruent (stop and sibilant) consonants than English (Fourcin 2017: 266). There often remains, however, a wariness of clearly and correctly articulating long consonants for fear of jeopardising *legato* or 'line', used to mean a smooth connection through a musical phrase without interruption of sound.

The *tenuto* effect created by short consonants fits well with the common understanding of *legato*, perhaps most notably within the context of the Michelangelo effect, where it disguises the division of the bar line (measure line). It may well be that the prevalence of the Michelangelo effect is in part responsible for the overall impression of smoothness and flow so often associated with sung Italian.

In contrast, the *staccato* and *martellato* effects and inevitable interruption to vowels created by correctly articulated long consonants, in particular stop consonants, would seem to render *legato* singing and correct diction mutually exclusive. For some, line and *legato* have therefore become synonymous with removing long consonants in sung Italian, thus compromising the quality of diction and expression.

With this in mind, it is useful to revisit the original use of the term *legato* and the evolution of the concept as recorded in centuries of Italian-language literature on the subject of singing.

The concept of *legato* in Italian vocal literature

In the works of Pier Francesco Tosi (1723), Giambattista Mancini (1774), Domenico Corri (1811), Nicola Tacchinardi (1833), Francesco Lamperti (1864) and other leading Italian educators of the eighteenth and nineteenth centuries, it is universally clear that correct diction was deemed the fundamental foundation for expressive sung Italian.

In the guidance given on Italian pronunciation, there is a particular focus on the correct rendering of long and short consonants. Tosi advises that singers practise their pronunciation without making what he calls the common 'erroracci ridicoli' [horrible and ridiculous mistakes] of reducing the length of double consonants and adding length to short consonants (1723: 35). Tacchinardi (1833: 9–10) similarly refers to the importance of mastering consonant length correctly, and Lamperti (1864: 13) points out that consonant length must be respected in order to achieve correct pronunciation, even in vocalising practice.

At the same time, *legato* is also described as a key quality in many of these methods. It is widely described as an important tool for good, expressive singing and considered essential for any student of singing to master. Nevertheless, there is inconsistency in terminology alongside incomplete explanations of what *legato* means in practice, which are further confused in the translations of various methods from Italian into other languages.

In his highly regarded treatise *Opinioni de' cantori antichi, e moderni, o sieno Osservazioni sopra il canto figurato* [Opinions of ancient and modern singers; or, Observations on *canto figurato*] (1723), described by tenor and author John Potter (2006: 524) as 'the bible of early eighteenth-century singing',[25] Tosi does not make reference to the term *legato* as such. He does, however, describe the two universally accepted ways that singers can move from one note to the next: either *battuto*, meaning that each note is articulated distinctly, or *scivolato*,

---

25. John Potter, 'Beggar at the Door: The Rise and Fall of Portamento in Singing', *Music and Letters*, 2006, 87, 4, 523–50, by permission of Oxford University Press.

whereby notes are connected with a slide (1723: 30). It is not clear exactly what the nature of this slide should be – as Potter explains, 'Tosi uses various terms to describe the artistic joining of notes, and we cannot be absolutely sure of the meaning of any of them' (2006: 524).[26] In their translations of Tosi's work, both Johann Ernst Galliard (Tosi 1743) and Johann Friedrich Agricola (Tosi 1757) sought to clarify Tosi's ideas and 'expanded on the Italian original sufficiently to gain some idea of what later generations thought he meant even if his original remains opaque' (Potter 2006: 525).[27] Galliard explains that the singer should learn to 'glide with the vowels' (Tosi 1743: 29) while Agricola's equivalent is translated by Julianne Baird as 'the art of slurring from one note to another' (Agricola 1995: 86).[28] Baird adds a note that both Tosi and Agricola are referring here to 'the *portamento*' (Agricola 1995: 266).[29]

Notably, in the subsequent methods of Mancini, Corri, Tacchinardi, Lamperti and others, the term *legato* is also frequently used in the context of *portamento* or *portamento di voce* [carriage of the voice]. In some occurrences, *legato* is used as a synonym for *portamento*, while in others it is considered a form of *portamento*. In all cases, there is consensus that *legato* involves the smooth transition from one note to the next, created by a rapid, continuous slide on the vowel, with no hesitation on intermediate tones.

While there are references to avoiding the interruption of an inbreath during the slide from one note to the next (Mancini 1774: 91, 95; Lamperti 1864: 10), in all of the Italian methods reviewed, the teaching of *legato* as a form of *portamento* did not include any reference to shortening or softening consonants to facilitate the smooth connection of notes. In Lesson 1 of his *Metodo pratico di canto italiano* (1837: 4), Nicola Vaccaj

---

26. John Potter, 'Beggar at the Door: The Rise and Fall of Portamento in Singing', *Music and Letters*, 2006, 87, 4, 523–50, by permission of Oxford University Press.
27. See note 27 above.
28. Johann Friedrich Agricola, *Introduction to the Art of Singing by Johann Friedrich Agricola*, trans. and ed. by Julianne C. Baird, © Cambridge University Press 1995. Reproduced with permission of Cambridge University Press through PLSclear.
29. See note 28 above.

outlines a division of syllables that addresses the placement (and, seemingly, pitching) of all consonants by moving them to the beginning of each syllable and allowing the vowel to take the duration of each note. He mentions here that this will help singers to master *canto legato* (singing with *legato*), as it was known, and subsequently in Lesson 13, that this will make it easier to learn the correct way to apply *portamento di voce* (1837: 29). Manuel García Jr. (1847: II. 4) later proposes the opposite approach to Vaccaj, instead advising singers to place consonants at the end of each syllable. Mauro Uberti, professor and musicologist, observes that García's approach produces 'risultati oggettivamente migliori' [clearly better results] (2004: 47) than that of Vaccaj. However, neither approach considers the precise placement and pitching of consonants according to their length. When consonant length is taken into account, it is clear that their placement and pitching are subject to their duration, and that the duration of preceding vowels must therefore adapt accordingly.

Canto legato was considered a fundamental tool for conveying and heightening emotion. Acclaimed singer and singing teacher Tacchinardi defines three qualities of operatic singing: 'La Scuola del Canto che serve al teatro, è di tre qualità. Di Canto di forza, o declamato: Di Canto affettuoso, o legato, e di Canto brillante, o di agilità' [The School of Singing that serves theatre has three qualities. Forceful, or declamatory Singing, affectionate, or *legato* Singing, and bright, or *coloratura* Singing] (1833: 15). Here, Tacchinardi uses *canto legato* synonymously with *canto affettuoso*, meaning 'affectionate' or 'tender' singing. He goes on to explain how the singer should create *canto affettuoso*, stating that this should always be *legato* (1833: 22–23).

The dictionary definition of *canto legato* given in 1869 by composer and musicologist Luigi Felice Rossi in the renowned Tommaseo-Bellini *Dizionario della lingua italiana* [Dictionary of the Italian language] (the most comprehensive Italian dictionary of the nineteenth century) is based on Tacchinardi's words: *canto legato* is defined as 'lo stesso che

Canto affettuoso' [the same as *canto affettuoso*] (Rossi 1869: 1789). In turn, the definition of *canto affettuoso* is as follows:

> Che tramezza il brillante e il declamato. [...] Non ti sorprende, non ti scuote, ma dolcemente ti muove. Si eseguisce sempre con quella unione e morbidezza che viene dal portamento della voce, ond'è chiamato ancora Canto legato.
>
> [It is between coloratura and declamatory singing. [...] It does not startle or shake you, it gently moves you. It is always executed with that connection and smoothness that comes from *portamento di voce*, which is why it is also called *canto legato*.] (Rossi 1861: 227)

Taking into consideration the teachings in the Italian vocal literature discussed in this section, the concept of *legato* is therefore understood in the Melofonetica Method as the use of *portamento* to heighten expression – while preserving correct diction.

The use of *portamento* as an expressive tool

> *Endeavour to attain this high qualification of the Portamento, and I must again repeat, deliver your words with energy and emphasis, articulate them distinctly, let the countenance be adapted to the subject, and fear not your success.*
>
> — DOMENICO CORRI (1811: 4)

When skilfully executed, *portamento* was widely regarded during the eighteenth and nineteenth centuries as one of the ways to achieve excellence as a singer. At this time, it was common practice for singers to use *portamento* instinctively in expressive singing, so composers did not need to mark every opportunity for them to do so. Deborah Kauffman remarks:

> It is not surprising that the writers of [singing treatises in the nineteenth century] do not explain in detail where and how *portamento* is applied, since, while it generally highlights important elements of the text and music, it is left to the singer to apply as he or she sees fit, according to his or her training and experience. (1992: 158)

This is similar to the intuitive use of *appoggiatura* which Lorenzo Bianconi (2005: 196) describes as a standard practice in the eighteenth and nineteenth centuries, so taken for granted that it was unnecessary to notate (he adds that omitting the use of *appoggiatura* due to a misplaced sense of scrupulous loyalty to the written score would be a mistake).

Portamento should not be used excessively but applied selectively. The singer and composer Bernardo Mengozzi (1804: 17) advises that, rather than overusing *portamento* to the point of rendering singing monotonous and cloying, it is essential that the singer knows how to inject variety by alternating the use of *portamento* and the connection of notes without *legato*.

There is also emphasis in several Italian vocal methods that *legato* as a form of *portamento* should not be confused with *glissando*, the slower, freer form of *portamento* that can involve hesitation on intermediate tones and was meant to be used more sparingly as a form of ornamentation. This was referred to as *strascino* (P. Tosi, 1723: 31), *striscio* (Lamperti 1864: 8) or *strascicato* (Tacchinardi 1833: 23).

Kauffman observes that 'in [the twentieth] century *portamento* has been viewed with suspicion' (1992: 139), noting the views of music critic and scholar William J. Henderson (1938: 86) who believed that *portamento* could be a very effective expressive tool when used prudently, but that its habitual use could result in scooping, i.e. dropping down to a lower tone before beginning an upward slide (or vice versa).

It is to such misuses that the decline in popularity of *portamento* may perhaps be attributed. However, as Kauffman points out:

> Even a cursory listening of recordings from the turn of the century reveals an entirely different attitude toward portamento. Rather than viewing it with suspicion, singers from the end of the nineteenth century introduced portamento frequently, and with considerable care and delicacy [...] portamento seems to have been an indispensable part of their expressive vocabulary. (1992: 139)

Indeed, a detailed analysis of recordings of great singers, even into the twenty-first century, is revealing: voices differ according to timbre, tempo and interpretation, but the skilled application of *portamento* is often evident.

Where to apply *portamento*

Portamento is applicable in all types of Italian vocal repertoire, from all eras. *Portamento* is usually used instinctively to connect notes in melismatic passages, but its use in syllabic passages was originally an expressive choice made by singers. As such, *portamento* in syllabic passages has only been marked in scores (with a slur) from the nineteenth century onwards. Where it is not notated, the singer may still choose to add *portamento* in syllabic passages to heighten emotional impact. This will depend on the nature of the piece and the singer's interpretation. In the same way that the singer decides where to apply the agogic accent to heighten expressive effect, they may also identify appropriate points to use *portamento* by looking for words that drive the drama or emotion. The composer is likely to have highlighted such words or syllables through the use of tonic, dynamic and/or agogic accents; tempo markings; and/or other expressive indications.

The use of *portamento* is more common in slower tempi and/or on notes of long duration, but its frequency and placement can vary according to preference. The use of *portamento* on the approach to an unstressed beat that forms part of the Michelangelo effect is particularly effective.

How to apply *portamento*

The use of *portamento* in syllabic passages involves a rapid, continuous slide on the vowel (or priority vowel in a group of vowels), without hesitation on intermediate tones, to transition to the pitch of the next note before the onset of the phoneme that follows. This slide can occur in any interval, whether descending or ascending in pitch, and can, in some instances, be barely perceptible.

In the correct application of *portamento* in the Melofonetica Method, the slide on the vowel must always start at a specific point, while the full duration of the slide will depend upon whether there is a long consonant, or not, before the note that follows. The *portamento* slide will be shorter where it precedes a long consonant or group of consonants containing a long consonant, and longer where it precedes a short consonant or group of two short consonants. Due to its specific starting point and length, this type of *portamento* is distinct from *glissando* and 'French' *portamento* – so called here since it was described by Manuel García Sr. (1830: 7) as 'l'ancienne manière Française' [the old French style]. Like *glissando*, French *portamento* can be considered a form of ornamentation where, across two notes, the pitch of the first note is carried to the second syllable before a quick slide to reach the pitch of the second note on the vowel of the second syllable. While García advises against using this type of *portamento* in Italian repertoire (1830: 7), Vaccaj simply refers to it as a lesser used form (1833: 29).

The correct placement of the *portamento* slide is illustrated, in Figures 177 to 188, across two crotchets (quarter notes). The length of the slide will be proportionately shorter in faster tempi. For each example that follows, the same notes are also shown without the use of *portamento*.

For simplicity, rhythmic variants are not included in the examples provided here. However, regardless of the length of the consonant that follows, the *portamento* slide will always start at the point where the onset of a long consonant would normally occur (see Section 1.9, 'Long consonants in notation').

IN MELOPHONETIC TRANSCRIPTION

A *portamento* slide is indicated with a forward slash [/] immediately after the relevant vowel, or priority vowel in a group of vowels. This applies in any interval, whether descending or ascending in pitch.

Applying *portamento* before a short consonant
or group of two short consonants

Where a *portamento* slide is applied before a short consonant or group of two short consonants, the slide on the vowel begins on the last quaver (eighth note) of the first crotchet (quarter note). It is a quaver of continuous sound that reaches the pitch of the second crotchet immediately prior to the onset of the short consonant, as shown in Figures 177 and 178.

🎧 Figure 177. *Portamento* slide applied to the vowel *a*, prior to the short consonant *m* in *amo*.

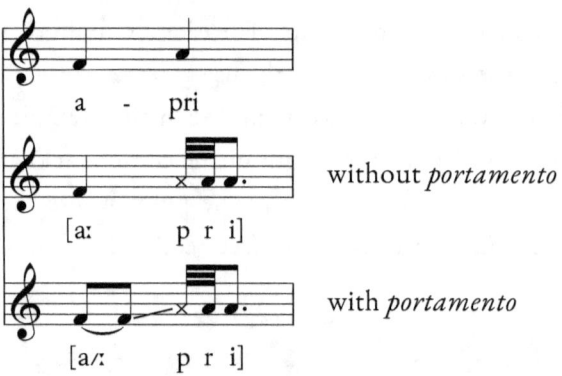

🎧 Figure 178. *Portamento* slide applied to the vowel *a*, prior to the group of two short consonants *pr* in *apri*.

APPLYING *PORTAMENTO* BEFORE A LONG CONSONANT

Where a *portamento* slide is applied before a long consonant, the slide on the vowel still begins on the last quaver (eighth note) of the first note. It is a semiquaver (sixteenth note) of continuous sound that reaches the pitch of the second note immediately prior to the onset and hold of the long consonant; together the onset and hold take the remaining semiquaver of the first note, as shown in Figures 179 to 181. The *portamento* slide begins where the onset of the long consonant would normally occur, so the hold of the long consonant is proportionally shortened to accommodate the length of the slide.

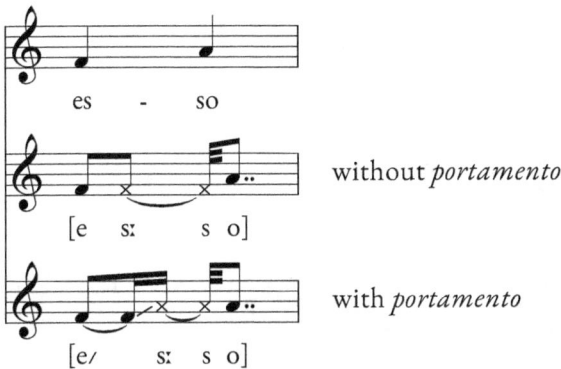

🎧 Figure 179. *Portamento* slide applied to the vowel *e*, prior to the long sibilant consonant *s* in *esso*.

As a consequence of the slide on the vowel, the onset and hold of all sonorant consonants (which would normally be pitched on the first note, as explained in 'Sonorant consonants' in Section 1.9) are pitched on the second note when *portamento* is used, as shown in Figure 180.

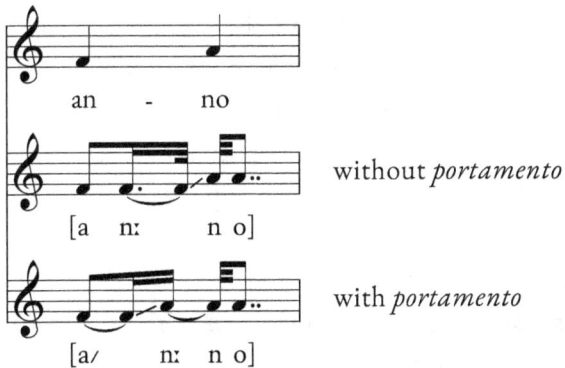

🎧 Figure 180. *Portamento* slide applied to the vowel *a*, prior to the long sonorant consonant *n* in *anno*.

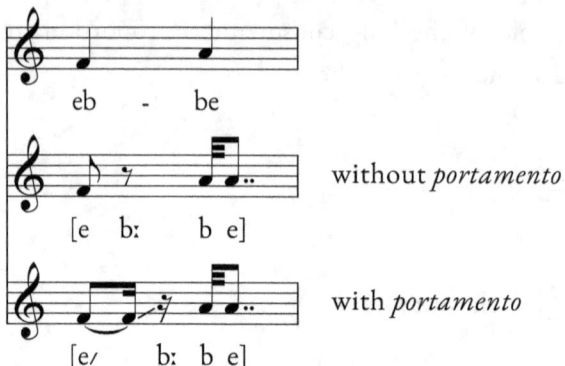

🎧 Figure 181. *Portamento* slide applied to the vowel *e*, prior to the long stop consonant *b* in *ebbe*.

APPLYING *PORTAMENTO* BEFORE A GROUP OF CONSONANTS CONTAINING A LONG CONSONANT

Where a *portamento* slide is applied before a group of consonants that contains a long consonant, the position and length of the slide are the same as those before a long consonant between vowels. The *portamento* slide starts where the onset of the first consonant in the group would normally occur (see 'Groups of consonants in notation' in Section 1.10). As mentioned previously, there is a proportional shortening of the hold of the long consonant to accommodate the length of the *portamento* slide. As a consequence of the slide on the vowel, all consonants in the group that would normally be pitched on the first note are instead pitched on the second note when *portamento* is applied, as shown in Figures 182 to 185.

To clarify the placement of groups of consonants in notation, the examples in Figures 182 to 185 show how *portamento and* melo-gemination are applied independently or in combination.

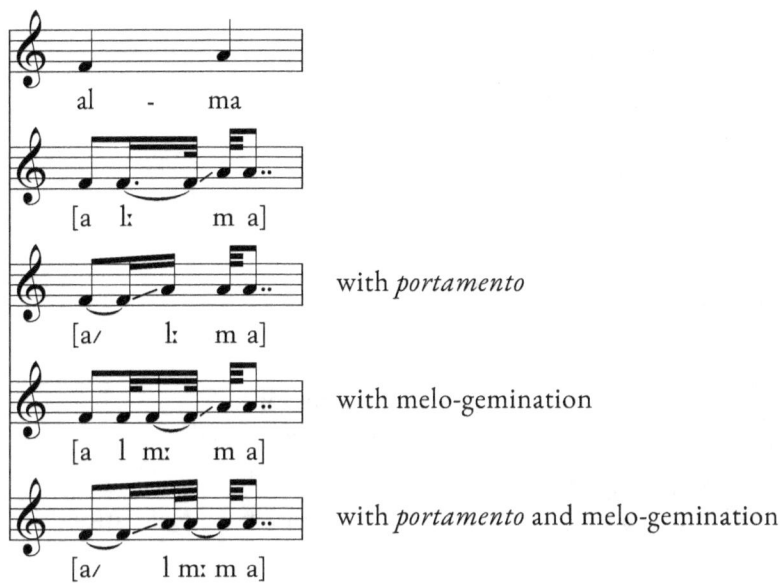

🎧 Figure 182. *Portamento* slide applied to the vowel *a*, prior to the group of consonants *lm* in *alma*, shown with and without the additional use of melo-gemination.

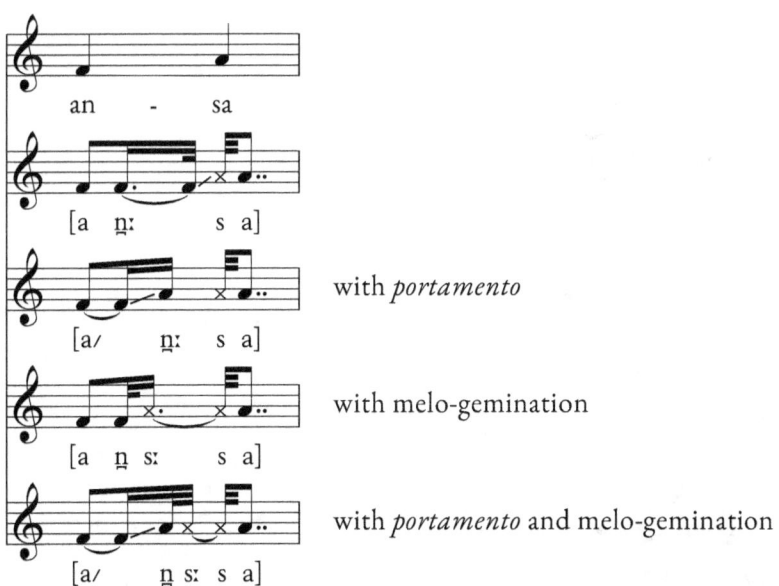

🎧 Figure 183. *Portamento* slide applied to the vowel *a*, prior to the group of consonants *ns* in *ansa*, shown with and without the additional use of melo-gemination.

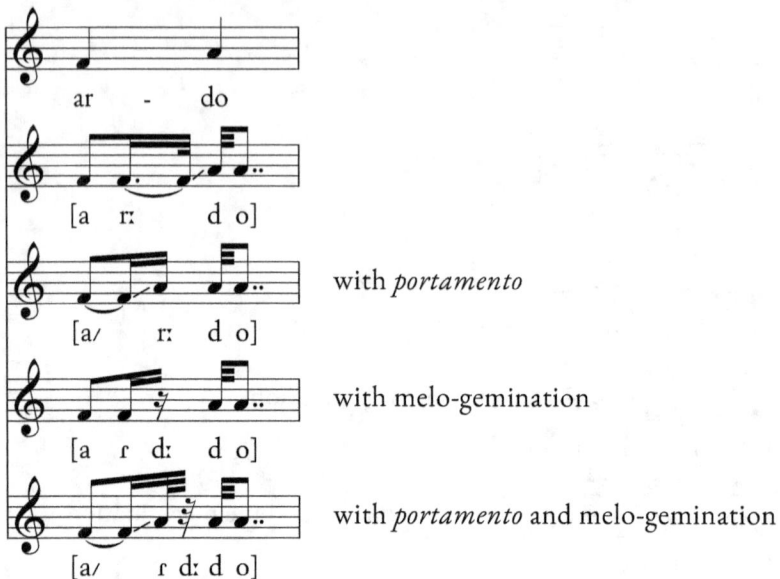

🎧 Figure 184. *Portamento* slide applied to the vowel *a*, prior to the group of consonants *rd* in *ardo*, shown with and without the additional use of melo-gemination.

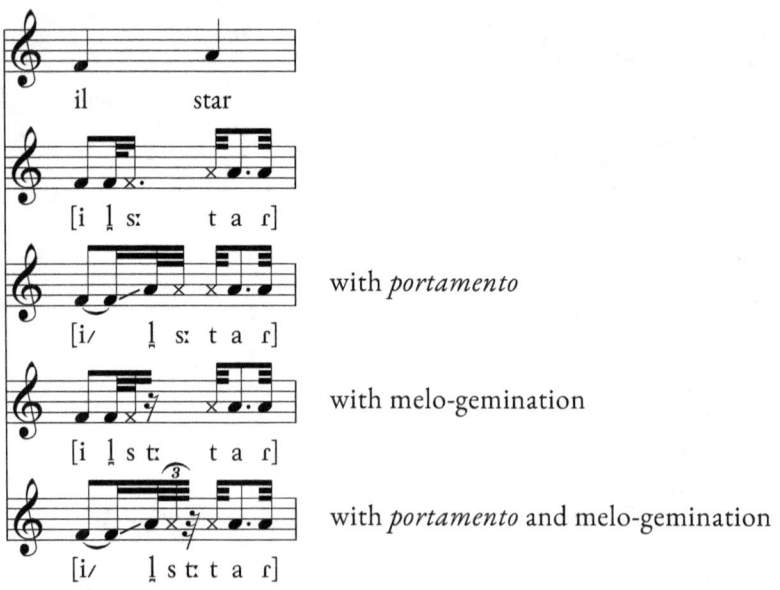

🎧 Figure 185. *Portamento* slide applied to the vowel *i*, prior to the group of consonants *lst* in *il star*, shown with and without the additional use of melo-gemination.

Applying portamento before a vowel

Where a *portamento* slide is applied before a vowel, i.e. there is no consonant between notes one and two, the slide is placed in exactly the same way as it would be before a short consonant. The slide on the vowel begins on the last quaver (eighth note) of the first crotchet (quarter note). It is a quaver of continuous sound that reaches the pitch of the second crotchet immediately prior to the onset of the vowel on the second crotchet, as shown in Figure 186.

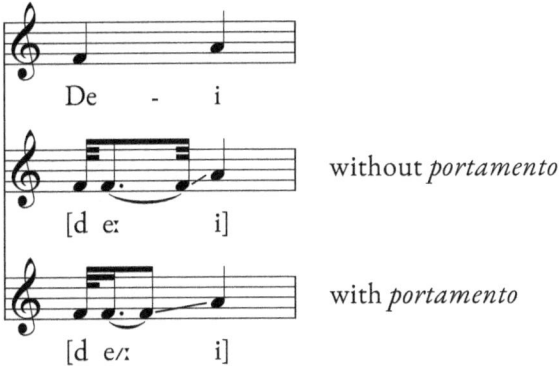

🎧 Figure 186. *Portamento* slide applied to the vowel *e*, prior to the vowel *i* in *dei*. Note that even where *portamento* is not applied, there is still a very quick, instinctive slide at the end of the first vowel, shown here as a demisemiquaver (thirty-second note), in order to connect to the vowel on the next note.

Applying portamento within a group of vowels

Where a group of vowels occurs on the first note, the *portamento* slide is always applied to the priority vowel (see Section 2.4, 'Groups of vowels and vowel prioritisation'). The preceding or subsequent vowels are placed accordingly: any preceding vowels are pitched on the first note, while subsequent vowels are pitched on the second note, as shown in Figures 187 and 188.

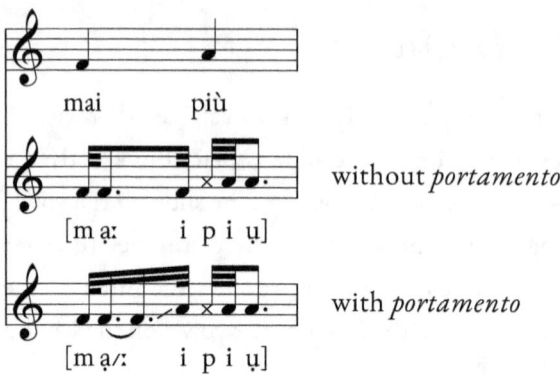

🎧 Figure 187. *Portamento* slide applied to the vowel *a* (priority vowel) in *mai più*.

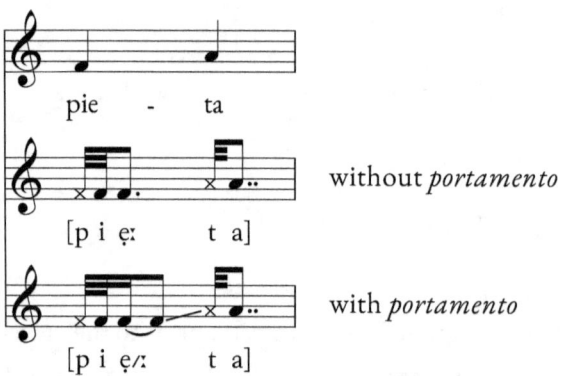

🎧 Figure 188. *Portamento* slide applied to the vowel *e* (priority vowel) in *pietà*.

Portamento and the use of the suspensive agogic accent

The singer should never apply a suspensive agogic accent during a *portamento* slide since this would create *glissando*. Where there is a *portamento* slide before a short consonant, a group of two short consonants or a vowel, it is necessary to reach the end of the slide and the pitch of the second note before applying the suspensive agogic accent. Where there is a *portamento* slide before a long consonant or a group of consonants that contains a long consonant, the suspensive agogic accent must only be applied to the hold of the long consonant. See also 'How to apply the suspensive agogic accent' in Section 3.3.

3.10 Line, phrasing and anchoring

In instrumental music, the concept of line can reasonably be understood as the production of sound without interruption, but in vocal music the same definition cannot apply since the singer needs to articulate text. For singers, any concept of line must retain clear diction at its core. In the Melofonetica Method, the concept of line is therefore understood as *fraseggio*, meaning the shape of melophonetic phrasing that the singer gives to each line of text.

The librettist crafts each line in accordance with the metric rules of Italian opera libretti. While arias and ensembles are traditionally written with a variety of poetic metres (rhythmic structures), the vast majority of *secco* and *accompagnato* recitatives are written only with hendecasyllables (lines of eleven syllables) or septenaries (lines of seven syllables). In music, the composer adds caesuras, enjambment and repetition and, in many cases, uses a slur to denote each line or section of a line (the *legatura di frase* [phrasal slur] or *legatura di espressione* [expressive slur]). Finally, the singer completes the shaping and interpretation of each phrase. Specifically, it is through the clear and expressive use of consonants that the singer manages the way in which vowels fit into the musical rhythm, revealing micro-rhythm within the notated rhythm.

García Jr. reminds the singer of the importance of consonants in phrasing, pacing and indicating when the orchestra should re-enter to accompany the voice (1847: II. 7). In this regard, it is particularly useful for the singer to identify those syllables that are energised by the release of long consonants. In each phrase, one or more of these syllables can function as anchoring points that help the singer to structure the musical line. These points are where the use of expressive tools, including the agogic accent, *portamento* and micro-dynamics, will often be appropriate.

When identified early in the process of learning new repertoire, anchoring points help the singer to embed clear and expressive diction firmly into the muscle memory. These expressive 'hotspots' create a map through the score, helping the singer to shape each line decisively, communicate clearly with their pianist or orchestra, and support the creative work of conductor and director.

CHAPTER SUMMARY

▶ The term '*attacco del suono*' [start of the sound] refers to beginning each line with clear musical and dramatic intention. In the Melofonetica Method, this is usually achieved by applying a long consonant whenever starting a new line or beginning singing again after an in-breath.

▶ In order to highlight a word or syllable that begins with a short consonant, in some instances it is possible to apply expressive emphasis by geminating the short consonant. In the Melofonetica Method this is termed 'melo-gemination'.

▶ The agogic accent adds emphasis by extending or shortening the duration of a note. Agogic accents may be notated by the composer but may also be added by the singer to highlight moments of particular significance in the text.

▶ In the Melofonetica Method, the term 'suspensive agogic accent' is used to define an accent that emphasises a syllable not by lengthening the note that the syllable occurs on, but instead by further lengthening the *preceding long phoneme* (vowel or consonant). This builds suspense on the approach to the syllable in focus and is used instinctively in the expressive articulation of text, often resulting in *rubato*.

▶ There is sometimes a misconception that singers need to add volume or length to accentuate stressed syllables. While this can work in other languages, the correct lengths of long and short consonants must be preserved in sung Italian. In music, the composer will have aligned primary stressed syllables to stressed beats to maintain their accentuation and there is nothing further that singers need to do.

▶ In order to enhance connection through words and phrases, it is often effective to incorporate rests of short duration and punctuation marks into sung Italian diction. The way this is achieved will depend on the phonemes that precede and follow the rest.

CHAPTER SUMMARY CONT.

▶ The 'Michelangelo effect' is a term used in the Melofonetica Method to describe a particular sequence of text in music. This sequence occurs so often in sung Italian that it may be considered the defining melophonetic characteristic at the heart of 'Italian style' in vocal music. The sequence consists of a syllable that belongs to an unstressed beat and begins with the release of any long consonant, followed by a syllable that belongs to a stressed beat and begins with a short consonant, or no consonant, and is preceded by the continuity of a long vowel, or a long sibilant or sonorant consonant in a group. The resulting syncopation is surprising and unpredictable: we hear an accented (emphasised) note where we are expecting an unaccented note and vice versa.

▶ The Michelangelo effect can occur through the correct articulation of long and short consonants, before any expressive emphasis is added. The singer may also choose to create or avoid the Michelangelo effect by using melo-gemination and/or de-gemination, for different expressive results.

▶ The practice of *notes inégales* (literally meaning 'unequal notes') in instrumental music involves a freedom in the performance of smaller note values, originally inspired by vocal music. Inequality of rhythm is often evident in sung Italian, particularly across notes of smaller value, due to the sequencing of long and short consonants and the use of the agogic accent. This is at its most striking in the Michelangelo effect.

▶ The sung Italian language gives singers the freedom to colour vowels in the way that is right for their voice and the expressive qualities they wish to deliver in each line.

▶ Despite the apparent fluidity of the sung language, Italian has fewer vowels and more stop and sibilant consonants than English. There often remains, however, a wariness of clearly and correctly articulating long consonants for fear of jeopardising *legato* or 'line', used to mean a smooth connection through a musical phrase without interruption of sound.

> **CHAPTER SUMMARY CONT.**

▶ In eighteenth- and nineteenth-century Italian vocal treatises, *legato* is frequently described as a form of *portamento di voce* that involves a smooth connection between notes and is used to heighten emotional impact. While there are references to avoiding the interruption of an in-breath during the slide from one note to the next, the teaching of *legato* as a form of *portamento* did not include any reference to shortening or softening consonants to facilitate the smooth connection of notes. In the Melofonetica Method, the concept of *legato* is therefore understood as the use of *portamento* to heighten expression – while preserving correct diction.

▶ In the Melofonetica Method, *portamento* is achieved through the use of a rapid, continuous slide on the vowel to transition to the pitch of the following note immediately prior to the onset of the consonant. The slide must always start at a specific point and its duration will be dependent upon the phoneme(s) that follow(s).

▶ While in instrumental music the concept of 'line' can reasonably be understood as the production of sound without interruption, in vocal music the same definition cannot apply since the singer needs to articulate text. In the Melofonetica Method, the concept of line is therefore understood as *fraseggio*: the shape of melophonetic phrasing that the singer gives to each line of text.

▶ In shaping each phrase, it is through the clear and expressive use of consonants that the singer manages the way in which vowels fit into the musical rhythm, revealing micro-rhythm within the notated rhythm.

▶ Syllables that are energised by the release of long consonants can function as anchoring points that help the singer to structure the musical line and are often where the use of expressive tools will be appropriate. These expressive 'hotspots' create a map through the score, helping the singer to shape each phrase decisively.

Vocalising exercises

🎧 1. The *attacco del suono*

1.	me - ra	- vi -	glia al		cor
2.	so - li	- tu -	di -	ni	
3.	ram - men	- tar	al -	lor	
4.	ca - ro a	- mi	-	co	
5.	te - me	- ra	-	ri	
6.	spi - ra il	ven	-	to	
7.	sì	brin - dia	-	mo	
8.	ec - cel	- len	-	te	
9.	sma - nie e	fu	-	rie	
10.	a - mor	mi	-	o	

Transcriptions:
1. *meraviglia al cor* [m: me: ɾa: viʎ: ʎal: koɾ]
2. *solitudini* [s: so: li: tu: di: ni]
3. *rammentar allor* [ɾam: men̪: ta: ɾal: loɾ]
4. *caro amico* [k: ka: ɾo a: mi: ko]
5. *temerari* [t: 'te: me: ɾa: ɾi]
6. *spira il vento* [sp: pi: ɾal: ven̪: to]
7. *sì brindiamo* [sib: bɾin̪: di̯a: mo]
8. *eccellente* [etʃ: tʃel: len̪: te]
9. *smanie e furie* [sm: ma: ni̯ef: fu: ɾi̯e]
10. *amor mio* [ʔ: ʔa: mor: mi̯o]

🎧 2. Melo-gemination

Apply melo-gemination to highlight the word(s) in brackets:

1.	fi	- da	- ti	del	co	- re	(*core*)
2.	ca	- ra	spo	- sa, a	- man	- te	(*sposa*)
3.	un	bra	- ma	- to ar	- do	- re	(*bramato* and *ardore*)
4.	i	per	- du	- ti i	- stan	- ti	(*perduti* and *istanti*)
5.	lu	- sin	- ghi e	- ra	spe	- me	(*lusinghiera* and *speme*)
6.	ma	la	gran	de im	- pre	- sa	(*grande* and *impresa*)

Transcriptions:
1. *fidati del core* [f: fi: da: ti: delk: ko: ɾe]
2. *cara sposa, amante* [k: ka: ɾasp: po: sa: maṉ: te]
3. *un bramato ardore* [umb: bɾa: ma: toa̱ɾd: do: ɾe]
4. *i perduti istanti* [ip: per: du: tist: taṉ: ti]
5. *lusinghiera speme* [l: lu: siŋg: gi̱ẹ: ɾasp: pe: me]
6. *ma la grande impresa* [mal: la: gɾaṉd: dẹimp: pɾe: sa]

⏎ 3. Suspensive agogic accent

Apply a suspensive agogic accent to complement the *fermata* in the following lines:

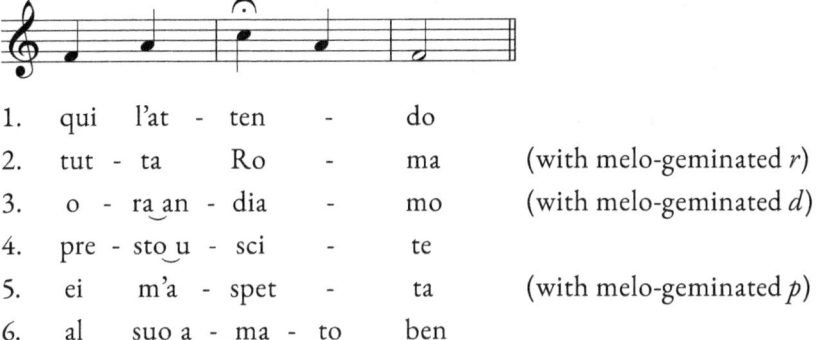

1.	qui	l'at -	ten	-	do	
2.	tut - ta		Ro	-	ma	(with melo-geminated *r*)
3.	o -	ra‿an -	dia	-	mo	(with melo-geminated *d*)
4.	pre -	sto‿u -	sci	-	te	
5.	ei	m'a -	spet	-	ta	(with melo-geminated *p*)
6.	al	suo‿a -	ma -	to	ben	

Transcriptions*:
1. *qui l'attendo* [kuiˑlː latˑː tenː do]
2. *tutta Roma* [tutː tarˑː roː ma]
3. *ora andiamo* [ʔː ʔoː randˑː diaː mo]
4. *presto uscite* [pː presː touʃˑː ʃiː te]
5. *ei m'aspetta* [ʔː ʔei: maspˑː petˑː ta]
6. *al suo amato ben* [al̹ː suaˑː maː toː ben]

*The choice of anticipation and/or delay as shown in the transcriptions for numbers 1 to 5 and the use of *rubato* in all examples may be varied according to the singer's preference.

🎧 4. The incorporation of rests into diction (between lines and sections of lines)

1. u - na   stel - la   nel   ciel
2. che si   pos - sa   be - ar
3. dal mio se - no,   scac - ciar
4. a   sal - var - la...   io   vo
5. scel-le - ra - to!   che   fai?
6. già la ce - na   ser - vir

Transcriptions:
1. *una stella nel ciel* [ʔː ʔuː nasː telː lanː nel̪ː tʃel]
2. *che si possa bear* [kesː siː posː sabː beː aɾ]
3. *dal mio seno, scacciar* [dː dalː mio̞ː seː noskː katʃː tʃaɾ]
4. *a salvarla... io vo* [asː salː varː laː io̞ː vo]
5. *scellerato! che fai?* [ʃelː leː ɾaː tokːː kefː fa̞i]
6. *già la cena servir* [dʒalː laː tʃeː nasː serː viɾ]

🎧 5. The incorporation of rests into diction (between and within words)

1. eb - ben chi   bat - te   las - sù
2. in - co - min - cia - mo_a can - tar
3. ah for - se_è lui   che   nel   cor
4. ca - ro_e - li - sir   di   bel - tà
5. so - spi - ro_e pal - pi - to_or sì
6. sen - ti - lo   bat - te - re   qui

Transcriptions:
1. *ebben chi batte lassù* [ebˑ beŋkˑ kibˑ batˑ telˑ lasˑ su]
2. *incominciamo a cantar* [iŋkˑ koˑ miɲtʃˑ tʃaˑ moa̯kˑ kaɲtˑ tar]
3. *ah forse è lui che nel cor* [afˑ forsˑ selˑ lu̯ikˑ kenˑ nelkˑ kor]
4. *caro elisir di beltà* [kˑ kaː ro̯ẹ liː sirdˑ dibˑ beḽtˑ ta]
5. *sospiro e palpito or sì* [sospˑ piː ro̯ẹpˑ palpˑ piː torsˑ si]
6. *sentilo battere qui* [seṉtˑ tiˑ lobˑ batˑ teː rekˑ kui̯]

🎧 6. The incorporation of punctuation into diction

1.   cre - di,   par - la   col   cor
2.   qui   nel   sen;   ma da al - lor
3.   dor - mi...   dor - mi...   te - sor
4.   ciel!   ma   co - me?   lan - guir
5.   con   un   brin - di - si,   sì!
6.   or   tu   dim - mi: 'ei   vien'

Transcriptions:
1. *credi, parla col cor* [kː kɾeː dipˑː parː laː kolː koɾ]
2. *qui nel sen; ma da allor* [kː ku̯inː ne̯lsː semˑː madː dalː loɾ]
3. *dormi... dormi... tesor* [dː dorː midˑː dorː mitˑː teː soɾ]
4. *ciel! ma come? languir* [ʧelmˑː makː koː melˑː laŋː gu̯iɾ]
5. *con un brindisi, sì!* [kː koː numː brin̠ː diː sisˑː si]
6. *or tu dimmi: 'ei vien'* [ʔː ʔorː tudː dimː miʔˑː ʔei̯ː vi̯en]

7. The Michelangelo effect

1. oh, se Flo-rin-do è fe-del
2. pie-ni di gio-ia e d'a-mor
3. sa-rà cru-de-le co-sì
4. cre-di, sa-pran-no sa-lir
5. re del-l'a-bis-so a li-brar
6. or un ne-mi-co non è
7. il gran po-e-ma can-tar
8. se me-sta vo-ce e-gli a-vrà
9. so-lo il suo a-mor può col-mar
10. là ci da-re-mo la man
11. per ven-di-car-mi qui vien
12. sol col-l'o-nor vin-ce-rà

Transcriptions:
1. *oh, se Florindo è fedel* [oːʰ seʳː floː rin̠ː doe̯fʳː feː del]
2. *pieni di gioia e d'amor* [pː pi̯eː nidʳː diː dʒoː i(a̯)edʳː daː moɾ]
3. *sarà crudele così* [sː saː ɾakʳː kɾuː deː lekʳː koː si]
4. *credi, sapranno salir* [kː kɾeː disʳː saː pɾanː nosʳː saːʳ liɾ]
5. *re dell'abisso a librar* [ɾedʳː delʳː laː bisʳː soa̯lʳː liː bɾaɾ]
6. *or un nemico non è* [ʔː ʔoː ɾunʳː neː miː konʳː noː ˈne]
7. *il gran poema cantar* [ʔː ʔil: gɾampʳː poːʳ eː makʳː kan̠ʳː taɾ]
8. *se mesta voce egli avrà* [semʳʳ mestʳː taːʳ voː t͡ʃeʎʳː ʎaː vɾa]
9. *solo il suo amor può colmar* [sː soː lol̩ːs su̯aːʳ moɾː pu̯okʳː kolʳː maɾ]
10. *là ci daremo la man* [lat͡ʃːʳ t͡ʃidʳː daːʳ ɾeː molʳː laː man]
11. *per vendicarmi qui vien* [pː peɾː ven̠dː diː kaɾː mikʳː ku̯iː vi̯en̠]
12. *sol coll'onor vincerà* [sː solː kolʳː loː noɾː vin̠t͡ʃː t͡ʃeːʳ ɾa]

8. Portamento

Apply *portamento* where indicated by the slurs in the following lines:

1. a - mo - re - vo - le
2. sof - fio e - te - si - o
3. mil - le e tren - ta - tré
4. ah, non più pe - nar
5. se ar-dor bra - mi al - fin
6. mai lo sia per me

Transcriptions:
1. *amorevole* [ʔː ʔa/ː moː ɾe/ː voː le]
2. *soffio etesio* [so/f: fioe̯ː te/ː siː o]
3. *mille e trentatré* [mi/lː leː tɾe/n̪ tː taː tɾe]
4. *ah, non più penar* [a/n: nom: piu̯/p: peː naɾ]
5. *se ardor brami alfin* [s: sea̯/r: doɾb: bɾa/ː mia̯lf: fin]
6. *mai lo sia per me* [m: ma̯/i: los: si̯/ːa: perː me]

APPENDIX A

The Italian melophonetic alphabet and notes on pronunciation

The following table assigns each letter in the Italian alphabet to its corresponding symbol(s) in melophonetic transcription and provides details on articulation. Specific guidance on pronunciation, where applicable, is provided in the notes that follow the table. This list is based on the symbols used in the International Phonetic Alphabet (International Phonetic Association 2020), the ^{can}IPA Natural Phonetics framework (Canepari 2009) and the principles of the Melofonetica Method. Refer to the glossary at the end of this book for full explanations of phonetic terminology.

Each phoneme marked with an asterisk (*) is an allophone, i.e. a phonetic variant that occurs when certain consonants are coarticulated. For more information about allophones, see Section 1.11, 'Coarticulation of consonants'.

Table 5. The Italian melophonetic alphabet.

Letter	Symbol	Articulation
a, à	[a]	Archi-vowel – see Note 1
b	[b]	Voiced bilabial occlusive
c	[k]	Unvoiced velar occlusive – see Notes 5 and 6
c (+ e, è, é, i or ì)	[tʃ]	Unvoiced post-alveolar occlu-constrictive – see Notes 5 and 6
ch	[k]	Unvoiced velar occlusive – see Notes 5 and 6
d	[d]	Voiced denti-alveolar occlusive – see Note 2
e, è, é	[e]	Archi-vowel – see Note 1
f	[f]	Unvoiced labio-dental; non-grooved constrictive when short, non-grooved occlu-constrictive when long – see Note 3
g	[g]	Voiced velar occlusive – see Notes 5 and 6
g (+ e, è, é, i or ì)	[dʒ]	Voiced post-alveolar occlu-constrictive – see Notes 5 and 6
gh	[g]	Voiced velar occlusive – see Notes 5 and 6

THE ITALIAN MELOPHONETIC ALPHABET AND NOTES ON PRONUNCIATION

Letter	Symbol	Articulation
gl	[ʎ] or [gl]	Voiced palatal lateral or [g] + [l] as a group of two consonants – see Notes 4 and 6
gn	[ɲ]	Voiced palatal nasal
h	Mute or [ʔ]	Diacritic symbol or unvoiced glottal occlusive consonant – see Note 5
i, ì	[i]	Archi-vowel or diacritic symbol (*i* only) – see Notes 1 and 6
j	[i]	Archi-vowel – see 'Approximant consonants [j] and [w]' in Section 2.4, and Note 1
l	[l]	Voiced alveolar lateral
l (+ *c* [tʃ], *g* [dʒ] or *sc* [ʃ])	[l̠]*	Voiced post-alveolar lateral
l (+ *d, s, t* or *z*)	[l̪]*	Voiced denti-alveolar lateral
l (+ *gl* [ʎ] or *gn*)	[ʎ]*	Voiced palatal lateral
m	[m]	Voiced bilabial nasal
m (+ *c* [k], *g* [g] or *q*)	[ŋ]*	Voiced velar nasal
m (+ *c* [tʃ] or *g* [dʒ])	[n̠]*	Voiced post-alveolar nasal
m (+ *d, s, t* or *z*)	[n̪]*	Voiced denti-alveolar nasal

*Denotes an allophone, see 'Coarticulation of consonants' in Section 1.11.

Letter	Symbol	Articulation
m (+ *f* or *v*)	[ɱ]*	Voiced labio-dental nasal
m (+ *gl* [ʎ] or *gn*)	[ɲ]*	Voiced palatal nasal
m (+ *l*, *n* or *r*)	[n]*	Voiced alveolar nasal
n	[n]	Voiced alveolar nasal
n (+ *b*, *m* or *p*)	[m]*	Voiced bilabial nasal
n (+ *c* [k], *g* [g] or *q*)	[ŋ]*	Voiced velar nasal
n (+ *c* [tʃ], *g* [dʒ] or *sc* [ʃ])	[ɲ̟]*	Voiced post-alveolar nasal
n (+ *d*, *s*, *t* or *z*)	[n̪]*	Voiced denti-alveolar nasal
n (+ *f* or *v*)	[ɱ]*	Voiced labio-dental nasal
n (+ *gl* [ʎ] or *gn*)	[ɲ]*	Voiced palatal nasal
o, ò, ó	[o]	Archi-vowel – see Note 1
p	[p]	Unvoiced bilabial occlusive
q	[k]	Unvoiced velar occlusive
r	[ɾ]	Voiced alveolar vibrant (tap) – see Note 7
	[r]	Voiced alveolar vibrant (trill) – see Note 7

*Denotes an allophone, see 'Coarticulation of consonants' in Section 1.11.

THE ITALIAN MELOPHONETIC ALPHABET AND NOTES ON PRONUNCIATION

Letter	Symbol	Articulation
s	[s]	Unvoiced denti-alveolar grooved constrictive – see Notes 8 and 9
	[z]	Voiced denti-alveolar grooved constrictive – see Notes 2 and 8
sc	[ʃ] or [sk]	Unvoiced post-alveolar grooved constrictive or [s] + [k] as a group of two consonants – see Notes 6 and 10
t	[t]	Unvoiced denti-alveolar occlusive – see Note 11
u, ù	[u]	Archi-vowel – see Note 1
v	[v]	Voiced labio-dental; non-grooved constrictive when short, non-grooved occlu-constrictive when long – see Note 3
z	[ts]	Unvoiced denti-alveolar occlu-constrictive – see Note 12
	[dz]	Voiced denti-alveolar occlu-constrictive – see Note 12
n/a	[ʔ]	Unvoiced glottal occlusive consonant
n/a	[h]	Unvoiced glottal constrictive consonant

Notes on pronunciation

1. Archi-vowels

In the Melofonetica Method, a sung Italian vowel can be anywhere within a range of sound that corresponds to one of the five written vowels: *a, e, i, o* or *u*. These five spectra of vowel sounds are therefore referred to as archi-vowels. They also comprise all vowels that carry accents in spelling, i.e. *à, è, é, ì, ò, ó* and *ù*. See Section 2.1, 'The five archi-vowels', for further information. The five sung Italian archi-vowels are represented simply with the five symbols [a], [e], [i], [o] and [u].

2. *d, s, t* and *z* as denti-alveolar consonants

In spoken *italiano neutro*, *d, s, t* and *z* are all considered dental consonants. In sung Italian, however, it is advisable to instead articulate these as denti-alveolar consonants. The high back tongue resting position required in Italian, which is even more prominent in singing (See 'Optimisation of the tongue position and pharyngeal space' in Section 1.13), means it is mechanically more comfortable for the blade of the singer's tongue to touch the upper gum as well as the teeth. This is evident particularly in the articulation of long consonants, where the singer needs to anchor the tongue in a more stable position, i.e. a laminal place of articulation rather than apical.

3. Long *f* and *v* as stop consonants

In spoken *italiano neutro*, long *f* and *v* are labio-dental non-grooved constrictive consonants, and as such the singer may assume they would be categorised as sibilant and sonorant consonants respectively. In sung Italian, however, it is advisable to instead produce both long *f* and *v* as occlu-constrictive (stop) consonants, particularly from the middle register upwards.

Observation shows that the increased air pressure required during singing can make it uncomfortable to control continuous voiced or unvoiced frication through the narrow fissure between the upper teeth and lower lips, a requirement in the articulation of labio-dental constrictive consonants. This type of constrictive sound is easier to produce in the lower register, but overall both long *f* and *v* sound clearer and more idiomatic in sung Italian when they are produced with a stop before their constriction, i.e. when they are occlu-constrictive. To achieve this correctly, it helps to close the lips during the labio-dental articulation.

4. *gl* as [ʎ] or [g] + [l]

As a general rule, where *gli* occurs within a word and is intervocalic, the *i* is diacritic, signalling that the *gl* is pronounced [ʎ], for example in *pagliacci* [paʎ: 'ʎatʃ: tʃi]. Where *gl* + *i* occur at the *end* of a word, the *i* is not diacritic, so they are pronounced instead as [ʎi], for example in *figli* ['fiʎ: ʎi]. Note that the article or pronoun *gli* is always pronounced [ʎi], for example in *per gli Dei*.

In combinations of *gli* + consonant, the *i* is not diacritic so *gl* is usually pronounced [ʎi], for example in *biscaglina* [bis: kaʎ: ʎi: na]. However, the *gl* can sometimes be pronounced as a group of two distinct consonants, [g] + [l], for example in *glicine* [gli: tʃi: ne] or *anglicano* [aŋ: gli: ka: no]. It is advisable to consult a good Italian dictionary to determine the correct pronunciation of words containing *gli* followed by a consonant.

5. *h* as a diacritic symbol or mute

In Italian, the letter *h* is a diacritic symbol where it is preceded by the consonants *c* or *g*. In these cases, the *h* signals a different pronunciation of the *c* or *g*, as follows:
- *che* is [ke], while *ce* is [tʃe]
- *chi* is [ki], while *ci* is [tʃi]
- *ghe* is [ge], while *ge* is [dʒe]

- *ghi* is [gi], while *gi* is [dʒi]
- *sche* is [ske], while *sce* is [ʃe]
- *schi* is [ski], while *sci* is [ʃi]

Where the letter *h* is not diacritic, it is always mute when it occurs within a word, for example in *ahimè* [aːi ˈme]. Where *h* occurs at the beginning of an Italian or non-Italian word, it is a glottal occlusive consonant, for example in *ho* [ˈʔo] or *Harry* [ˈʔaːri].

6. Diacritic *i*

The letter *i* is sometimes a diacritic symbol where it is preceded by the consonants *c, g, gl* or *sc*. In these cases, the *i* signals a different pronunciation of the *c, g, gl* or *sc*, as follows:
- *cia* is [tʃa], while *ca* is [ka]
- *cie* and *ce* are both [tʃe]
- *cio* is [tʃo], while *co* is [ko]
- *ciu* is [tʃu], while *cu* is [ku]
- *gia* is [dʒa], while *ga* is [ga]
- *gie* and *ge* are both [dʒe]
- *gio* is [dʒo], while *go* is [go]
- *giu* is [dʒu], while *gu* is [gu]
- *glia* is [ʎa], while *gla* is [gla]
- *glie* is [ʎe], while *gle* is [gle]
- *glio* is [ʎo], while *glo* is [glo]
- *gliu* is [ʎu], while *glu* is [glu]
- *scia* is [ʃa], while *sca* is [ska]
- *scie* and *sce* are both [ʃe]
- *scio* is [ʃo], while *sco* is [sko]
- *sciu* is [ʃu], while *scu* is [sku]

There are some instances of the above combinations where the *i* is not diacritic. This occurs where the *i* is accented, for example in *Lucia* [luːˈtʃia] or *magia* [maːˈdʒia], or where the *i* is at the end of a word, for example in *amici* [aːˈmiːtʃi]. The singer should consult a good Italian dictionary to determine whether an *i* is diacritic or not.

7. When and how to roll *r*

In sung Italian, when *r* is a long consonant, for example in *terra* ['ter: ra], it should be rolled as a trill. To practise achieving a long rolled *r* in sung Italian, see Exercise 7: 'Improving the rolled *r*', in Chapter 1. A short intervocalic *r*, for example those in *per ora* [pe: 'ro: ɾa], should instead simply be tapped (flicked once) and not rolled. Note the difference between the symbols for long *r* [r] and short *r* [ɾ].

Where the *r* is short within a group of consonants, this should also simply be tapped, for example in *altro*. If some rolling does occur here, this is not incorrect as long as the rolled *r* is not given as much length as the long consonant in the group.

Where a word ending with *r* also ends the line or is followed by an in-breath, the *r* should remain short unless the singer wishes to finish the line more dramatically. In this case, the *r* may be rolled with a few flicks but should not be as long as a fully rolled *r*.

Where *r* occurs at the beginning of a word and at the beginning of a line, in many cases the *attacco del suono* should be applied and the *r* should therefore be long and rolled. If an exception to the *attacco del suono* applies, the *r* will remain short and simply be tapped. See Section 3.1, 'The *attacco del suono*'.

Note that the Italian *r* should be articulated as an alveolar vibrant consonant. This is distinct from the English *r*, a post-alveolar approximant consonant, and the French *r*, an uvular vibrant consonant.

8. *s* as unvoiced [s] or voiced [z]

In spoken *italiano neutro*, *s* is almost always pronounced as unvoiced [s]. It is only pronounced as voiced [z] if it is intervocalic, in the middle of a word, and not part of or adjacent to a prefix or suffix or followed by another voiced consonant. For example, in *risuona* [ɾi: 'suǫ: na] and *vedasi* ['ve: da: si], the *s* is unvoiced, while in *casa* ['ka: za] and *sleale* [z: le: 'a: le], the *s* is voiced [z]. There are, however, many instances where it is equally acceptable to articulate a voiced [z] as unvoiced [s].

In sung Italian, it is usually advisable to produce all instances of *s* (long and short) as unvoiced [s]. In the creation of the short voiced *s* [z], there is naturally, in any case, a combination of voiced and unvoiced sound, but the unvoiced sound prevails when a greater volume is required (see Elie and Laprie 2017: 209). Attempting to fully voice a short *s* as [z] produces a sound that is too long, while fully unvoicing it instead makes the sound easier to produce and more audible (see Elie and Laprie 2017: 209). This is noticeable particularly when *s*, a denti-alveolar consonant, needs to be articulated with the high air pressure involved in singing.

The only instance of a long voiced *s* [z] in spoken Italian occurs where this is followed by another voiced consonant, for example in *disdetta*. In sung Italian, it is also preferable to produce the long voiced *s* as an unvoiced [s] since this is the most comfortable way to articulate a longer fricative sound with enough volume (see Elie and Laprie 2017: 209).

IN MELOPHONETIC TRANSCRIPTION

Given the above and for simplicity, all instances of short and long *s* are indicated with the symbol [s].

9. Long Italian *s*

When making the long sibilant *s*, singers sometimes 'squeeze' the sound by positioning the tip of the tongue too high behind the upper teeth. To make a correct long *s* in Italian, there should be a larger resonating space for the outward airstream. This is created by moving the tip of the tongue forward towards the lower gum to make a larger channel (groove) between the centre of the tongue and the upper alveolar ridge (the ridge that protrudes between the upper gum and the beginning of the hard palate). In contrast, the English *s* is produced via a smaller channel and, as a result, has a higher-frequency sound.

10. sc as [ʃ] or [s] + [k]

Where *sc* is followed by *e, è, é, i* or *ì*, it is pronounced [ʃ], for example in *scena* [ˈʃeː na] or *esci* [ˈeʃː ʃi].

Where *sc* is within a word and is followed by *i* + another vowel, the *i* is diacritic, signalling that the *sc* should be pronounced [ʃ], for example in *lascia* [ˈlaʃː ʃa] or *scienza* [ˈʃen̪ː tsa].

However, where *sc* is followed by *a, o* or *u*, or diacritic *h* + *e* or *i*, it is pronounced as a group of two distinct consonants, [s] + [k], for example in *fresco* [ˈfrɛsː ko] or *scherzo* [sː ˈkɛrː tso].

11. Italian *t*

The correct articulation of the Italian *t* is often a challenge for singers whose first language is English, and it can also prove difficult for other singers whose first language uses an occlu-constrictive and/or post-alveolar *t*. When *t* is articulated as an occlu-constrictive consonant, as it is in English, it produces a sound that is often described as 'wet'. This is because upon the release of the sound, the tongue causes a constriction that audibly obstructs the airflow, similar to the constriction made when the English *ch* [tʃ] sound is articulated.

The 'dry' Italian *t* is an occlusive consonant, meaning that following the occlusion of the airflow, there is a clean release without any audible obstruction. Additionally, when the place of articulation is post-alveolar, as it is in the production of the English *t*, this means that the tongue touches the alveolar ridge. This is further back than the tongue position needed for the articulation of the Italian *t*, making it harder to seal the airflow (particularly important in the articulation of a long stop *t*) and reducing pharyngeal space.

In the articulation of the Italian *t*, the correct place of articulation is denti-alveolar, meaning that the blade of the tongue is against the teeth and upper gum, i.e. further forward than the post-alveolar position. The denti-alveolar position makes it more comfortable to effectively seal the airflow and creates greater pharyngeal space for the production of the vowel that follows.

Sometimes singers try to resolve a wet *t* by articulating a *d* instead. This may avoid constriction upon the release of the sound (since, in the case of English, *d* is an occlusive consonant like the Italian *t*), but the voicing of the release jeopardises comprehension in Italian, for example *noto* (well known) becomes *nodo* (knot). Furthermore, the English *d* does not employ the same place of articulation as the Italian *t*, since the English *d* is articulated as a post-alveolar rather than denti-alveolar consonant.

12. *z* as unvoiced [ts] or voiced [dz]

In spoken *italiano neutro*, *z* can either be unvoiced [ts] or voiced [dz]. The rules vary and there are many instances where it is equally acceptable to articulate voiced [dz] as unvoiced [ts].

In sung Italian, it is advisable to produce all occurrences of *z* as unvoiced [ts]. Whether it is a short or long consonant, we only hear the voicing or unvoicing of *z* in its release (when *z* is long, it is a stop consonant with a silent hold before its release). There is naturally, in any case, a combination of voiced and unvoiced sound in the short voiced *z* [dz], but the unvoiced sound prevails when a greater volume is required (see Elie and Laprie 2017: 209). Attempting to fully voice a short *z* [dz] produces a sound that is too long, while fully unvoicing it as [ts] makes the sound easier to produce and more audible (see Elie and Laprie 2017: 209). This is noticeable particularly when *z*, a denti-alveolar consonant, needs to be articulated with the high air pressure involved in singing.

> ### IN MELOPHONETIC TRANSCRIPTION
>
> Given the above and for simplicity, all instances of short and long *z* are indicated with the symbol [ts].

APPENDIX B

Guide to melophonetic transcription

Melophonetic transcription is the concise visual representation of clear and expressive sung Italian based on the symbols used in the International Phonetic Alphabet (International Phonetic Association 2020), the *can*IPA Natural Phonetics framework (Canepari 2009) and the elements created as part of the Melofonetica Method. The list that follows provides full explanations of each symbol used in melophonetic transcription.

Square brackets [ ]

Each line, or section of a line, starts with an open square bracket and ends with a closed square bracket. The text inside the brackets represents a line sung with one breath, i.e. the singer would usually breathe before the opening bracket and again after the closing bracket. The position of the brackets may easily be adjusted in accordance with the singer's preferences regarding breathing.

Division of phonic syllables [ˈviːs siːd daː ˈmoː ɾe]

A space is used to separate each phonic syllable from the next. A phonic syllable belongs to one note (or group of notes in a melisma). Note that the division of syllables used in melophonetic transcription differs from that traditionally used in scores. Even though the chain of sounds in each line should still be considered connected, melophonetic transcription assigns each phonic syllable (each group of sounds that together form a sung syllable) to its corresponding note and shows, in particular, where the onset, hold and release of each long consonant are placed.

Stressed syllables [ˈ]

Where melophonetic transcription is not used in conjunction with notation, primary stressed syllables (ictuses) are preceded by a superscript vertical line, [ˈ], to indicate correct accentuation. Where melophonetic transcription is used together with notation, primary stressed syllables are not marked, since they are aligned to stressed beats (see Section 3.4, 'Stressed syllables').

Chroneme [ː]

The chroneme [ː] is a colon with triangular dots. It indicates that the preceding sound is long.

Short consonants [ˈaː li] [ˈaː pɾe]

A short consonant is represented with a single symbol, denoting both its onset and release. Where there is a short consonant between vowels, or a group of two short consonants between vowels, the preceding vowel is always long and denoted with a chroneme.

Long consonants [ˈatː to] [ˈebː bɾi]

A long consonant between vowels that spans two phonic syllables is represented with two identical symbols. The first symbol is placed at the end of the first syllable and is followed by a chroneme; these represent the onset and hold. The second symbol is placed at the beginning of the second syllable and represents the release.

In some groups of consonants, the long consonant does not cross two syllables, so it is represented with a single symbol followed by a chroneme, denoting its onset, hold and release, all occurring on one note.

Archi-vowels: [a], [e], [i], [o] and [u]

The five sung Italian archi-vowels are represented with the five symbols [a], [e], [i], [o] and [u]. As explained in Chapter 2, 'Vowels', there is a wide spectrum of sung sound that corresponds to each written vowel and the choices that the singer makes within each are driven by the requirements of resonance, dynamics and timbre. As such, the archi-vowels used in melophonetic transcription indicate each overarching area of vowel sound rather than specifying closed, intermediate or open vowel sounds.

Priority vowels [no̞i]

A dot is placed beneath the priority vowel in each group of vowels.

Suspensive agogic accent [ˑː] [ːˑ] [ˑːˑ]

A suspensive agogic accent is indicated with a half chroneme [ˑ], which is placed in one of the following positions:
- Before the chroneme already in place [ˑː] where the hold of a long consonant is anticipated
- After the chroneme already in place [ːˑ] where the release of a long consonant or long vowel is delayed
- Before and after the chroneme already in place [ˑːˑ] where the hold of a long consonant is both anticipated and delayed

The extent of anticipation and/or delay will depend on tempo, note duration and the amount of emphasis that the singer wishes to add.

Portamento [ˈaɹː moɾ]

A *portamento* slide is indicated with a forward slash [/] immediately after the relevant vowel, or priority vowel in a group of vowels. This applies in any interval, whether descending or ascending in pitch.

APPENDIX C

How to prepare Italian text: a quick guide

For readers who wish to start applying the Melofonetica Method quickly to any Italian repertoire, the following guide provides the key practical steps to take to improve diction and expression, with section references for further reading.

For readers who are approaching this section before reading Chapters 1 to 3, it is important to note that the phonetic backbone of sung Italian is based on its sequences of long and short consonants. This is a guiding principle of the Melofonetica Method and the foundation upon which clear and expressive sung Italian is built. A number of terms mentioned here may be unfamiliar to the new reader; full explanations can be found in the glossary at the end of this book and the sections referenced.

1. Identify long consonants

This means:

- All **written double consonants** within or across words, for example, *mm* in *fiamma* or *ll* in *al lato*

Plus all of the following 'hidden' long consonants:

- The ***attacco del suono*** [start of the sound]: in the Melofonetica Method, in order to achieve a good *attacco del suono* and set a clear musical and dramatic intention, the singer should lengthen the first consonant of each new line and when beginning singing again after an in-breath (see Section 3.1, 'The *attacco del suono*')
- **Self-geminated consonants**: the consonants *gl, gn, sc* and *z* are always pronounced as long consonants where they occur between vowels (see 'Self-gemination' in Section 1.6)
- **Co-geminated consonants** (phrasal doubling): certain words that end with a vowel, in particular monosyllabic words, activate a lengthening of the short consonant at the beginning of the following word to create a long consonant (see 'Co-gemination' in Section 1.6)
- **Gemination in groups of consonants** (consonant clusters): in most groups of two or more consecutive consonants, one consonant is lengthened when pronounced (see 'Gemination in groups of consonants' in Section 1.10)
- **Melo-geminated consonants**: see point 5, 'Enhance expression'

2. Differentiate long from short consonants

Long consonants should be articulated with adequate length, rather than strength. To create enough distinction between long and short consonants in sung Italian, it is helpful to think of a long consonant as up to five times the length of a short consonant (depending on note duration). See Section 1.2, 'Short vs. long consonants', and Section 1.3, 'The onset, hold and release of consonants'.

The correct articulation of a long consonant will always shorten the preceding vowel. See Section 1.9, 'Long consonants in notation'. Short consonants, on the other hand, are as short as possible, allowing the preceding vowel to be long and sustained. See Section 1.5, 'Short consonants in notation'.

3. Identify priority vowels

Find all groups of vowels that occur on one note and identify the vowels that should take the greatest length. As a general rule (barring some exceptions), vowels should be prioritised in the following order: *a*, *e/o* and *i/u*.

Where both *e* and *o*, or both *i* and *u*, occur in the same group, priority should be given to whichever of the two vowels occurs last. Likewise, if the same vowel appears more than once in the group, priority should be given to the last occurrence of that vowel. See Section 2.4, 'Groups of vowels and vowel prioritisation'.

4. Enjoy the freedom of sung Italian vowels

Allow vowels to be shaped by the requirements of resonance, dynamics and timbre rather than trying to conform to the rules of the spoken language or to an idea of what constitutes an 'Italian vowel'. See Section 2.1, 'The five archi-vowels'; Section 2.2, 'Vowel modification'; and Section 2.3, 'Open and closed vowels'.

5. Enhance expression

Look for opportunities to add expressive emphasis to important words through the use of:
- **Melo-gemination**: the optional lengthening of a short consonant at the beginning of a syllable (see Section 3.2, 'Melo-gemination: the lengthening of short consonants for emphasis')
- **The suspensive agogic accent**: the further lengthening of a long phoneme (vowel or consonant) to build suspense and enhance expressive effect (see Section 3.3, 'The agogic accent')

These tools are often appropriate where the composer has musically highlighted words or syllables. It is particularly effective to apply melo-gemination to consonants that release on unstressed beats, in order to create the sequence described as the 'Michelangelo effect'. See Section 3.6, 'The Michelangelo effect: the essence of Italian style'.

6. Map the score

Identify one or more syllables in each line that are energised by the release of a long consonant and use these as anchoring points to create a clearly defined phrasing map through the score. These points are often where the use of expressive tools, including the agogic accent, *portamento* and micro-dynamics, will be appropriate. Anchoring points also help to enhance collaboration with the pianist or orchestra, conductor and director. See Section 3.10, 'Line, phrasing and anchoring'.

APPENDIX D

Melophonetic transcriptions of Italian arias

The expressive choices indicated in the arias that follow are the suggestions of the author and should not be considered prescriptive. They are intended to show the expressive potential of all of the elements in the Melofonetica Method and their visual representation in transcription. Specifically, the use of melo-gemination, de-gemination, the suspensive agogic accent, the incorporation of rests and punctuation into diction, the Michelangelo effect and *portamento* can be varied according to performers' preferences.

🔊 1. Giunse alfin il momento... Deh vieni non tardar

From Mozart, *Le nozze di Figaro*, Bärenreiter (2001: 456–60)

🎵 2. Una voce poco fa

From Rossini, *Il barbiere di Siviglia*, Ricordi (2014: 127–37)

MELOPHONETIC TRANSCRIPTIONS OF ITALIAN ARIAS 217

🎧 3. Che gelida manina

From Puccini, *La bohème*, Ricordi (1961: 64–69)

4. Bella siccome un angelo

From Donizetti, *Don Pasquale*, Ricordi (2006: 13–16)

THE MELOFONETICA METHOD

GLOSSARY

A-gemination: A rule inherited from Latin whereby certain monosyllabic words that end with a vowel (including articles, pronouns and prepositions) do not allow the consonant that follows to be lengthened. This is opposite to co-gemination.

Agogic accent: An accent created by extending or shortening the duration of a note. Rhythmic duration is fixed in the score, but the singer may add agogic accents for expressive reasons. This can often result in *rubato*.

Allophone: A phonetic variant of a phoneme that does not change the meaning of a word. In Italian, allophones exist for the consonants *l*, *m* and *n* where these directly precede other specific consonants. See also 'coarticulation'.

Alveolar: A consonant articulated with the blade of the tongue against the upper gum, between the upper teeth and upper alveolar ridge. In sung Italian, all alveolar consonants should be produced using the blade of the tongue (laminal), as opposed to using the tip of the tongue (apical).

Alveolar ridge (upper): The ridge that protrudes between the upper gum and the hard palate.

Anchoring point: A term used in the Melofonetica Method to describe one or more syllables in each line that are energised by the release of a long consonant. Anchoring points help the singer to shape each phrase and are often where the use of additional expressive tools will be appropriate, including the agogic accent, *portamento* and micro-dynamics.

Apical: A consonant articulated with the tip of the tongue, as opposed to the blade of the tongue (laminal). *See also* 'laminal'.

Approximant: A consonant articulated with two articulators in close proximity but not touching one another, creating only a slight obstruction to the airflow.

Archi-vowel: The spectrum of sung sound that corresponds to each of the five written Italian vowels, *a, e, i, o* and *u*, including all those that carry accents in spelling.

Attacco del suono: This phrase literally means 'start of the sound' and refers to beginning each line with clear musical and dramatic intention. In the Melofonetica Method, this is usually achieved by applying a long consonant whenever starting a new line or beginning singing again after an in-breath.

Back (of tongue): The rear area on the upper surface of the tongue, between the centre and root.

Bilabial: A consonant articulated with the upper and lower lips touching one another.

Blade (of tongue): The area on the upper surface of the tongue just beyond the tip.

Co-gemination: A rule inherited from Latin whereby certain words, particularly monosyllabic words, that end with a vowel activate a lengthening of the short consonant at the beginning of the word that follows, creating a long consonant. Also known as *raddoppiamento* or *rafforzamento (fono)sintattico*, or phrasal doubling.

Centre (of tongue): The central part of the upper surface of the tongue, between the front and back.

Chroneme: The symbol [ː], used in phonetics to denote that the preceding phoneme is long.

Coarticulation: A phenomenon in all languages whereby the articulation of certain sounds changes due to the nature of preceding or subsequent sounds. In Italian pronunciation, coarticulation occurs when the consonants *l*, *m* or *n* directly precede other specific consonants. In these instances, the first consonant assumes the place of articulation of the second. This also results in phonetic variants ('allophones') of *l*, *m* and *n*.

Constrictive: A consonant articulated with a constriction in the vocal tract, which releases air through a narrow opening and produces audible friction. Constrictive consonants can be grooved or non-grooved. Also known as 'fricative'.

Contoid: A consonant sound. A consonant symbol in spelling can represent different contoids, for example, *c* can be pronounced as [tʃ] or [k]. A contoid may also be represented by more than one consonant symbol in spelling, for example *gl* [ʎ].

De-gemination: The optional shortening of a long consonant (to a short consonant) for specific expressive reasons only. De-gemination can only be applied to co-geminated consonants, geminated consonants in groups of consonants or the written double *l* in an articulated preposition.

Denti-alveolar: A consonant articulated with the blade of the tongue against the teeth and upper gum. In sung Italian, all denti-alveolar consonants should be produced using the blade of the tongue (laminal), as opposed to using the tip of the tongue (apical).

Diacritic: A symbol or sign that signals a different pronunciation of a letter. In Italian, the letters *h* and *i* are sometimes diacritic symbols, which means that they are not pronounced in their own right, but instead signal a specific pronunciation of the preceding consonant.

Dynamic accent: An accent created through a change in volume: *piano, forte, crescendo* or *diminuendo*.

Elision: The omission of a phoneme.

Euphonic: In Italian, *d* is added to the preposition *a* [at/to] and the conjunctions *e* [and] and *o* [or] where they precede a word starting with a vowel. The *d* is called 'euphonic' because it makes these words easier to articulate and clearer before the vowel that follows.

Evanescent vowel: A brief vowel sound created between consonants while the tongue transitions from one place of articulation to another but voicing of the sound continues. Also known as a 'ghost vowel' or 'shadow vowel'.

Formant: A peak of acoustic energy that is concentrated around a particular frequency and gives each resonant sound its characteristic quality.

Front (of tongue): The forward central area on the upper surface of the tongue, just beyond the blade.

Gemination: The term 'gemination' comes from the Latin *gemini* and refers to the twinning or doubling of a consonant. In practice, a geminated consonant in spoken or sung Italian often has a greater duration than the combined length of two single consonants.

Glissando: A free form of *portamento* used as ornamentation. This involves a slide on the vowel that has no restrictions on its starting point or length, and can include hesitation on intermediate tones.

Glottal: A consonant articulated with an occlusion to the airflow created by the glottis.

Grooved: A consonant articulated with a groove in the tongue during the channelling of the outward airstream. Also known as 'with sulcalisation'.

Group of consonants: Two, three or four consonants occurring consecutively, either within a word or across two words. Also known as a 'consonant cluster'.

Group of vowels: Two, three or (rarely) four consecutive vowels occurring on the same note. These can occur within a word or across two or three words.

Half chroneme: The symbol [·], used in the Melofonetica Method to denote the additional length given to a long phoneme where a suspensive agogic accent is used.

Hold (of a consonant): The sustaining of sound between the onset and release of a sibilant or sonorant consonant, or the suspense of sound between the onset and release of a stop consonant.

Intervocalic: A phoneme that occurs between two vowels.

Italiano neutro (neutral, standard Italian): A standardised, 'accent-free' version of spoken Italian. This has been defined by Canepari and Giovannelli (2012: 24–29) according to the phonological structure of standard Italian as it is spoken in the 'phono-linguistic centre' of Italy (specific provinces in the regions of Tuscany, Umbria, Le Marche, Lazio and Abruzzo), where the language remains closest to its Latin phonetic roots, but also encompasses acceptable phonetic variants. The Melofonetica Method is based on *italiano neutro*.

Labio-dental: A consonant articulated with the upper teeth touching the lower lip.

Laminal: A consonant articulated with the blade of the tongue, as opposed to the tip of the tongue (apical). In Italian, alveolar and denti-alveolar consonants are all produced using the laminal place of articulation. This is the most natural way to articulate these types of consonants due to the high back tongue resting position required in Italian. The laminal place of articulation also creates the most comfortable and stable anchoring position for long consonant production.

Lateral: A consonant articulated with either the centre or blade of the tongue raised to touch the hard palate, directing the outward airstream along both sides of the tongue. Also known as 'liquid'.

Long consonant: A geminated consonant. In practice, a geminated consonant in spoken or sung Italian often has a greater duration than the combined length of two single consonants. In sung Italian, a long consonant can be any of the following: a written double consonant, a self-geminated consonant, a co-geminated consonant, a post-geminated consonant, a geminated consonant in a group of consonants, a consonant that creates the *attacco del suono* or a melo-geminated consonant. Long consonants have a much earlier onset than short consonants, and a hold between their onset and release.

Long vowel: A term used in the Melofonetica Method to describe a vowel (or priority vowel in a group of vowels) that is sustained for the duration of a note because it is not followed by a long consonant.

Manner of articulation: The way that the air is diverted or constricted as it flows out of the vocal tract. The manners of articulation referred to in the Melofonetica Method are constrictive, lateral, nasal, occlusive, occlu-constrictive and vibrant.

***Martellato* effect**: One of the three musical effects identifiable in sung Italian. This is created where a vowel is followed by a long sonorant or sibilant consonant and a sudden, natural *diminuendo*.

Melisma: The singing of one single syllable of text across two or more notes, usually of different pitch.

Melo-gemination: The lengthening of a short consonant at the beginning of a word or syllable to add expressive emphasis.

Melophonetic alphabet (Italian): The melophonetic symbols that correspond to each letter of the Italian alphabet. These are based on the symbols used in the International Phonetic Alphabet (International Phonetic Association 2020), the ^{can}IPA Natural Phonetics framework (Canepari 2009) and the principles of the Melofonetica Method.

Melophonetic notation: The representation of the precise placement, length and pitch (where applicable) of sung phonemes in notation.

Melophonetic transcription: A system of phonetic transcription that provides a concise visual representation of clear and expressive sung Italian based on the symbols used in the International Phonetic Alphabet (International Phonetic Association 2020), the ^{can}IPA Natural Phonetics framework (Canepari 2009) and the elements created as part of the Melofonetica Method.

Melophonetics: A term coined during the research for the Melofonetica Method to define the study and transcription of sounds in sung language (*melofonetica* in Italian).

Michelangelo effect: A term used in the Melofonetica Method to describe a particular sequence of text in music. This occurs so often in sung Italian that it may be considered the defining melophonetic characteristic at the heart of 'Italian style' in vocal music. The sequence consists of a syllable that belongs to an unstressed beat and begins with the release of any long consonant, followed by a syllable that belongs to a stressed beat and begins with a short consonant, or no consonant, and is preceded by the continuity of a long vowel, or a long sibilant or sonorant consonant in a group. The resulting syncopation is surprising and unpredictable: we hear an accented (emphasised) note where we are expecting an unaccented note and vice versa.

Nasal: A consonant articulated with the soft palate lowered to form an occlusion at the back of the oral cavity, causing the airstream to flow out through the nose instead. Also known as 'liquid'.

Non-grooved: A constrictive consonant articulated with no groove in the tongue during the channelling of the outward airstream. Also known as 'without sulcalisation'.

Occlu-constrictive: A consonant articulated with a temporary complete blockage (occlusion) to the airflow in the vocal tract, followed by its release through a narrow opening, which produces audible friction. The occlusion in a short occlu-constrictive consonant is so short and rapid that it is almost imperceptible, while the occlusion in a long occlu-constrictive consonant is fully discernible as a stop. Also known as 'affricate'.

Occlusive: A consonant articulated with a temporary complete blockage (occlusion) to the airflow in the vocal tract. The occlusion in a short occlusive consonant is so short and rapid that it is almost imperceptible, while the occlusion in a long occlusive consonant is fully discernible as a stop. Also known as 'plosive'.

Onset (of a consonant): The point at which a consonant starts, either immediately after a preceding phoneme or following an in-breath.

Palatal (place of articulation): With the centre of the tongue touching the hard palate.

Phoneme: A unit of sound in a language, i.e. a consonant sound (contoid) or vowel sound (vocoid).

Phonetics: The study and transcription of sounds in spoken language.

Phonic syllable: A group of sounds that, together, form a spoken or sung syllable.

Place of articulation: The place in the mouth or vocal tract where an obstruction is created by one of the articulators (glottis, gums, hard palate, lips, soft palate, teeth or tongue) in order to produce a specific phoneme. Places of articulation referred to in the Melofonetica Method are alveolar, bilabial, denti-alveolar, glottal, labio-dental, palatal, post-alveolar and velar. Also known as 'point of articulation'.

***Portamento* (*di voce*)**: The smooth transition from one note to the next, created by a rapid, continuous slide on the vowel, with no hesitation on intermediate tones. This is distinct from *glissando*.

Post-alveolar: A consonant articulated with the front of the tongue touching the alveolar ridge.

Post-gemination: A lengthening of the final single consonant of certain words where the following word begins with a vowel. This only applies to onomatopoeic or non-Italian words.

Priority vowel: A vowel that should be given the greatest length in a group of vowels. Where a group of vowels occurs on a note of short duration and/or in faster tempi, prioritisation becomes obsolete.

Release (of a consonant): The final part of a consonant that releases into the phoneme that follows or the silence at the end of a line.

Self-gemination: The lengthening of certain consonant sounds when they occur between two vowels. In Italian, *gl*, *gn*, *sc* and *z* are always self-geminated when they occur between two vowels.

Short consonant: A consonant that is so fleeting that it creates almost no interruption between the preceding and subsequent sounds. The onset and release of a short consonant occur consecutively and are perceived as a single event, with no audible sustaining of the sound.

Sibilant (consonant): A consonant that has a continuous hissing sound and is unpitched (unvoiced). In the Melofonetica Method, long consonants are categorised as sibilant, sonorant or stop.

Sonorant (consonant): A consonant that has a continuous sound and is pitchable (voiced). In the Melofonetica Method, long consonants are categorised as sibilant, sonorant or stop.

***Staccato* effect**: One of the three musical effects identifiable in sung Italian. This is created where a vowel is followed by a stop consonant or by a group of consonants that contains a stop consonant. The *staccato* effect of stop consonants gives sung Italian an energised rhythm.

Stop (consonant): A consonant that starts when it is positioned with an instant closure at its place of articulation (onset) but instead of an immediate release of the sound, there is a silence (hold). The air pressure is then released with the final sound, which can be voiced or unvoiced. In the Melofonetica Method, long consonants are categorised as sibilant, sonorant or stop. Also known as 'plosive'.

Suspensive agogic accent: A term used in the Melofonetica Method to define an accent that emphasises a syllable not by lengthening the note that the syllable occurs on, but instead by further lengthening the *preceding long phoneme* (vowel or consonant). This builds suspense on the approach to the syllable in focus and is used instinctively in the expressive articulation of text, often resulting in *rubato*.

***Tenuto* effect**: One of the three musical effects identifiable in sung Italian. This is created where two vowels are bridged by a short consonant or a group of two short consonants. The first vowel occupies the full duration of the note value and the short consonant, or group of two short consonants, is articulated rapidly at the beginning of the following note. There seems to be almost no interruption between the two vowels, creating an effect of *tenuto*, meaning 'held'. This effect also occurs where there are two or more consecutive vowels across two notes.

Tonic accent: An accent created through the use of an interval that is significantly higher or lower in pitch. Tonic accents are usually created by the composer, but they may be added by the singer through the use of *appoggiatura* or other ornamentation.

Type of phonation: The way a consonant is produced either with vibration of the vocal folds (voiced) or without vibration of the vocal folds (unvoiced or voiceless).

Unvoiced: A consonant produced with no vibration of the vocal folds. Also known as 'voiceless'.

Velar: A consonant articulated with the back of the tongue touching the soft palate.

Vibrant: A consonant produced with a very quick and light tap of the blade of the tongue against the upper gum. A series of these taps in rapid succession is known as a trill, which is used in the production of the long rolled *r* in Italian. Also known as 'liquid'.

Vocoid: A vowel sound. A vowel symbol in spelling can represent different vocoids.

Voiced: A consonant produced with vibration of the vocal folds.

BIBLIOGRAPHY

Music examples

BELLINI, VINCENZO. 2003. *I Capuleti e i Montecchi: tragedia lirica in two acts by Felice Romani*, reduction for voice and piano based on the critical edition of the orchestral score edited by Claudio Toscani (Milan: Ricordi)

—— 2009. *I puritani: versione per Napoli*, a cura di Raffaello Monterosso, riduzione per canto e pianoforte [Naples version, edited by Raffaello Monterosso, reduction for voice and piano], ed. by Leslie Howard (Cremona: Fondazione Claudio Monteverdi)

—— 2010. *La sonnambula: melodramma in two acts by Felice Romani*, reduction for voice and piano based on the critical edition of the orchestral score edited by Alessandro Roccatagliati and Luca Zoppelli (Milan: Ricordi)

DONIZETTI, GAETANO. 2005. *L'elisir d'amore: melodramma in due atti di Felice Romani* [*Melodramma* in two acts by Felice Romani] (Milan: Ricordi) [Vocal score]

—— 2006. *Don Pasquale: dramma buffo in tre atti*, libretto di Michele Accorsi [*Dramma buffo* in three acts, libretto by Michele Accorsi], vocal score ed. by Mario Parenti 1960 (Milan: Ricordi)

—— 2022. *Lucia di Lammermoor: dramma tragico in tre atti di Salvadore Cammarano* [*Dramma tragico* in three acts by Salvadore Cammarano], vocal score based on the critical edition of the orchestral score edited by Gabriele Dotto and Roger Parker (Milan: Ricordi)

GLUCK, CHRISTOPH WILLIBALD. 1962. *Orfeo ed Euridice (Vienna version of 1762): azione teatrale per musica in three acts*, libretto: Raniero de' Calzabigi, vocal score based on the Urtext of the Gluck Complete Edition by Heinz Moehn (Kassel: Bärenreiter)

HANDEL, GEORGE FRIDERIC. 1998. *Rinaldo: opera seria in tre atti* [*Opera seria* in three acts] (1711), HWV 7^a, vocal score based on the Urtext of the Halle Handel Edition by Michael Rot (Kassel: Bärenreiter)

―― 2002. *Rodelinda, Regina de' Longobardi: dramma per musica in tre atti* [*Dramma per musica* in three acts], libretto: Nicola Haym, HWV 19, vocal score based on the Urtext of the Halle Handel Edition by Michael Rot (Kassel: Bärenreiter)

―― 2005. *Giulio Cesare in Egitto: opera in tre atti* [Opera in three acts], libretto: Nicola Francesco Haym after Giacomo Francesco Bussani, HWV 17, piano reduction based on the Urtext of the Halle Handel Edition by Karl-Heinz Müller (Kassel: Bärenreiter)

LEONCAVALLO, RUGGERO. 1981. *Pagliacci: dramma in due atti*, parole e musica di Ruggero Leoncavallo, riduzione per canto e pianoforte, edizione critica a cura di Giacomo Zani [*Dramma* in two acts, libretto and music by Ruggero Leoncavallo, reduction for voice and piano, critical edition by Giacomo Zani] (Milan: Sonzogno)

MONTEVERDI, CLAUDIO. 2007. *Il ritorno d'Ulisse in patria: tragedia di lieto fine in un prologo e tre atti.* [The Return of Ulysses: Tragedy with happy ending in one prologue and three acts], libretto: Giacomo Badoaro, piano reduction based on the Urtext edition by Rinaldo Alessandrini (Kassel: Bärenreiter)

―― 2016. *L'orfeo: edizione critica di Anna Maria Vacchelli,* testo poetico di Alessandro Striggio, riduzione per canto e pianoforte di Anna Maria Vacchelli [Critical edition by Anna Maria Vacchelli, libretto by Alessandro Striggio, reduction for voice and piano by Anna Maria Vacchelli] (Cremona: Fondazione Claudio Monteverdi)

―― 2017. *L'incoronazione di Poppea*, ed. by Hendrik Schulze (Kassel: Bärenreiter) [Libretto: Gian Francesco Busenello]

MOZART, WOLFGANG AMADEUS. 2001. *La clemenza di Tito: opera seria in due atti* [*Opera seria* in two acts], libretto: Caterino Mazzolà after Pietro Metastasio, KV 621, vocal score based on the Urtext of the New Mozart Edition by Eugen Epplée (Kassel: Bärenreiter)

―― 2001. *Le nozze di Figaro: opera buffa in quattro atti* [*Opera buffa* in four acts], libretto: Lorenzo Da Ponte, KV 492, piano reduction based on the Urtext of the New Mozart Edition by Eugen Epplée (Kassel: Bärenreiter)

―― 2005. *Idomeneo: dramma per musica in tre atti* [*Dramma per musica* in three acts], libretto: Giambattista Varesco, KV 366, piano reduction based on the Urtext of the New Mozart Edition by Hans-Georg Kluge (Kassel: Bärenreiter)

―― 2005. *Il dissoluto punito ossia il Don Giovanni: dramma giocoso in zwei akten* [*Dramma giocoso* in two acts], libretto: Lorenzo Da Ponte, KV 527, piano reduction based on the Urtext of the New Mozart Edition by Hans-Georg Kluge (Kassel: Bärenreiter)

―― 2006. *Così fan tutte ossia La scuola degli amanti: dramma giocoso in zwei akten* [*Dramma giocoso* in two acts], libretto: Lorenzo Da Ponte, KV 588, piano reduction based on the Urtext of the New Mozart Edition by Rasmus Baumann (Kassel: Bärenreiter)

PUCCINI, GIACOMO. 1896. *La bohème (scene dalla Vie de Bohème di Henry Murger): quattro quadri di Giuseppe Giacosa e Luigi Illica*, riduzione per canto e pianoforte di Carlo Carignani [Four scenes by Giuseppe Giacosa and Luigi Illica, reduction for voice and piano by Carlo Carignani], ed. by Mario Parenti 1961 (Milan: Ricordi)

―― 1907. *Madama Butterfly: tragedia giapponese in tre atti di Luigi Illica e Giuseppe Giacosa (da John L. Long e David Belasco)*, riduzione per canto e pianoforte di Carlo Carignani [Japanese tragedy in three acts by Luigi Illica and Giuseppe Giacosa (based on the work of John L. Long and David Belasco), reduction for voice and piano by Carlo Carignani], ed. by Mario Parenti 1964 (Milan: Ricordi)

―― 1912. *La fanciulla del West: opera in tre atti di Guelfo Civinini e Carlo Zangarini*, dal dramma di David Belasco, riduzione per canto e pianoforte di Carlo Carignani [Opera in three acts by Guelfo Civinini and Carlo Zangarini, based on the drama by David Belasco, reduction for voice and piano by Carlo Carignani], ed. by Mario Parenti 1963 (Milan: Ricordi)

―― 1917. *La rondine: commedia lirica in tre atti di Giuseppe Adami*, opera completa per canto e pianoforte, riduzione di Carlo Carignani [*Commedia lirica* in three acts by Giuseppe Adami, complete opera for voice and piano, reduction by Carlo Carignani] (Milan: Sonzogno)

―― 1926 *Turandot: dramma lirico in tre atti e cinque quadri di G. Adami e R. Simoni*, l'ultimo duetto e il finale dell'opera sono stati completati da F. Alfano, riduzione per canto e pianoforte di Guido Zuccoli [*Dramma lirico* in three acts and five scenes by G. Adami and R. Simoni, the last duet and the finale of the opera were completed by F. Alfano, reduction for voice and piano by Guido Zuccoli], ed. by Mario Parenti 1963 (Milan: Ricordi)

―― 1959. *Gianni Schicchi: opera in one act*, libretto by Giovacchino Forzano (Milan: Ricordi) [Vocal score]

―― 1995. *Tosca: melodramma in three acts by Luigi Illica and Giuseppe Giacosa*, based on the drama by Victorien Sardou, reduction for voice and piano of the revised edition of the full score based on the original sources, edited by Roger Parker (Milan: Ricordi)

ROSSINI, GIOACHINO. 2014. *Il barbiere di Siviglia (Almaviva o sia l'inutile precauzione): commedia in two acts by Cesare Sterbini*, volume I, reduction for voice and piano based on the critical edition of the orchestral score published by the Fondazione Rossini of Pesaro in collaboration with Casa Ricordi of Milan, ed. by Alberto Zedda (Milan: Ricordi)

VERDI, GIUSEPPE. 1893. *Falstaff: commedia lirica in tre atti di Arrigo Boito*, riduzione per canto e pianoforte di Carlo Carignani [*Commedia lirica* in three acts by Arrigo Boito, reduction for voice and piano by Carlo Carignani], ed. by Mario Parenti 1964 (Milan: Ricordi)

—— 1996. *Nabucodonosor: dramma lirico in four parts by Temistocle Solera*, reduction for voice and piano based on the critical edition of the orchestral score edited by Roger Parker (Chicago and London: University of Chicago Press; Milan: Ricordi)

—— 2001. *La traviata: melodramma in three acts by Francesco Maria Piave*, volume I, reduction for voice and piano based on the critical edition of the orchestral score, ed. by Fabrizio Della Seta (Chicago and London: University of Chicago Press; Milan: Ricordi)

—— 2002. *Il trovatore: dramma in four parts by Salvadore Cammarano*, reduction for voice and piano based on the critical edition of the orchestral score edited by David Lawton (Chicago and London: University of Chicago Press; Milan: Ricordi)

—— 2004. *Simon Boccanegra (seconda versione): melodramma in un prologo e tre atti*, libretto di Francesco Maria Piave con aggiunte e modifiche di Arrigo Boito [(Second version): Melodrama in a prologue and three acts, libretto by Francesco Maria Piave with additions and modifications by Arrigo Boito] (Milan: Universal Music MGB Publications)

Works cited

ABRAMOV-VAN RIJK, ELENA. 2009. *Parlar cantando: The Practice of Reciting Verses in Italy from 1300 to 1600* (Oxford: Peter Lang)

AGRICOLA, JOHANN FRIEDRICH. 1995. *Introduction to the Art of Singing by Johann Friedrich Agricola*, trans. and ed. by Julianne C. Baird (Cambridge: Cambridge University Press)

APPELMAN, DUDLEY RALPH. 1986. *The Science of Vocal Pedagogy: Theory and Application*, First Midland Book edition (Bloomington: Indiana University Press)

ARTUSI, GIOVANNI MARIA. 1600. *L'Artusi, overo delle imperfettioni della moderna musica* [The Artusi, or imperfections of modern music] (Venice: Giacomo Vincenti)

BALDELLI, IGNAZIO, and RAFFAELLO MONTEROSSO. 1970. 'Canzone' [Song], in *Enciclopedia dantesca* [The Dante encyclopedia], ed. by Umberto Bosco, 6 vols (Rome: Istituto della Enciclopedia Italiana), I, 796–809. Material used with kind permission of Enciclopedia Italiana Treccani. Any reproduction and/or use of this material that is not strictly for personal and private purposes is forbidden. Onward transmission online, or in any other form, is strictly forbidden.

BANZINA, ELINA. 2016. 'Consonant Lengthening for Persuasiveness in L1 and L2 English', in *International Journal of Applied Linguistics*, 26, 3 (November): 403–19 <https://doi.org/10.1111/ijal.12137>

BELTRAMI, PIETRO G. 2011. *La metrica italiana* [Italian metrics], 5th edn (Bologna: Il Mulino)

BERTINETTO, PIER MARCO. 2010. 'Fonetica' [Phonetics], in *Enciclopedia dell'italiano* [Encyclopedia of Italian], ed. by Raffaele Simone, 2 vols (Rome: Istituto della Enciclopedia Italiana), I <https://www.treccani.it/enciclopedia/fonetica_%28Enciclopedia-dell%27Italiano%29> [accessed 15 March 2023]. Material used with kind permission of Enciclopedia Italiana Treccani. Any reproduction and/or use of this material that is not strictly for personal and private purposes is forbidden. Onward transmission online, or in any other form, is strictly forbidden.

BIANCONI, LORENZO. 2005. 'Sillaba, quantità, accento, tono' [Syllable, duration, accent, tone], in *Il saggiatore musicale*, 12, 1: 183–218 <https://www.saggiatoremusicale.it/wp-content/uploads/2021/05/Bianconi-2005b.pdf> [accessed 15 March 2023]

BJÖRKNER, EVA. 2008. 'Musical Theater and Opera Singing: Why So Different? A Study of Subglottal Pressure, Voice Source, and Formant Frequency Characteristics', in *Journal of Voice*, 22, 5: 533–40 <https://doi.org/10.1016/j.jvoice.2006.12.007>

CACCINI, GIULIO. 1601/2. *Le nuove musiche* [The new music] (Florence: Marescotti)

CANEPARI, LUCIANO. 2007. *Natural Phonetics & Tonetics: Articulatory, Auditory, & Functional* (Munich: Lincom)

—— 2009. *Dizionario di pronuncia italiana: Il DiPI* [Dictionary of Italian pronunciation: The DiPI] (Bologna: Zanichelli)

CANEPARI, LUCIANO, and BARBARA GIOVANNELLI. 2012. *La buona pronuncia italiana del terzo millennio: Manualetto d'italiano neutro con sonori, esercizi e test* [Good Italian pronunciation for the third millennium: Handbook of neutral Italian with audio examples, exercises and tests], 4th edn (Rome: Aracne)

CASTEL, NICO. 2000. *Verismo Opera Libretti*, ed. by Scott Jackson Wiley, 2 vols (New York: Leyerle), I. Material used with the permission of Leyerle Publications, www.leyerlepublications.com © Copyright 2000 Leyerle Publications.

CHAPMAN, JANICE L., and RON MORRIS. 2017. 'Breathing and Support', in Janice L. Chapman, *Singing and Teaching Singing: A Holistic Approach to Classical Voice*, 3rd edn (San Diego: Plural Publishing), 41–63

Coffin, Berton. 2002. *Coffin's Sounds of Singing: Principles and Applications of Vocal Techniques with Chromatic Vowel Chart*, 2nd edn (Lanham, MD: Scarecrow Press), all rights reserved

Corri, Domenico. 1811. *The Singer's Preceptor, or Corri's Treatise on Vocal Music* (London: Chappell & Co.)

Dalle Fratte, Matteo. 2003. 'Gilda Dalla Rizza, la cantante che ispirò Puccini: Un soprano fra Toscanini, Zandonai e la "Giovane scuola"' [Gilda Dalla Rizza, the singer who inspired Puccini: A soprano amid Toscanini, Zandonai and the 'Young School'] (unpublished master's thesis, University of Padua, 2003)

Elie, Benjamin, and Yves Laprie. 2017. 'Glottal Opening and Strategies of Production of Fricatives', in *Proceedings of Interspeech 2017*: 206–09 <https://doi.org/10.21437/Interspeech.2017-1039>

Elwert, W. Theodor. 1984. *Italienische Metrik* [Italian metrics], 2nd edn (Wiesbaden: Franz Steiner)

Foscolo, Ugo. 1823. *Essays on Petrarch* (London: John Murray)

Fourcin, Adrian. 2017. 'Hearing and Singing', in Janice L. Chapman, *Singing and Teaching Singing: A Holistic Approach to Classical Voice*, 3rd edn (San Diego: Plural Publishing), 257–70

Freitas, Roger. 2002. 'Towards a Verdian Ideal of Singing: Emancipation from Modern Orthodoxy', in *Journal of the Royal Musical Association*, 127, 2: 226–57 <https://doi.org/10.1093/jrma/127.2.226>

Galeazzi, Francesco. 1791. *Elementi teorico-pratici di musica* [Theoretical and practical elements of music] (Rome: Pilucchi Cracas)

García Jr., Manuel. 1847. *Traité complet de l'art du chant en deux parties* [A complete treatise on the art of singing, in two parts] (Paris: Troupenas)

García Sr., Manuel. 1830. *Exercises pour la voix* [Exercises for the voice] (Paris: Ph. Petit)

Gardiner, John Eliot. 2018. 'The Return of Ulysses to his Homeland', sleeve note for Monteverdi: *Il ritorno d'Ulisse in patria*, Monteverdi Choir and English Baroque Soloists, cond. by John Eliot Gardiner (Monteverdi Productions, SDG730, 2018), 6–11

Garrett, Margo. 2018a. 'The Art and the Skills of Vocal Coaching: Martin Isepp on German Consonants', in *Journal of Singing* (National Association of Teachers of Singing, https://www.nats.org/), 75, 1 (September): 81–87

—— 2018b. 'The Art and the Skills of Vocal Coaching: Pierre Vallet on l'accent d'insistance and Singing in French', in *Journal of Singing* (National Association of Teachers of Singing, https://www.nats.org/), 75, 2 (November): 207–10

HENDERSON, WILLIAM J. 1938. *The Art of Singing* (New York: Dial Press)

INTERNATIONAL PHONETIC ASSOCIATION. 2020. *The International Phonetic Alphabet and the IPA Chart* <https://www.internationalphoneticassociation.org/content/ipa-chart> [accessed 15 March 2023]

JOHNSON, KEITH. 2012. *Acoustic and Auditory Phonetics*, 3rd edn (Chichester: Wiley-Blackwell)

KAUFFMAN, DEBORAH. 1992. 'Portamento in Romantic Opera', in *Performance Practice Review*, 5, 2: 139–58 <https://doi.org/10.5642/perfpr.199205.02.03> This work is licensed under the Creative Commons Attribution 4.0 International License. To view a copy of this license, visit http://creativecommons.org/licenses/by/4.0/ or send a letter to Creative Commons, PO Box 1866, Mountain View, CA 94042, USA.

KÜHNERT, BARBARA, and FRANCIS NOLAN. 1999. 'The Origin of Coarticulation', in *Coarticulation: Theory, Data and Techniques*, ed. by William J. Hardcastle and Nigel Hewlett (Cambridge: Cambridge University Press), 7–30

KUIJKEN, BARTHOLD. 2013. *The Notation Is Not the Music: Reflections on Early Music Practice and Performance* (Bloomington and Indianapolis: Indiana University Press)

LAMPERTI, FRANCESCO. 1864. *Guida teorico-pratica-elementare per lo studio del canto* [A theoretical, practical and elementary guide for the study of singing] (Milan: Ricordi)

LÖFQVIST, ANDERS. 1975. 'A Study of Subglottal Pressure During the Production of Swedish Stops', in *Journal of Phonetics*, 3, 3 (July): 175–89 <https://doi.org/10.1016/S0095-4470(19)31366-X>

MACE, DEAN T. 1969. 'Pietro Bembo and the Literary Origins of the Italian Madrigal', in *Musical Quarterly*, 55, 1 (January): 65–86 <https://doi.org/10.1093/mq/LV.1.65>

MANCINI, GIAMBATTISTA. 1774. *Pensieri, e riflessioni pratiche sopra il canto figurato* [Thoughts and practical reflections on *canto figurato*] (Vienna: Ghelen)

MANNI, PAOLA. 2003. *Il Trecento toscano: la lingua di Dante, Petrarca e Boccaccio* [The Tuscan fourteenth century: The language of Dante, Petrarch and Boccaccio], Storia della lingua italiana [History of the Italian language], ed. by Francesco Bruni, 10 vols (Bologna: Il Mulino), x

McCoy, Scott. 2019. *Your Voice: An Inside View*, 3rd edn, e-book version (Gahanna: Inside View Press)

Mengozzi, Bernardo. 1804. *Méthode de chant du Conservatoire de Musique: Contenant les principes du chant, des exercices pour la voix, des solfèges tirés des meilleurs ouvrages anciens et modernes et des airs dans tous les mouvemens et les différens caractères* [Method of singing of the Conservatoire of Music: With principles of singing and exercises for the voice, solfège exercises taken from the best old and modern works, and arias from all movements and for different characters] (Paris: Impr. du Conservatoire de musique)

Metastasio, Pietro. 1792. *Lettere del sig. abate Pietro Metastasio* [Letters of Abbot Pietro Metastasio], 2 vols (Naples: Lieto), II, ETH-Bibliothek Zürich, Rar 6515 <https://doi.org/10.3931/e-rara-25829> Public Domain Mark

Migliorini, Bruno. 2019. *Storia della lingua italiana* [History of the Italian language], intro. by Ghino Ghinassi, afterword by Massimo Fanfani, nuova edizione riveduta e corretta [new revised and corrected edition] (Florence and Milan: Giunti/Bompiani)

Miller, Richard. 1986. *The Structure of Singing: System and Art in Vocal Technique* (New York: Schirmer Books)

—— 2004. *Solutions for Singers: Tools for Performers and Teachers* (New York: Oxford University Press)

Monteverdi, Claudio. 1638. *Basso continuo: Madrigali guerrieri et amorosi, libro ottavo* [Basso continuo: Madrigals of war and love, eighth book] (Venice: Alessandro Vincenti)

—— 1994. *Lettere* [Letters], ed. by Éva Lax, Studi e testi per la storia della musica [Studies and texts on the history of music], 15 vols (Florence: Leo S. Olschki), x

—— 2014. *L'Orfeo, L'Arianna, Il lamento di Olimpia: Edizione critica di Anna Maria Vacchelli* [Critical edition by Anna Maria Vacchelli] (Cremona: Fondazione Claudio Monteverdi)

Monteverdi, Giulio Cesare. 1607. 'Dichiaratione della lettera stampata nel quinto libro de suoi madregali' [Declaration based on a letter printed in the fifth book of his madrigals], in *Scherzi musicali a tre voci di Claudio Monteverde, raccolti da Giulio Cesare Monteverde suo fratello, e novamente posti in luce* [Musical *scherzi* for three voices by Claudio Monteverde, collected by his brother Giulio Cesare Monteverde, and newly brought to light] (Venice: Ricciardo Amadino)

Moore, F. Richard. 1983. 'A General Model for Spatial Processing of Sounds', in *Computer Music Journal*, 7, 3 (Autumn): 6–15 <https://doi.org/10.2307/3679589>

Morris, Ron, and Janice L. Chapman. 2017. 'Articulation', in Janice L. Chapman, *Singing and Teaching Singing: A Holistic Approach to Classical Voice*, 3rd edn (San Diego: Plural Publishing), 105–37

Néron, Martin. 2018. 'Phonetic [L]Imitation', in *Journal of Singing* (National Association of Teachers of Singing, https://www.nats.org/), 75, 2 (November/December), 175–81

Nix, John. 2004. 'Vowel Modification Revisited', in *Journal of Singing* (National Association of Teachers of Singing, https://www.nats.org/), 61, 2 (November/December): 173–76

Pirrotta, Nino. 1966. 'Ars nova e stil novo' [New art and new style], in *Rivista italiana di musicologia*, 1, 1: 3–19 <https://www.jstor.org/stable/24315286> [accessed 15 March 2023]

Potter, John. 2006. 'Beggar at the Door: The Rise and Fall of Portamento in Singing', in *Music and Letters*, 87, 4 (November): 523–50 <https://doi.org/10.1093/ml/gcl079>

Rossi, Luigi Felice. 1861. '(Canto) affettuoso' [Affectionate (singing)], in *Dizionario della lingua italiana* [Dictionary of the Italian language], ed. by Nicolò Tommaseo and Bernardo Bellini, 8 vols (Turin: Unione Tipografico-Editrice), i, pt. 1, 227, section 8

—— 1865. 'Chiaroscuro', in *Dizionario della lingua italiana* [Dictionary of the Italian language], ed. by Nicolò Tommaseo and Bernardo Bellini, 8 vols (Turin: Unione Tipografico-Editrice), i, pt. 2, 1389, section 4

—— 1869. '(Canto) legato' [Legato (singing)], in *Dizionario della lingua italiana* [Dictionary of the Italian language], ed. by Nicolò Tommaseo and Bernardo Bellini, 8 vols (Turin: Unione Tipografico-Editrice), ii, pt. 2, 1789, section 18

Tacchinardi, Nicola. 1833. *Dell'opera in musica sul teatro italiano e de' suoi difetti* [Opera: Italian theatre and its defects], 2nd edn (Florence: Giovanni Berni)

Titze, Ingo R. 2007. 'Resurrection from the Coffin', in *Journal of Singing* (National Association of Teachers of Singing, https://www.nats.org/), 64, 2 (November/December): 199–201

Tosi, Arturo. 2001. *Language and Society in a Changing Italy* (Clevedon: Multilingual Matters)

Tosi, Pierfrancesco. 1723. *Opinioni de' cantori antichi, e moderni, o sieno Osservazioni sopra il canto figurato* [Opinions of ancient and modern singers; or, Observations on *canto figurato*] (Bologna: Lelio dalla Volpe)

—— 1743. *Observations on the Florid Song; or, Sentiments on the Ancient and Modern Singers*, trans. by [John Ernest] Galliard (London: J. Wilcox)

—— 1757. *Anleitung zur Singkunst: Aus dem italiänischen, des Herrn Peter Franz Tosi, mit Erläuterungen und Zusätzen von Johann Friedrich Agricola* [Instructions in the art of singing: from the Italian, by Mr. Peter Franz Tosi, with explanations and additions by Johann Friedrich Agricola], trans. by Johann Friedrich Agricola (Berlin: G. L. Winter) [A German translation of Tosi 1723; see Agricola 1995 for Julianne C. Baird's English translation of this German translation]

UBERTI, MAURO. 2004. 'Il "Metodo pratico di canto" di Nicola Vaccaj' [Nicola Vaccaj's *Practical method of singing*], in *Nuova rivista musicale italiana*, 1 (January–March): 43–67

VACCAJ, NICOLA. 1837. *Metodo pratico di canto italiano per camera, diviso in quindici lezioni, testo italiano e francese, nuova edizione riveduta* [Practical method of Italian chamber singing, in fifteen lessons, with Italian and French text, new revised edition] (Milan: Ricordi)

VERDI, GIUSEPPE, GAETANO CESARI, and ALESSANDRO LUZIO. 1913. *I Copialettere di Giuseppe Verdi* [Giuseppe Verdi's Letter Book] (Milan: Stucchi Ceretti)

ZULIANI, LUCA. 2011. 'Elena Abramov-van Rijk, *Parlar Cantando: The Practice of Reciting Verses in Italy from 1300 to 1600*', in *Lingua e Stile: Rivista di storia della lingua italiana*, 1 (June): 123–30 <https://doi.org/10.1417/34820>

Other works consulted

ADAMS, DAVID. 2008. *A Handbook of Diction for Singers: Italian, German, French*, 2nd edn (New York: Oxford University Press)

ADLER, KURT. 1967. *Phonetics and Diction in Singing: Italian, French, Spanish, German* (Minneapolis: University of Minnesota Press)

ALGAROTTI, FRANCESCO. 1763. *Saggio sopra l'opera in musica* [Essay on opera] (Livorno: Marco Coltellini)

ARTEAGA, STEFANO (ESTEBAN DE). 1783. *Le rivoluzioni del teatro musicale italiano dalla sua origine fino al presente* [Revolutions in Italian opera from its origins to the present day], 2 vols (Bologna: Carlo Trenti)

BELLOTTO, FRANCESCO. 1997. 'Gli appunti di teoria musicale di Giovanni Simone Mayr: Acquisizioni per lo studio della semiografia donizettiana' [Notes on music theory by Giovanni Simone Mayr: Learnings for the study of Donizetti's notation], in *Studi su Gaetano Donizetti nel Bicentenario della nascita (1797–1997)* [Studies on Gaetano Donizetti in the bicentennial year of his birth (1797–1997)], ed. by Marcello Eynard (= *Bergomum: Bollettino della Civica Biblioteca Angelo Mai di Bergamo* [Bergomum: Bulletin of the Angelo Mai Civic Library of Bergamo], 1 (January–March): 31–64)

BENELLI, ANTONIO. 1814. *Regole per il canto figurato* [Rules for *canto figurato*] (Dresden: the author; Leipzig: Breitkopf & Härtel)

BILANCIONI, GUGLIELMO. 1923. *La voce parlata e cantata, normale e patologica: Guida allo studio della fonetica biologica* [The spoken and sung voice, normal and pathological: A guide to the study of natural phonetics] (Rome: Pozzi)

BISMANTOVA, BARTOLOMEO. 1677. *Compendio musicale* [Compendium of music] (Ferrara: the author)

BOZEMAN, KENNETH W. 2013. *Practical Vocal Acoustics: Pedagogic Applications for Teachers and Singers* (Hillsdale, NY: Pendragon Press)

BRUNI, FRANCESCO. 2001. *L'italiano letterario nella storia* [Literary Italian in history] (Bologna: Il Mulino)

CANEPARI, LUCIANO. 2006. *Avviamento alla fonetica* [Introduction to phonetics] (Turin: Einaudi)

CASELLA, FABRIZIO. 1848. *Compendio dell'opera sulle teorie per l'arte del canto* [Compendium of theories of the art of singing in opera] (Rome: Puccinelli)

CHAPMAN, JANICE L. 2017. *Singing and Teaching Singing: A Holistic Approach to Classical Voice*, 3rd edn (San Diego: Plural Publishing)

COFFIN, BERTON. 1980. *Coffin's Overtones of Bel Canto: Phonetic Basis of Artistic Singing with 100 Chromatic Vowel-Chart Exercises* (Lanham, MD: Scarecrow Press)

COLORNI, EVELINA. 1970. *Singers' Italian: A Manual of Diction and Phonetics* (New York: Schirmer; London: Collier Macmillan)

CRESCENTINI, GIROLAMO. 1812. *Raccolta di esercizi per il canto all'uso del vocalizzo* [Collection of vocalising exercises for singing] (Milan: Ricordi)

CRIVELLI, DOMENICO. 1841. *L'arte del canto* [The art of singing] (London: the author)

DONI, GIOVAN BATTISTA. 1647. *De praestantia musicae veteris: Libri tres* [The excellence of ancient music: Book three] (Florence: Amatore Massa)

Drusi, Riccardo. 2014. 'Pietro Bembo "super partes"' ['Impartial' Pietro Bembo], in *Acta Histriae*, 22, 1: 41–56 <https://zdjp.si/wp-content/uploads/2015/08/drusi.pdf> [accessed 15 March 2023]

Ermagora, Fabio. 1839. *Teorica del canto per servire al Musicale Istituto eretto in Venezia dal Signor Giuseppe Camploy coll'approvazione dell'Eccelso I.R. Governo* [Theory of singing for the use of the Institute of Music in Venice established by Mr Giuseppe Camploy with the approval of the Excellent Imperial Royal Government] (Venice: Andreola)

Fabbri, Paolo. 2007. *Metro e canto nell'opera italiana* [Metre and song in Italian opera] (Turin: EDT)

Ferrero, Franco, Arturo Genre, Louis-Jean Boë, and Michel Contini. 1979. *Nozioni di fonetica acustica* [Notions of acoustic phonetics] (Turin: Omega)

Florimo, Francesco. 1840. *Metodo di canto* [Method of singing] (Milan: Ricordi)

Fox, Margalit. 2015. 'Nico Castel, Tenor and Diction Coach at the Met, Dies at 83', *New York Times*, 3 June <https://www.nytimes.com/2015/06/04/arts/music/nico-castel-tenor-and-diction-coach-at-the-met-dies-at-83.html> [accessed 15 March 2023]

Garaudé, Alexis De. 1854. *Méthode complète de chant* [Complete method of singing], 2nd edn (Paris: the author)

Gervasoni, Carlo. 1800. *La scuola della musica* [The teaching of music] (Piacenza: Orcesi)

Goldschmidt, Jenny Lind, and V.M. Holmstrom. 1917. 'Jenny Lind's Singing Method', in *Musical Quarterly*, 3, 4 (October): 548–51 <http://www.jstor.org/stable/737988> [accessed 15 March 2023]

Grasso Caprioli, Leonella, Roberta Ziosi, and Sergio Durante. 2015. *Lessico italiano del canto* [Italian lexicon of singing] (Naples: Liguori) <http://www.liguori.it/schedanew.asp?isbn=5259> [accessed 15 March 2023]

Halle, Morris, Gary W. Hughes, and Jean-Pierre A. Radley. 1957. 'Acoustic Properties of Stop Consonants', in *Journal of the Acoustical Society of America*, 29, 1: 107–16 <https://doi.org/10.1121/1.1908634>

Harris, Ellen T. 1980. 'The Italian in Handel', in *Journal of the American Musicological Society*, 33, 3 (Autumn): 468–500 <https://www.jstor.org/stable/831303> [accessed 15 March 2023]

—— 2001. 'Portamento (i) (It.)', in *Grove Music Online* <https://doi.org/10.1093/gmo/9781561592630.article.40990>

HILES, JOHN. 1873. *Dictionary of 12,500 Italian, French, German, English and other Musical Terms, Phrases and Abbreviations*, 2nd edn (London: Brewer & Co.)

JUVARRA, ANTONIO. 2006. *I segreti del Belcanto: Storia delle tecniche e dei metodi vocali dal Settecento ai nostri giorni* [The secrets of Belcanto: History of vocal techniques and methods from the eighteenth century to nowadays] (Milan: Curci)

LEPSCHY, ANNA LAURA, and GIULIO LEPSCHY. 1988. *The Italian Language Today*, 2nd edn (Chicago: New Amsterdam)

LIVERZIANI, GIUSEPPE. 1797. *Grammatica della musica* [The grammar of music] (Rome: Pilucchi Cracas)

MANECA, CONSTANT. 1965. 'Considerazioni sopra la prostesi vocalica in italiano' [Considerations on vowel prothesis in Italian], in *Revue roumaine de linguistique*, 10, 5: 499–507 <http://dspace.bcu-iasi.ro/handle/123456789/11835> [accessed 15 March 2023]

MARAFIOTI, PASQUAL MARIO. 1922. *Caruso's Method of Voice Production: The Scientific Culture of the Voice* (New York: D. Appleton)

MEYNADIER, YOHANN, ANITA EL HAJJ, MICHEL PITERMANN, THIERRY LEGOU, and ANTOINE GIOVANNI. 2018. 'Estimating Vocal Effort from the Aerodynamics of Labial Fricatives: A Feasibility Study', in *Journal of Voice*, 32, 6 (November): 771.e15–771.e24 <https://doi.org/10.1016/j.jvoice.2017.08.010>

MURATORI, LODOVICO ANTONIO. 1706. *Della perfetta poesia italiana, spiegata, e dimostrata con varie osservazioni* [On the perfection of Italian poetry, explained, and demonstrated with various observations] (Modena: Bartolomeo Soliani)

MYERSCOUGH, MARIE. 2008. *Preparing an Operatic Role: Legendary Italian Coach Ubaldo Gardini and Leading Opera Artists on the Approach to a Convincing Vocal Performance* (London: WHZ Books)

NIVERS, GUILLAUME-GABRIEL. 1665. *Livre d'orgue contenant cent pièces de tous les tons de l'Église* [Book for the organ with one hundred pieces in all the keys of the Church] (Paris: the author and R. Ballard)

PAYNE, ELINOR. 2006. 'Non-durational Indices in Italian Geminate Consonants', in *Journal of the International Phonetic Association*, 36, 1 (June): 83–95 <https://doi.org/10.1017/S0025100306002398>

PELLEGRINI CELONI, ANNA MARIA. 1810. *Grammatica, o siano regole per ben cantare* [The grammar, or rules of, good singing] (Rome: Piale and Martorelli)

PEROTTI, GIOVANNI AGOSTINO. 1846. *Guida per lo studio del canto figurato* [A guide to the study of *canto figurato*] (Milan: Ricordi)

PERRINO, MARCELLO. 1810. *Osservazioni sopra il canto* [Observations on singing] (Naples: Trani)

QUADRO, FRANCESCO-SAVERIO. 1744. *Della storia e della ragione d'ogni poesia* [On the history and reason of all poems], 3 vols (Milan: Agnelli)

QUANTZ, JOHANN JOACHIM. 1789. *Versuch einer Anweisung die Flöte traversiere zu spielen* [Essay on a method for playing the transverse flute] (Breslau: Korn)

ROSENBLUM, SANDRA P. 1994. 'The Uses of Rubato in Music, Eighteenth to Twentieth Centuries', in *Performance Practice Review*, 7, 1: 33–53 <https://doi.org/10.5642/perfpr.199407.01.03>

SANTLEY, CHARLES. 1908. *The Art of Singing and Vocal Declamation* (London: Macmillan and Co.)

STOWELL, ROBIN T. 2001. 'Portamento (ii) (It.)', in *Grove Music Online* <https://doi.org/10.1093/gmo/9781561592630.article.53856>

TOFT, ROBERT. 2013. *Bel Canto: A Performer's Guide* (Oxford: Oxford University Press)

TOMASIN, LORENZO. 2009. 'Carducci, Ascoli e la questione della lingua' [Carducci, Ascoli and the language question], in *La lingua italiana: Storia, strutture, testi*, 5: 81–94

TRISSINO, GIOVANNI GIORGIO. 1529. *Epistola de le lettere novamente aggiunte ne la lingua italiana* [Epistle on the letters newly added to the Italian language] (Vicenza: Tolomeo Janiculo)

ZACCONI, LODOVICO. 1596. *Prattica di musica* [Music practice] (Venice: Bartolomeo Carampello)

ZARLINO, GIOSEFFO. 2011. *L'istituzioni armoniche* [The fundamentals of harmony], ed. by Silvia Urbani (Treviso: Diastema)

INDEX

a
 notes on pronunciation 194
 as activator of co-gemination (preposition) 27
abdominal muscles 66
Abramov-van Rijk, Elena 4, 5
accelerando 119, 130
 in the Michelangelo effect 146
accent d'insistance 118
accent markings 119, 151
accented vowels 84, 94
Accent Method 66
affricate consonants *see* occlu-constrictive consonants
a-gemination **29**, 223
 activators of **30–31**, 126–27
 superseded by melo-gemination 125
agogic accent 118–19, **129**, 153, 177, 223
 and inequality of rhythm 159
 suspensive *see* suspensive agogic accent
 three types 130–31
Agricola, Johann Friedrich 164
Alfredo, *La traviata* 136
Alice, *Falstaff* 139
allophones 23, 33, **51**, 189, 191, 192, 223
alveolar consonants 22, 23, 32–33, **223**, 228
 coarticulation 51, 53, 56
 rolled *r* 78, 197
alveolar ridge 223, 231 (*see also* post-alveolar consonants)
 s articulation 198
 t articulation 199
Amelia, *Simon Boccanegra* 157
Amina, *La sonnambula* 146
anchoring **177**, 223

Annio, *La clemenza di Tito* 121
apical place of articulation 223, **224**, 225
Appelman, Dudley Ralph xv, 92, 112
appoggiatura xxiii, 129, 166–67, 233
approximant consonants 14, **106**, 197, 224
archi-vowels 14, **84–86**, 194, 224
 transcription 203
Argante, *Rinaldo* 127
Artusi, Giovanni Maria 9
Ascoli, Graziadio Isaia 12
aspiration 35
assimilation *see* coarticulation of consonants
attacco aspirato 117
attacco del suono **113**, 224
 exceptions 116–17
 in the Michelangelo effect 147–49
 in notation 114–15
 vocalising exercises 181

Badoer, Paolo xiii
Baird, Julianne 164
Bardi, Giovanni 8–9
Bartolo, *Le nozze di Figaro* 156
Basilio, *Il barbiere di Siviglia* 126, 140
battuto 163
Bella siccome un angelo, transcription 220–22
Bellini, Bernardo, dictionary 88, 165–66
Bellini, Vincenzo
 I Capuleti e i Montecchi 123, 151–52, 154
 I puritani 125
 La sonnambula 146
Beltrami, Pietro G. 92
Bembo, Pietro 6–7
Bertarido, *Rodelinda* 143
Bertinetto, Pier Marco 90–91

Bianconi, Lorenzo 166–67
bilabial consonants 22, 23, 32–34, **224**
  coarticulation 51, 53, 60–61
Boccaccio, Giovanni 3, 6
brackets (square), in transcription 202
breath support 66–67

c, notes on pronunciation 195, 196
Caccini, Giulio 8–9, 10
cadences 119, 131
Camerata de' Bardi 8–9
Canepari, Luciano xv, 13, 30, 52
*can*IPA Natural Phonetics framework 189, 201
  vocograms 85
canto affettuoso 165–66
canto legato 165–66 (*see also legato*)
canzone 4–5
Canzoniere (Petrarch) 5
Capellio, *I Capuleti e i Montecchi* 154
Castel, Nico 89
Castilian 6
Cavaradossi, *Tosca* 132
Chapman, Janice L. 65, 66, 67
Che gelida manina, transcription 217–19
Cherubino, *Le nozze di Figaro* 136
chiaroscuro 88, 91, 161
chorus pieces
  I Capuleti e i Montecchi 154
  L'Orfeo 155
  Michelangelo effect in 153–56
  Nabucodonosor 140
chroneme 24, 36, 46, 202, 203, 225
  half chroneme 132
coarticulation 51–52, 90–91
  of consonants **51–61**, 137, 225
  vocalising exercises 81
Coffin, Berton 87
co-gemination **27–28**, 127, 224
  activators of 30–31
Commedia (Dante) 3–4, 5
comprehension of text 89–90

consonant clusters *see* groups of consonants
consonants (*see also* long consonants; short consonants)
  activation of breath support 66–67
  affricate *see* occlu-constrictive consonants
  allophones 23, 33, 51, 189, 223
  alveolar *see* alveolar consonants
  approximant 14, **106**, 197, 224
  bilabial *see* bilabial consonants
  bridging rests 137
  clusters *see* groups of consonants
  coarticulation **51–61**, 81, 137, 225
  constrictive *see* constrictive consonants
  creation of pharyngeal space 67–68
  denti-alveolar *see* denti-alveolar consonants
  distinctive duration 16
  double 26
  and formant frequencies 68–69
  fricative *see* constrictive consonants
  gemination *see* gemination of consonants
  glottal *see* glottal stops
  grooved *see* grooved consonants
  groups *see* groups of consonants
  hold **18**, 227
  importance for phrasing and pacing 177
  intervocalic 19, 195, 197, 227
  labio-dental *see* labio-dental consonants
  laminal 194, 223, 225, **228**
  lateral *see* lateral consonants
  length, not strength **35**, 113
  liquid *see* lateral consonants; vibrant consonants
  long vs. short **17**, **18**, 77, 163
  manner of articulation 21, **228**
  nasal *see* nasal consonants
  non-grooved 194, 225, **230**
  occlu-constrictive *see* occlu-constrictive consonants
  occlusive *see* occlusive consonants
  onset **18**, 230
  palatal *see* palatal consonants
  phrasal doubling *see* co-gemination

place of articulation 21, **231**
post-alveolar *see* post-alveolar consonants
raddoppiamento (fono)sintattico see co-gemination
rafforzamento (fono)sintattico see co-gemination
release **18**, 231
sibilant *see* sibilant consonants
sonorant *see* sonorant consonants
stop *see* stop consonants
unvoiced (voiceless) *see* unvoiced consonants
velar *see* velar consonants
vibrant *see* vibrant consonants
voiced *see* voiced consonants
word-final 19–20
word-initial 19 (*see also* co-gemination)
constrictive consonants 22, 23, 32, 66, 69, 117, **225**
  f and *v* as stop consonants 14, 194–95
Contessa, *Le nozze di Figaro* 132
contoids 225
Cornelia, *Giulio Cesare* 149
Corri, Domenico 163, 164, 166

d
  euphonic 20, 128, **226**
  notes on pronunciation 194
Dalla Rizza, Gilda xiii, 113
Dante Alighieri **3–5**, 7
Decameron, The (Boccaccio) 6
de-gemination **29**, 225
  and *attacco del suono* 116
  in groups of consonants 121
  in the Michelangelo effect 146, 156
Deh vieni non tardar, transcription 211–12
denti-alveolar consonants 22, 23, 32, 33–34, **225**, 228
  coarticulation 53, 54, 58
  d articulation 194
  rolled *r* 78
  s articulation 194, 198
  t articulation 194, 199

z articulation 194, 200
Despina, *Così fan tutte* 138
De vulgari eloquentia (Dante) 4, 7
diacritics 225
h **195**, 199
i **100–01**, 196, 199
diction
  and the concept of line 177
  and *legato* 162–66
  views on the importance of 8–11
diminuendo 63, 88, 136, 137–38, 140, 156
diphthongs *see* prioritisation of vowels
dissonance 119
distinctive duration 16
Donizetti, Gaetano
  Don Pasquale 220–22
  L'elisir d'amore 120
  Lucia di Lammermoor 136
Donna Anna, *Don Giovanni* 137, 147
Don Ottavio, *Don Giovanni* 125
Dorabella, *Così fan tutte* 141
dotted notes 119, 152–53, 158–59
double consonants 26
double vowels 101
dynamic accent 119, 129, 131, 168, **226**
  in the Michelangelo effect 146
dynamics 84, 113, 119, 129, 146, 177
  balancing with resonance and timbre 161
  effect on vowels 88

e
  notes on pronunciation 194
  open and closed 84, 89–93
Elder, Sir Mark xvi
elision of vowels 20, 94–95, **103–05**, 226
Elvira, *I puritani* 125
Elwert, W. Theodor 92
emphasis
  and a-gemination 125–27
  applied correctly to long consonants 35
  of short consonant-initial syllables *see attacco del suono*; melo-gemination

using agogic accent *see* agogic accent; suspensive agogic accent
using portamento *see portamento di voce*
of vowel-initial syllables 127–28
English
  evolution of 2, 6
  lengthening of consonants 118
  d articulation 200
  r articulation 197
  s articulation 198
  t articulation 199
  vowels and obstruent consonants vs. Italian 162
ensembles 153–56
Ericlea, *Il ritorno d'Ulisse in patria* 142
euphonic *d* 20, 226
  melo-gemination 128
evanescent vowels 51, 226

f, notes on pronunciation 194–95
fermata 130
Ferrando, *Così fan tutte* 62
Fiordiligi, *Così fan tutte* 139
Florentine dialect 12
formant frequencies 68–69, 226
Fortuna, *L'incoronazione di Poppea* 126
Foscolo, Ugo 5
Fourcin, Adrian 162
fraseggio 177
Frederick II 2
Freitas, Roger 11
French
  accent d'insistance 118
  evolution of 2, 6
  portamento 169
  r 197
fricative consonants *see* constrictive consonants
frottola 6

g, notes on pronunciation 195, 196
Galliard, Johann Ernst 164

García, Manuel Jr. 88, 118, 129, 165, 177
García, Manuel Sr. 169
Gardiner, Sir John Eliot xvi, 155
Garrett, Margo 65, 118
gemination of consonants 17, **26–31**, 226
  (*see also* a-gemination; de-gemination)
  in *attacco del suono* 113
  co-gemination *see* co-gemination
  in groups of consonants 42–43
  hidden 26–28
  post-gemination **28**, 139, 231
  self-gemination **27**, 231
  short consonants for emphasis *see* melo-gemination
  written 26
German
  evolution of 6
  lengthening of consonants 65, 118
ghost (evanescent) vowels 51, 226
Giovannelli, Barbara 13, 52
Giulietta, *I Capuleti e i Montecchi* 151
Giunse alfin il momento, transcription 210
gl
  and formant frequencies 68
  notes on pronunciation 195
  self-geminated 27
glissando 167, 169, 176, 226
glottal stops 34, 101, 196, 226
  in *attacco del suono* 115, 117
  to interpret rests 137–38
  to interpret punctuation 143
  before syllable-initial vowels 127–28
Gluck, Christoph Willibald, *Orfeo ed Euridice* 117
gn
  and formant frequencies 68
  self-geminated 27
grooved consonants 23, 32, 225, 227
  and formant frequencies 69
groups of consonants 21, **42–50**
  attacco del suono 115
  coarticulation in 51–61

gemination in 42–43
melo-gemination in 121–23
in notation 43–50
portamento applied before 169, 172–74
vocalising exercises 80, 81
groups of vowels 227
  approximant consonants in 106
  diacritic *i* in 100–01
  mute *h* in 99
  portamento applied within 175
  prioritisation in **94–106**, 109, 203, 231
  punctuation in 102, 143
  vowel elision in 103–05
Guglielmo, *Così fan tutte* 148

h
  as diacritic **195**, 199
  mute 99, **196**
Handel, George Frideric
  Giulio Cesare 142, 149
  Rinaldo 127
  Rodelinda 143
Henderson, William J. 167
hold of consonants **18**, 227

i
  as an approximant consonant 106
  as diacritic **100–01**, 196, 199
  notes on pronunciation 194
ictus 90–91, 156, 134, 202
Ilia, *Idomeneo* 128
inequality of rhythm 158–59
instruments, imitating the voice 158–59
International Phonetic Alphabet xiii, 189, 201
intervocalic consonants 227
  single consonants 19
  gli 195
  r 197
Isepp, Martin 65
Italian
  evolution of 1–7
  loanwords in 20, 28

standardisation 12–13
  vowels and obstruent consonants vs. English 162
italiano neutro xv, xxii, **13**, 14, 227
  approximant consonants 106
  coarticulated consonants 52
  vowels 84–85, 90
  vowel elision 103

j, as an approximant consonant 106
Johnson, *La fanciulla del West* 130

Kauffman, Deborah 166, 167
Kühnert, Barbara 51–52
Kuijken, Barthold 133, 158, 159

l
  coarticulation 53–55
  and formant frequencies 68
  labio-dental consonants 22, 23, 33, 34, 227
  coarticulation 53, 60
  f and *v* articulation 194–95
  laminal place of articulation 194, 223, 225, **228**
Lamperti, Francesco 16, 163, 164
lateral consonants 22, 32–33, **228**
  and formant frequencies 68–69
  and sound-damping 69
Latin
  a-gemination 29
  co-gemination 27
  distinctive duration 16
  as official language 1, 6
  rhyming of vowels in poetry 92
legato 162–66
Le nozze di Tetide (Monteverdi) 10
Le nuove musiche (Caccini) 8–9, 10
Leoncavallo, Ruggero, *Pagliacci* 133
Leporello, *Don Giovanni* 116, 160
libretti
  clarity of words 8, 10–11

metrics in 92, 177
line 177
liquid consonants *see* lateral consonants; vibrant consonants
Liù, *Turandot* 127
loanwords
  post-gemination 28
  word-final consonants 20
loft resonance 67
long consonants 17, **26–41**, 228 (*see also* gemination of consonants)
  activation of breath support 66–67
  categories 32–34
  de-gemination 29
  emphasis 35
  and formant frequencies 68–69
  hidden 26–28
  identification 26
  interruption of sound 162
  in notation 36–41
  onset, hold and release 18
  portamento applied before 170–72
  vs. short consonants 17, 18, 77, 163
  sibilant 32
  sonorant 32–33
  stop 33–34
  suspensive agogic accent applied to 131–32
  technical benefits 65–69
  transcription 203
  vocalising exercises 75–81, 181–86
long vowels 18, 83, 228
  in the Michelangelo effect 145
  suspensive agogic accent 131
Lucia, *Lucia di Lammermoor* 136
L'umana fragilità, *Il ritorno d'Ulisse in patria* 130
Luther, Martin 6

m
  coarticulation 53, 56–60
  and formant frequencies 68–69
  loosening tongue root tension 68

Macchiavelli, Niccolò 7
Mace, Dean T. 7
madrigal 6, 8, 9
Magda, *La rondine* 64
Malatesta, *Don Pasquale* 220–22
Mancini, Giambattista 163, 164
manner of articulation 21, 228
Manni, Paola 1
Manrico, *Il trovatore* 63
Manzoni, Alessandro 12
marcato markings 119, 151
Marcellina, *Le nozze di Figaro* 116, 126
Marcello, *La bohème* 142
martellato effect **63**, 64, 136, 156, 162, 228
McCoy, Scott 84, 90
melismas 37–38, 119, 168, 202, 229
  groups of vowels in 105
melo-gemination 14, 46, **118–28**, 229
  in groups of consonants 121–25, 172
  to interpret rests 135–37, 139
  to interpret punctuation 142
  to create the Michelangelo effect 146
  vocalising exercises 182
melophonetics 14, 229
  notation 229
  origin of word xv
  transcription xxiv, 189–93, **201–04**, 229
  transcription of arias 209–22
Mengozzi, Bernardo 167
Metastasio, Pietro 11
metrics 92, 177
Michelangelo effect 120, 125, **144–56**, 229–30
  avoiding 156
  creating 146, 148
  enhancing 146
  in ensembles 153–56
  identifying 145, 149
  and *marcato* markings 151
  and *notes inégales* 159
  in *Sì, mi chiamano Mimì*, case study 152–53
  smoothness and flow 162

and *staccato* markings 150–51
stressed/unstressed beats 144–45
tenuto effect in 145, 151
vocalising exercises 187
micro-dynamics 146, 153, 177, 223
micro-rhythm 149, 177
Miller, Richard 65, 66, 67–68, 69
Mimì, *La bohème* 117, 151, 171
minimal pairs
  distinctive duration 16
  open and closed vowels 89
modulation 119, 131
Monterosso, Raffaello 4–5
Monteverdi, Claudio 9–10, 158
  Il ritorno d'Ulisse in patria 130, 142
  L'incoronazione di Poppea 126, 138
  L'Orfeo 155
  Le nozze di Tetide 10
Monteverdi, Giulio Cesare 9
Monteverdi 450 project xvi
Morris, Ron 65, 66, 67
Mozart, Wolfgang Amadeus
  Così fan tutte 62, 138, 139, 141, 148
  Don Giovanni 63, 116, 123, 137, 147, 160
  Idomeneo 128
  La clemenza di Tito 121
  Le nozze di Figaro 116, 126, 132, 136, 143, 145, 156, 210–12
muovere gli affetti **10**, 158
musical effects in sung Italian 62–64
mute *h* 99, **195–96**

n
  coarticulation 51, 53, 56–61
  and formant frequencies 68
nasal consonants 22, 32–33, **230**
  activation of breath support 66
  coarticulation 56–61
  and formant frequencies 68–69
  loosening tongue root tension 68
  and the *martellato* effect 63
  and sound-damping 69

Nemorino, *L'elisir d'amore* 120
Néron, Martin 70
Nix, John 87
Nolan, Francis 51–52
non-grooved consonants 194, 225, **230**
notation, melophonetic xxiv, 229
notes inégales 158–59

o
  notes on pronunciation 194
  open and closed 84, 89–93
occlu-constrictive consonants 22, 23, 32, 33–34, **230** (*see also* stop consonants)
  f and *v* articulation 194–95
  t articulation 199
occlusive consonants 22, 23, 32, 33–34, **230** (*see also* stop consonants)
  glottal *see* glottal stops
  t articulation 199–200
onomatopoeic words
  post-gemination 28
  word-final consonants 20
onset of consonants **18**, 230
opera
  clarity of words 10–11
  origins of 9
Opera Rara xvi
Orfeo, *Orfeo ed Euridice* 117
ornamentation 119, 129, 166–67, 169, 226, 233

pacing 177
palatal consonants 22, 32–33, 106, **230**
  coarticulation 53, 55, 59
parlar cantando (to speak in song) 4
Petrarch (Francesco Petrarca) 3, 5, 8
pharyngeal space 67–68
phonemes 230
phonetics 231
phonic syllables 42, 123, 144, 202, 231
  long consonants spanning 203
  division in transcription 202

phono-linguistic centre of Italy 13
phrasal doubling *see* co-gemination
phrasing 177
Pinkerton, *Madama Butterfly* 147
Pirrotta, Nino 4
place of articulation 21, 231
Plato 9
plosive consonants *see* occlusive consonants; stop consonants
poetry
  importance of hearing words 8
  metrics in 92, 177
  open and closed vowels in 92
  Sicilian School 1–3
  in sung form 4–6
  transcription 1–2, 3–4
  in Tuscany 3–4
polyphonic music 9
portamento di voce 153, 164, 165, **166–76**, 231
  transcription 204
  use, through the centuries 166–67
  vocalising exercises 188
post-alveolar consonants 22, 23, 32, 33, 34, **231**
  coarticulation 53, 56
  English *r* 197
  t and *d* articulation 199–200
post-gemination **28**, 139, 231
Potter, John 163–64
prima pratica 8
primary stressed syllables 90, 134
prioritisation of vowels 14, **94–106**, 203, 231
  vocalising exercises 109
Prose della volgar lingua (Bembo) 7
Puccini, Giacomo xiii
  Gianni Schicchi 137
  La bohème 117, 142, 151, 152–53, 217–19
  La fanciulla del West 130
  La rondine 64

Madama Butterfly 147
Tosca 132, 144
Turandot 127
punctuation 135, **142–43**
  in groups of vowels 102, 143
  vocalising exercises 186

questione della lingua 6–7

r
  when and how to roll 197
  activation of breath support 66
  loosening tongue root tension 67–68
  vocalising exercise 78
raddoppiamento (fono)sintattico see co-gemination
rafforzamento (fono)sintattico see co-gemination
rallentando 119, 130
recitar cantando 9
recitatives xxi, 84, 153, 177
release of consonants **18**, 231
resonance of vowels 87
resonance space 67–69
rests **135–41**
  vocalising exercises 184–85
rhyme 92
rhythm, inequality (*notes inégales*) 158–59
ritenuto 119
  in the Michelangelo effect 146
Rizzi, Carlo xvi
Rodolfo, *La bohème* 217–19
rolled *r* 197
  activation of breath support 66
  loosening tongue root tension 67–68
  vocalising exercise 78
Romeo, *I Capuleti e i Montecchi* 123, 154
Rosina, *Il barbiere di Siviglia* 213–16
Rossi, Luigi Felice 165–66
Rossini, Gioachino, *Il barbiere di Siviglia* 126, 140, 213–16
rubato 129–31

s
  activation of breath support 66
  and formant frequencies 69
  in groups of consonants (consonant clusters) 42, 47–50, 115, 123
  notes on pronunciation 194, 197–98
  in phonic vs. written syllables 42, 123
  voiced vs. unvoiced (voiceless) 14, 52, **197–98**
sc
  activation of breath support 66
  notes on pronunciation 199
  self-geminated 27
scivolato 163
seconda pratica 9
self-gemination **27**, 231
Sesto, *Giulio Cesare* 142
sforzato markings 119
shadow (evanescent) vowels 51, 226
short consonants 17, 22–23, 232
  in consonant clusters 21
  identification 19–23
  intervocalic 19
  vs. long consonants 17, 18, 77, 163
  melo-gemination 46, **118–28**
  in notation 24–25
  onset and release 18
  portamento applied before 169
  and the *tenuto* effect 62
  transcription 203
  vocalising exercises 74, 77, 79
  word-final 19–20
  word-initial 19
Sì, mi chiamano Mimì, case study 152–53
sibilant consonants **32**, 232
  activation of breath support 66
  as *attacco del suono* 114
  correct application of emphasis 35
  and formant frequencies 69
  and interpretation of rests 136
  in Italian vs. English 162
  and the *martellato* effect 63

  in the Michelangelo effect 145
  in notation 36–38
  vocalising exercises 74
Sicilian School 1–2
silence for dramatic tension 133
Silvio, *Pagliacci* 133
Simone, *Gianni Schicchi* 137
slides (*portamento di voce*) 153, 163–64, **166–76**
  transcription 204
slurs 168, 177 (*see also portamento di voce*)
Sommacampagna, Gidino di 4
sonnets 2, 5, 8
sonorant consonants **32–33**, 232
  activation of breath support 66
  as *attacco del suono* 114
  correct application of emphasis 35
  and interpretation of rests 136
  loosening tongue root tension 67–68
  and the *martellato* effect 63
  in the Michelangelo effect 145
  in notation 38–39
  portamento applied before 171
  vocalising exercises 75
sound-damping 69
speech xv, 10, 85, 112
  coarticulation in 51–52, 90–91
  marks 102
spelling
  of coarticulated consonants 51
  double consonants 26
  long consonants 17
spoken Italian
  standardisation 12–13
  vowels 84–85, 89–90, 103
squillo 91
staccato
  effect **62**, 64, 137, 138, 143, 162, 232
  markings 150–51
stop consonants **33–34**, 230, 232
  activation of breath support 66–67
  aspiration 35

as *attacco del suono* 114
correct application of emphasis 35
creating dramatic tension 133
f and *v* articulation 14, 194–95
and interpretation of rests 136
in Italian vs. English 162
and *legato* xiv, 162
in notation 40–41
creation of pharyngeal space 67
and the *staccato* effect 62, 64
vocalising exercises 75
Straka, George 70
strascino/strascicato 167
stress
  emphatic *see* melo-gemination
  in groups of vowels 94, 97–99, 101
  ictus 90–91, 134
  in the Michelangelo effect 144–45
  syllabic 84, 90, 134, 202
  transcription 202
  word-final 28
stressed beats 97, 134
  in the Michelangelo effect 144–46, 156, 159
stressed syllables *see* stress: syllabic
Striggio, Alessandro 10
striscio 167
sulcalisation 227, 230
Susanna, *Le nozze di Figaro* 143, 145, 210–12
suspensive agogic accent 120, **131–33**, 135, 232
  in the Michelangelo effect 146, 153
  and use of *portamento* 176
  transcription 204
  vocalising exercises 183
syllables
  division in transcription 202
  phonic *see* phonic syllables
  rests between 139
  stressed 84, 90, **134**, 202
syncopation 119, 144

t
  dry vs. wet 199–200
  notes on pronunciation 194, 199–200
Tacchinardi, Nicola 163, 164, 165–66
tap 17
  r 23, 197, 233
Tebaldo, *I Capuleti e i Montecchi* 154
tempo
  markings 119, 130, 168
  in the Michelangelo effect 146
tempo rubato 129–31
tenuto effect **62**, 64, 130, 232–33
  and *legato* 162
  in the Michelangelo effect 145, 150, 151
tenuto markings 130
text
  preparation 205–08
  vocalising with 70
timbre of vowels 65, 84, 88, 89–90, 161
Titze, Ingo R. 87
Tommaseo, Nicolò 88, 165–66
tongue
  anatomy 224, 226
  in articulation 224–28, 230, 231, 233
  Italianate setting 67
  resting position 67, 194, 228
  root tension 67–68
tonic accent 119, 129, 131, 143, 168, 233
  in the Michelangelo effect 146, 153
Tosca, *Tosca* 144
Tosi, Pier Francesco 10, 129, 163–64
transcription
  of arias 209–22
  melophonetic xxiv, 189–93, **201–04**
trills *see* vibrant consonants
triphthongs *see* prioritisation of vowels
Tuscan 3, 7
Tuscany 3, 13
type of phonation 21, 52, 233

u
  as an approximant consonant 106

notes on pronunciation 194
Uberti, Mauro 165
Una voce poco fa, transcription 213–16
unstressed beats
  and use of melo-gemination 120, 127
  in the Michelangelo effect 144–46, 152, 156, 159
  portamento applied before 168
  suspensive agogic accent applied before 133
unvoiced (voiceless) consonants 21, 22–23, 33–34, 36, **233** (*see also* voicing)

v, notes on pronunciation 194–95
Vaccaj, Nicola 164–65, 169
Vacchelli, Anna Maria 159
Vallet, Pierre 118
velar consonants 22, 23, 33–34, 106, **233**
  coarticulation 53, 57
Verdi, Giuseppe 11, 70
  Falstaff 139
  Il trovatore 63
  La traviata 136, 141, 150
  Nabucodonosor 140
  Simon Boccanegra 157
vernacular languages, transcription 1–2, 3
vibrant consonants 23, 32–33, 197, **233**
  activation of breath support 66
  loosening tongue root tension 67–68
Violetta, *La traviata* 141, 150
Virtù, *L'incoronazione di Poppea* 138
vocalising
  exercises 74–81, 109, 181–88
  with text 70
vocograms 85–86
vocoids 84, 85–86, 87, 233 (*see also* vowels)
voiced consonants 21, 22–23, 33–34, 38, 233 (*see also* voicing)
voiceless consonants *see* unvoiced consonants
voicing
  of *s* 14, 52, **197–98**

of short consonants 21
of stop consonants 33
of *z* 14, **200**
volgare illustre 7
volume, changes for emphasis *see* dynamic accent; dynamics
vowels
  archi-vowels 14, **84–86**, 194, 203, 224
  articulated as approximant consonants 106
  attacco del suono 115
  bridging rests 137
  bright and dark sounds 87, 88, 91, 161
  colour palette 161
  double 101
  dynamic variation 88
  elision 20, 94–95, **103–05**, 226
  emphasis applied to syllable-initial vowels 127
  evanescent 51, 226
  flexibility 84–86
  groups *see* groups of vowels
  learnt in isolation 70
  long 18, 83, 131, 145, 228
  open and closed 89–93
  portamento applied before 175
  portamento applied within groups of vowels 175
  prioritisation in groups of vowels 14, **94–106**, 109, 203, 231
  punctuation in groups of vowels 102, 143
  resonance 87
  slides 38, 163–64, **168–76**, 204
  sung vs. spoken 84, 92–93
  timbre 65, 84, 88, 89–90, 161

z
  notes on pronunciation 194, 200
  self-geminated 19, 27
  voicing 14, **200**
Zerlina, *Don Giovanni* 63

About the author

Dr. Matteo Dalle Fratte is an Italian language coach, musicologist and tenor. He studied singing in Italy with Paolo Badoer, a pupil of Gilda Dalla Rizza, Puccini's favourite soprano.

Since 2009, Matteo has conducted extensive research into sung Italian diction, including a research fellowship in Italian phonetics for opera at the Guildhall School of Music & Drama (GSMD) in London. He founded Melofonetica in 2014 to provide training in sung Italian and is Artistic Director of Melofonetica's Veneto Opera Summer School and Arte Lirica Festival in Italy.

Matteo is a Fellow of the Higher Education Academy and works with leading educational establishments around the world including the Royal College of Music, GSMD, the Royal Conservatoire of Scotland and National Opera Studio in the UK, the University of Melbourne and Melba Opera Trust in Australia, and the University of Oklahoma in the US.

Since 2010, he has coached for a wide range of renowned opera companies and record labels including the Royal Opera House, Monteverdi Choir & Orchestras, Opera North, Welsh National Opera, Grange Park Opera, The Mozartists, The English Concert, Opera Rara, Palau de les Arts Reina Sofía, Mecklenburgisches Staatstheater and Universal Music.

In 2024, Matteo was appointed as a board member of the Fondazione Monteverdi of Cremona. His musicological work includes publishing the biographies of the soprano Gilda Dalla Rizza and the tenor Giovanni Lunardi, and collaborating on critical editions of Monteverdi and Bellini operas with the Fondazione Monteverdi. Matteo previously worked as a music critic for *Rassegna Melodrammatica* and *Gazzettino*.

He holds a master's degree in Music in Performance from GSMD and a degree in Italian Literature and Musicology with distinction from the University of Padua.

Photo by Bertie Watson

Further guidance, resources and training

Online learning hub
Visit **melofonetica.com/online-learning** to access the 340+ audio recordings that accompany this book and a growing library of free and premium videos, exercises and materials to continue your learning.

Coaching
One-to-one coaching will give you tailored support to quickly and effectively build your skills and confidence in sung Italian. Matteo and a faculty of Melofonetica coaches provide sessions online for singers and other music professionals around the world.

Train the trainer
Matteo works with singing teachers, vocal coaches, répétiteurs, conductors and directors to develop their knowledge of sung Italian. Tailored training and resources can also be provided for staff in conservatoires, universities and other educational settings.

Courses, masterclasses and workshops
Courses in the Melofonetica Method take place regularly in the UK and Italy. Matteo also leads Italian repertoire masterclasses and workshops for opera companies and training organisations.

Connect
melofonetica.com
info@melofonetica.com
Sign up for email updates: melofonetica.com/subscribe
Follow us on Facebook and Instagram: @melofonetica

If you've found this book useful, please leave a brief review or rating online to let others know!

www.ingramcontent.com/pod-product-compliance
Lightning Source LLC
Chambersburg PA
CBHW071335080526
44587CB00017B/2844